Oklahoma's Atticus

An Innocent Man *and the* Lawyer Who Fought *for* Him

HUNTER HOWE CATES

University of Nebraska Press • *Lincoln*

A brief account of this story first appeared in *This Land* 4, no. 13 (July 2018): 17, 19.

Publication of this volume was assisted by a grant from the Friends of the University of Nebraska Press.

Library of Congress Cataloging-in-Publication Data
Names: Cates, Hunter Howe, author.
Title: Oklahoma's Atticus: an innocent man and the lawyer who fought for him / Hunter Howe Cates.
Description: Lincoln: University of Nebraska Press, 2019. | Includes bibliographical references.
Identifiers: LCCN 2019005310
ISBN 9781496200907 (cloth: alk. paper)
ISBN 9781496218339 (epub)
ISBN 9781496218346 (mobi)
ISBN 9781496218353 (pdf)
Subjects: LCSH: Youngwolfe, Buster, 1932–2008,—Trials, litigation, etc. | Trials (Murder)—Oklahoma—Texas—History—20th century. | Howe, Elliott, 1919–2007. | Public defenders—Oklahoma—Biography.
Classification: LCC KF224.Y68 C38 2019 | DDC 364.152/3092—dc23 LC record available at https://lccn.loc.gov/2019005310

Set in Minion Pro by Mikala R. Kolander.

For Mac and Bill

Ei incumbit probatio qui dicit, non qui negat.
(Proof lies on him who asserts,
not on him who denies.)

—JULIUS PAULUS PRUDENTISSIMUS

I wanted you to see what real courage is,
instead of getting the idea that courage is a
man with a gun in his hand. It's when you
know you're licked before you begin, but
you begin anyway and see it through
no matter what.

—ATTICUS FINCH, *To Kill a Mockingbird*

Contents

Illustrations

Acknowledgments

Oklahoma's Atticus is the result of years of instruction and inspiration from countless teachers, many of whom I know only through their work. As the written word is the transfer of ideas and virtues across time and space, cultures and generations, I have eternal gratitude for the authors of the past. They are as much my teachers as anyone who ever formally held the title.

However, one teacher did help me in a very literal way with this book—Professor Joli Jensen, formerly of the University of Tulsa. A few years after graduating from the university, I wrote a heavily condensed version of this story for This Land Press. Professor Jensen read the piece and encouraged me to expand it into a book, even going so far as to "coach" me during the writing. Dr. Jensen offered this act of altruism because she believed in the story and in me. So much so, she mentioned the book to the young woman who would become my agent and who found a publisher for this story. Had Dr. Jensen not done this, I don't know what would have happened to this story. Perhaps it would be collecting dust in a drawer somewhere. Thus, the book you hold in your hands right now is the result of a teacher living up to the highest standards of her profession. Words cannot describe how grateful I am.

I would also like to thank Michael Mason of This Land Press; Mark Brown, a former editor for *This Land*; and Michael Wallis. Transitioning from writing advertising copy to nonfiction is akin to changing sports for an athlete, so being coached by these skilled nonfiction writers was a tremendous help. However, their greatest contribution was the confidence they instilled simply by welcoming me into their hallowed ranks.

I would also like to thank Sheri Perkins of the Tulsa City-County

Library. This story is about everyday people caught up in extraordinary events in the early 1950s. As such, many of the participants' stories have been lost to time, particularly concerning their lives before and after the events this book details. Ms. Perkins kindly and diligently tracked down what happened to these people when I came up short. Libraries are gifts from one generation to the next, and librarians are the keepers of their treasures. This book is proof.

I would also like to thank the Youngwolfe and Howe families for their participation and involvement in this book, especially Kim Youngwolfe. After reading my article in *This Land*, she reached out to the magazine's editor, who contacted me. Ms. Youngwolfe connected me with other members of the family and tied up loose ends in the story. I am grateful not only for her contributions but also for her encouragement. I am also grateful to Buster's great-niece, Bessie Lee Youngwolfe, who filled in numerous gaps in his story. Unfortunately, Bessie passed away on May 19, 2018, just two months shy of her thirty-seventh birthday. I was blessed to be able to connect with her before her passing.

Though they are no longer around to accept my gratitude, I would like to extend my thanks to the journalists of the *Tulsa World* and *Tulsa Tribune* who covered this story, especially Troy Gordon and Tim Dowd, respectively. Their extensive coverage of the investigation and trial was absolutely invaluable to this book. I knew the story from my childhood, but I only realized how much I didn't know when I read these reporters' work.

History is not simply the passing down of knowledge from one person to another, such as recalling yesterday's events to someone who does not know them. So much of it is knowledge that has been forgotten. It's humbling, even frightening, really, to think about how much knowledge of the past is lost simply because nobody passes it down. I am lucky. I knew this story because of my mother, Nancy Haven Howe. It was important to her that her father's legacy be passed down to my brother and me, and for that I am proud and grateful. I cannot stress enough how important it is to know your family's history and share it with your loved ones. You never know—a book may be in there somewhere.

Oklahoma's Atticus

In the spring of 1953, an eleven-year-old girl named Phyllis Jean Warren was found raped and murdered in the slums of Tulsa, Oklahoma. When a young Cherokee man named Buster Youngwolfe confessed to killing her, the authorities thought the matter was settled—until Buster recanted his confession.

Nobody believed Buster when he said he had been threatened and abused by the police—nobody except his attorney, public defender Elliott Howe.

As Tulsa prepared for the grandest event in its young history—the International Petroleum Exhibition—the murder of Phyllis Warren and the trial of Buster Youngwolfe received national coverage from pulp magazines to *Redbook* and *Newsweek*.

Unfortunately, that is about the only place you will find the story—dusty, old magazines. With each passing year, those who remember it are lost to time. I am lucky. I only know this story because Elliott Howe was my grandfather.

1

The Forgotten City

Buster Youngwolfe could have seen the downtown Tulsa skyline if not for the trees that barricaded the horizon. Downtown was just a few miles from his home in the slums of north Tulsa, but in many ways it was a different city—a different world—from his. The steel and glass towers to the west were barely specks in the distance at Sixteen Hundred North Yale Avenue. This was the forgotten city. Its inhabitants were those left behind on the long march toward progress. Buster was one of them.

Just twenty-one years old, the young Cherokee man still acted as if he were a boy in many ways, making it hard for him to hold on to a job. While he could be immature and even reckless at times, he hid a sharp mind behind his shy, wary eyes. He was reticent and loved to read, when he could find a book, and hated more than anything to be thought of as a "dumb Indian." Whether people ever called him that or it was an internalized, prevailing fear, the specter haunted Buster all his days. Smart as he was, without steady work and with a wife and baby boy at home, Buster wasn't afforded the luxury of wondering what his life could have been. His life as it was kept him busy.

Buster spent his days seeking workman's wages as a journeyman roofer. As with the other residents of the forgotten city, life was hard for Buster. The pursuit of happiness, which had been embraced by millions, ended here, beyond the boundaries of the American Dream. The picket fences and lush green lawns of America in the 1950s that have been etched into our collective consciousness were nowhere to be found here. Only dry soil and damp swamp.

Ten homes total were in these slums. A handful sat on top of a tiny hill, while the rest were in the depths below. The neighborhood was surrounded by woods, with a wide, barren field in front, the final resting place for a few uprooted trees and shrubs.

Before statehood, this north Tulsa neighborhood was a little town called Dawson. It was named in honor of Wilbur A. Dawson, a Cherokee Indian and postmaster of the community's first post office, established in 1895. Dawson was the area's name, but it was known as Coal Bank. While Tulsa earned a global reputation for oil, the land was also pregnant with coal, and the most fertile area was in Dawson. Coal kept homes warm, trains running, and jobs plentiful. It put roofs over people's heads and food in their children's bellies. Coal was life here.

The Smith Brothers, the Leavell Coal Company, and the Hickory Coal Company owned the strip mines that made Dawson prosperous and kept mining a booming business from 1920 to 1950. It was only three years ago that the earth ran dry, within living memory for Dawson residents in 1953, but it might as well have been decades ago. Dawson had been absorbed into the city of Tulsa, and the strip mining industry left, taking its jobs with it.

The coal companies that had once made this area prosperous had abandoned it, leaving nothing behind but the strip pits. These strip pits formed scars in the land so wide and deep that they had gathered rainwater and become streams. You could ride a boat through them.

Just a few blocks to the east was a slaughterhouse, which on humid days scented the air with the stench of pig flesh. If you got close enough, you could hear the high-pitched screams of the pigs as they died.

The homes here were not houses but tar paper shacks. Though the city of Tulsa had condemned the shacks, people still lived in them, for they had no place else to go. The homes were nothing but two or three tiny rooms, with dirt floors and ceilings so low you had to slouch. The only heat came from stoves that burned wood, coal, or whatever else you could find. The kitchens were no more than six-by-six-foot enclosures. The bedrooms were slightly larger, with enough room for a few beds, where everyone slept beside each other like medieval serfs. People sat on rope-bottomed boxes or logs, with boards nailed across for their backsides. There were no sewers, so residents had to walk half a mile to reach the nearest drinking water, which came from an old hand pump. The whole family, sometimes two or three generations, slept together, ate together, did everything together.

Tulsans in 1953 were not hostile or even ambivalent about this place or its people; they were simply unaware. They knew the city was segregated by economic classes, the same as it was in many towns. But Tulsans could not have imagined the depths of poverty in their midst or that men, women, and children—families—could call the slums home.

The Tulsa most residents knew was nothing like this neighborhood. The city they lived in was a model of the 1950s American ideal. Watching newsreel footage from this era is similar to seeing images from a dream, blissful memories in fading technicolor. Tulsa was the centerpiece of a region known as Green Country, a halfway point between the golden plains to the west and the Ozark Mountains to the east. Verdant hills and lush trees existed alongside some of the most spectacular skyscrapers in the American southwest. With some of the nation's most elegant art deco and zigzag-style architecture, downtown Tulsa's buildings are the legacy to the oilmen who built them—for example, the Philtower and the Philcade Buildings financed by oil baron Waite Phillips and the Cosden Building, named for oilman Joshua Cosden, to name a few. In 1957 *Reader's Digest* magazine would christen Tulsa as "America's Most Beautiful City." The title was just as deserved in 1953 as well, though it did not extend to the north Tulsa slums.

"Burn 'em down," some city employees said. The problem was, people still lived there. Where were they supposed to go? Nobody had an answer. So the shacks stayed, sitting as if the area was a black stain on a new dress, an embarrassment to this blossoming, beautiful young city. But to the families who lived here, these eyesores were the only things they had besides each other. Multiple generations crowded together not so much in harmony but from inevitability. They were surprisingly cheerful, as there was no sense in being unhappy. It is the paradox of poverty: When everybody has it as bad as you do, you don't realize you are poor. It's just life.

All things considered, it was not a bad place to be a kid. Santa ran out of toys before he got to your house, and your birthday was no different from any other day, but none of that mattered when you didn't know what you didn't have. For a child, this neighborhood promised wide-open spaces. No fences. No boundaries. No prohibitions. Just lots of room to run, jump, and play any way you pleased. Simple and carefree as it was being a kid, it was a wonder why any child would have wanted to grow up too fast. But Phyllis Jean Warren wasn't like most children. She never had a chance.

· · ·

The north Tulsa slums were the only world Phyllis had ever known, but it was everything a tomboy such as she was could want. Trees were for climbing, fish and frogs were for catching, and dresses were for getting muddy. That was Phyllis. It was what you might expect from a girl who grew up with six brothers—Elmer, twenty-nine; Jimmy, twenty-eight; Kenneth Joe, twenty-five; E.J., twenty-three; Bobby, seventeen; and Billy Dale, thirteen. Phyllis was the baby, just eleven years old, and the only daughter born to Robert and Josie Warren. Bobby and Billy Dale still lived at home, while Elmer had joined the U.S. Army and was stationed in San Antonio, Texas. The other Warrens lived here and there but close to home.

Phyllis liked to play with the Youngwolfe kids, Eddie and Judy Mae. They were Buster Youngwolfe's nephew and niece and were both about Phyllis's age. Her daddy, Robert, didn't like her running around with those Cherokee kids, but living in a neighborhood as small as that, she didn't have much choice. Phyllis and her parents lived in one of the houses on top of the hill, while the Youngwolfes' place was on the bottom. Despite her daddy's protests, Phyllis would trot down the hill to play with them, making sure Robert wasn't home when she did.

"Stay away from those Youngwolfes," her old man would say, though no one knew exactly why. Maybe Robert Warren just needed to feel as if he was better than someone. Whatever a person's lot in life, everybody loves having somebody to look down on. Or maybe it was prejudice, plain and simple. That would be strange given that Robert's son Jimmy had married a Cherokee woman, the former Bessie Youngwolfe. Bessie was Eddie and Judy Mae's grandma and Buster's mother. Robert didn't seem to care that his son married a Cherokee or about Phyllis's safety, for that matter. He and his wife, Josie, would let her run off and play for hours, sometimes days at a time.

The most likely answer was the simplest: Robert was strange. Kids called him "ding-batty" and a "loony bird." A simple man with a slow mind, he was prone to acts of foolishness or outright lunacy. Robert once kept a full-grown mule in the house. He'd have to be crazy to do that, neighbors said. He was a drunk, too, and a mean one at that. There was more to Robert than he let on, though. He made good money working in the steel mills and even better money as a moonshine runner. Some even said he ran moonshine up to some pretty high places. Rumors are rumors, but everybody in the neighborhood knew Robert did well enough that he didn't have to keep his family here, with dirt floors and tar paper walls. Strange man, that Robert Warren. But whatever he was, he was the head of his household and demanded respect. No daughter of Robert Warren's was going to hang around those Youngwolfes. At least, not with him knowing about it.

Besides Robert's being a bit odd, not much happened out of the ordinary around the neighborhood. There was one time that a stranger hid behind a billboard and started firing his rifle at random people. He shot Bessie Warren in the hip, then hit another woman, and probably would have kept going if not for Clarence Youngwolfe, Buster's brother. Clarence told his son, Eddie, to go fetch his .22 rifle and some shells. Anytime the shooter poked his head out from behind the billboard, Clarence fired at him.

The police took their time getting there, but by the time they arrived, Clarence had stopped the madman. The police found him lying behind the billboard, bleeding to death. Clarence had gotten a few shots into him, close enough to his heart to stop him. Nobody ever figured out what the man wanted or even who he was. As far as anyone knew, he was just some nut who got it in his head that he wanted to shoot someone. Had Clarence not been there with his .22, there was no telling who else would have been hit.

That was about as interesting as things got around there until the spring of 1953.

Time faded slowly on that Thursday evening. It was March 12, 1953. The brutal summer weather was still some time away; that was a blessing, as the Oklahoma humidity could be cruel. Tonight the evening was crisp and cool. The setting sun painted the prairie sky pink. "The angels are baking cookies," folks said about such nights. Nobody was really sure what that meant, but it made perfect sense all the same.

Phyllis played in front of her parent's shack, twirling a purple wildflower through her stubby fingers. She had found it earlier by the creek bed where she liked to roam barefoot with her German shepherd, Smokey. If Phyllis was around, Smokey wasn't far behind. The two were inseparable.

With her curly blonde hair, blue eyes, and freckled face stained with mud and sweat, Phyllis was pretty but rough, resembling a rag doll that had been dropped in the dirt. She had the face of childish innocence, though the rumor among the adults and some of the older kids was that Phyllis was "experienced," an indirect way of saying she was no longer a virgin. If true, today they'd call this by its proper name—sexual assault and rape of a minor. There were rumors about who the culprit was, but nobody knew for sure. Maybe it was her daddy's good friend and fellow moonshine runner Gene Pruitt. Maybe it was one of the many convicted sex felons who were said to live in the neighborhood. Again nobody knew for sure, and nobody cared enough to do anything about it. What happened to Phyllis was nobody's concern. Young girls were to be seen, not heard. Phyllis just did what she was told, no matter what she was told to do.

It was a beautiful night, but Phyllis likely didn't come outside just to admire the twilight. She came to see Buster Youngwolfe, who wandered outside after lullabying his baby boy to sleep so he could catch his own last glimpse of the day. He lived two blocks away, give or take, from the Warrens. Buster was Phyllis's neighbor but also her stepnephew. As noted previously, her older brother Jimmy was married to Buster's mother, Bessie. Jimmy, Bessie, and Buster all lived together with Buster's wife, Betty, and the couple's eight-month-old son, Buster Jr.

Buster and Jimmy were the household's sole breadwinners, but work was scarce for Buster. Even paying the fifty cents a month it cost to keep a roof over his family's head was tough. His family helped with expenses, and the county helped with food. They managed.

Buster was turning twenty-one the next day, March 13, and he had been barhopping since noon with his father, his brother, and a neighbor. They only came home for a bite to eat and planned on going back out. Nothing special. Just a trip downtown to hit up a few more bars, a treat the young husband and father didn't get to enjoy often. Buster probably got restless cooped up in that house. It would be hard not to. There was no doubt he loved his mom, his wife, and his baby boy more than anything, but living in a shack with that many people would wear down anyone.

Buster was still young and virile, but he was now responsible for a wife and child. With no steady job to provide for them, Buster got reckless. Just a few months earlier, in the fall of 1952, Buster had been arrested for breaking into a grocery store. He could have been sent to prison but was placed on a two-year probation instead.

If other people treated Buster differently after his arrest, as though he was untrustworthy or worse, Phyllis likely wasn't one of them. She adored Buster. With his thick black hair, bronzed skin, and stern, brooding brown eyes, Buster cut an imposing figure. Buster could look so serious one moment but give off a glowing, boyish grin the next. It was easy to see how a young girl could develop a crush.

It wasn't just Buster's looks she liked; it was him. Buster didn't treat her as the other adults did, as if she were some silly little girl to be seen and not heard—or, worse, to be used and discarded. Buster treated her as a person. He teased her, joked with her, and had fun. He was playful and affectionate. If Buster had gone to prison, there's no doubt it would have broken the girl's heart.

Buster likely noticed her girlish crush and, being slightly immature, probably enjoyed it, but he always saw her as a little sister. Phyllis wanted to be more and was still young enough to think that wanting something was enough. For anyone who has ever suffered through an unrequited childhood crush, one can imagine Phyllis's feelings—a strange, frustrating sensation, painful at times, like a knot in the heart and stomach.

Phyllis perked up as soon as she heard the door slam against Buster's shack and saw him come outside. Buster didn't see her, or if he did, he didn't acknowledge her. The night was now as black as ink as the curtain closed on another long, dreary day in the slums. Buster lit a cigarette. The burning orange orb was all Phyllis could see of him, but it would have been enough to know he was there.

• • •

There was no light left to read and no TVs to watch or radios to listen to, so the families got together and talked. Being the patriarch and the matriarch of the clan, Robert and Josie Warren hosted these chats on their porch. Tonight the group discussed what they usually did—the Reverend Mrs. Leontine Bryant. Reverend Bryant was the seventy-two-year-old ordained minister of the Universal Church of the Master. She was a spiritualist and was said to commune with the spirit world. Her fantastic predictions were particularly appealing to Mae Ellen Warren, who was married to the Warrens' third-eldest son, Kenneth. Her stories of Reverend Bryant caused quite a stir among the ladies in the neighborhood.

Phyllis was not one of them. She didn't have anything to say about that "spiritualist woman," and nobody would have listened to her anyway. Her only concern was getting Buster's attention. She had changed her clothes after school into blue jeans, a red checkered shirt, and a yellow sweater. Robert may have raised his daughter in a squalid, tar paper shack, but every now and then he would treat her to nice clothes even if Phyllis inevitably got them filthy from playing outside.

Phyllis and Buster played in the field in front of the house. The eleven-year-old Phyllis and her twenty-one-year-old nephew goofed around as if they were two little kids. Buster gave her a toy rubber frog, the kind you'd find at a five-and-dime. It was a peculiar gift for a girl, but she appreciated it and put it in her pocket. It was getting late. The men were bored by all of the talk of the spiritualist woman, so they went their separate ways, with Buster, his family, and his friends leaving to celebrate Buster's birthday downtown. Talk on the porch began dying down. The conversation and darkness likely left everyone with an eerie feeling. Sister Bryant has a mighty strange power, someone said, breaking the silence. She said that Reverend Bryant could feel if something terrible was going to happen, even before it did.

Josie Warren shivered and asked the group to go inside. Someone mentioned Phyllis had disappeared, which she did when she got bored. Nobody had even noticed she was gone. Someone whistled for Smokey, for wherever Smokey was, Phyllis would be there too. But Smokey didn't come. Josie, tired of waiting out in the cold, said her daughter was probably at a friend's house. Phyllis's best friend, besides Smokey, was Gertrude Young, a classmate who lived a few blocks away. Phyllis spent the night there all the time, though she was supposed to tell her mother when she did.

The women went inside and kept talking. The chattering of voices was finally broken after a half hour by scratching on the door. It was Smokey, pleading to get inside.

Figuring Phyllis would be there too, Josie went to the door, ready to reprimand her daughter for running off without telling anybody. But Smokey was alone. The dog darted inside and curled up in his spot next to the stove. Phyllis had disappeared a million times before and Josie never worried, but Smokey's coming home by himself made this feel different. Maybe, Josie told herself, it was all just the conversation about Reverend Bryant and her talking to the dead.

The men returned an hour or so later. None of them had seen Phyllis, but they weren't worried, not even the girl's father, Robert. They figured this was just Phyllis being Phyllis. She'd turn up. Everyone went to their homes and crawled into their beds. While her husband slept, Josie stepped outside and stared into the night, alive with darkness. Her little girl was out there somewhere. But where? With whom?

Church bells tolled. Midnight. The church was only a few miles away, but the low, distant rumble of the bells could reverberate through bone. It was every bit as chilling as the midnight air.

Josie probably tried to console herself, for nobody else would. Her husband stayed in bed and barked at her to come inside. She did as she was told. Might as well try to get some sleep. Phyllis did things like this. She'd turn up.

Only she never did.

2

Magic City

Downtown Tulsa's skyline paled in comparison to that of New York City, or Philadelphia, or Boston, but this wasn't the East, where cities were built skyward. This was the West, where cities were built outward, as wide and as open as the American dream. Americans came from all corners of the country to the nation's heartland. Native Americans were forced here in exile. African Americans came to escape bondage. European Americans to reap the bounty of oil buried below. What brought them here was different, but what ultimately kept them here was the same—energy.

Tulsa is a city of energy, both literally and figuratively. Buried beneath these quiet plains, formed over billions of years, is the lifeblood of the modern world—oil. It is ironic that something so ancient and useless for so long should find its purpose in the present age. Oil powers industry. Oil powers transportation. Oil powers life. Its use extends to every corner of the globe, greasing the wheels of civilization. But it wasn't always this way.

Back when oil was still forming under the earth, before the buildings and the businesses, Tulsa was a nameless, endless wilderness. It had golden prairies, verdant valleys, grasses as tall as people, and trees towering like giants.

Besides the wild animals, this land was home to the original tribes, Native peoples who came here not by force but of their own accord. Seduced by the myth of the noble savage, we forget how hard life was on the unforgiving plains. There was nothing romantic about this life. The men slayed the bison. The women butchered the bodies. The children followed their preordained path. Nothing was wasted, and everything was earned. This was the way it was and always had been. But it would soon change.

• • •

The native had the land that the stranger wanted. This was not just America's story; it is humankind's story, recurring endlessly as our species soaks fields, forests, and deserts in blood. While the players and settings change, the story stays the same. It repeated itself in the new world, just as it had played out countless times in the old.

The problem was simple yet profound: European America was spreading, and Native America was in its way. What was the solution? Some of the more humanitarian settlers proposed "civilizing" the Natives by teaching them the ways of cultured European Americans. The commandments included converting to Protestant Christianity, learning to read and speak English, and, with time, practicing European-style economics, such as the private ownership of land and of people.

Five tribes—Choctaws, Creeks, Chickasaws, Cherokees, and Seminoles—adopted these ways. The "Five Civilized Tribes" were located in Florida, Georgia, Alabama, Mississippi, and the Carolinas, respectively. The tribes established towns under colonial legal systems of government. They tilled the soil; raised cattle, horses, and livestock; and grew cotton. Many owned businesses and became wealthy. Some even owned slaves and ran plantations. However, obedience to so-called civilized society wasn't what the strangers wanted from the Native. They wanted the Native's land.

Settlers poured into the fertile southern territory, pining for land to grow cotton, but the Native peoples occupied that land. The Louisiana Purchase temporarily solved this dilemma in 1803, providing the young nation with 828,000 square miles at a bargain of $11,250,000. The tribes could now start anew in the new lands west of the Mississippi.

Many tribes left, peacefully and of their own accord, beginning in 1812. Nearly two thousand Cherokee men, women, and children, or approximately one-fourth of the Cherokee Nation, voluntarily migrated from the southeastern United States. The "Old Settler" Cherokees ultimately settled between the White and Arkansas Rivers in northwest Arkansas.

The occupation of Native land continued in the southern states, escalating after the election of Andrew Jackson in 1828. The beloved war hero of 1812 had ridden a wave of angry populist resentment into the highest office in the land. That same year the Old Settler Cherokees and their descendants, who had moved peacefully nearly two decades before, were removed from the Arkansas Territory into the Indian Territory in present-day Oklahoma.

State governments joined the fight to remove Natives from their lands, passing laws that stripped Natives of their rights and permitting further encroachment into their territory. However, the U.S. Supreme Court ruled these anti-Indian laws were unconstitutional in *Cherokee Nation v. Georgia* (1831) and *Worcester v. Georgia* (1832), affirming that the tribes were sovereign nations "in which the laws of Georgia [and other states] can have no force." The law was final but feckless when unenforced. President Jackson had no intention of stopping the expansion, noting in 1832 that absent enforcement the Supreme Court's rulings would "[fall] . . . stillborn."

Andrew Jackson's view of Native tribes had been born on the frontier. While an army general, he had led campaigns that removed hundreds of thousands of acres of land from the Creeks in Georgia and Alabama and from the Seminoles in Florida. As president, he replaced the sword with the pen, signing the Indian Removal Act in 1830. The federal government now had the authority to exchange Indian lands east of the Mississippi for land in the west, or the "Indian colonization zone."

The Indian Removal Act required removal treaties to be negotiated fairly, voluntarily, and peacefully. Nevertheless, thousands of men, women, and children were forced from their homes, businesses, and farms. With the stroke of a pen, generations had to leave behind the only land they had ever known.

Facing invasion by the U.S. Army, the Choctaw people chose exile over extermination. They journeyed more than five hundred miles by foot from their homes in Mississippi to the eastern quarter of

Indian Territory. Some were even bound in chains and marched single file as if they were prisoners. Almost seventeen thousand began the journey, yet between twenty-five hundred and six thousand perished along the way. When they reached Little Rock, one Choctaw chief described their march with a simple phrase: it was, he said, "a trail of tears and death."

The French philosopher Alexis de Tocqueville, among the most insightful observers of America's greatness, also spoke about one of its darkest deeds: "In the whole scene there was an air of ruin and destruction, something which betrayed a final and irrevocable adieu; one couldn't watch without feeling one's heart wrung. The Indians were tranquil, but sombre and taciturn. There was one who could speak English and of whom I asked why the Chactas were leaving their country. 'To be free,' he answered, could never get any other reason out of him. We . . . watch the expulsion . . . of one of the most celebrated and ancient American peoples."

The Choctaws were the first to be removed, but they would not be the last. In 1832 Andrew Jackson was reelected in a landslide as president of the United States, inaugurating the most ambitious era in the history of Indian removal.

That same year several tribes ceded lands, many giving away their homes for a pittance: the Seminoles of Florida, the Chickasaws of Mississippi, the Wyandots or Hurons of Ohio, the Sauks and Foxes from east of the Mississippi River, the Prairie Band of Potawatomis of Indiana, the Shawnees and Delawares of Missouri, and the Kaskaskias, Peorias, Piankeshaws, and Weas of Illinois and Missouri. Even the small tribes of Stockbridges, Munsees, Brothertons, and New Yorks (Oneidas) ceded lands, relocating to the northeast corner of Indian Territory.

In 1833 the Kickapoos of Illinois and the Ottawas of Ohio were removed.

In 1834 the Caddos of Louisiana were removed beyond the limits of the United States to the Republic of Texas. That same year, the Muscogee-Creeks began their own trail of tears from Alabama into Indian territory. Thousands of people were forced from their old homes; many did not make it to their new one.

For years the Cherokee Nation negotiated with the federal government, hoping to avoid the same fate as other tribes. It was useless. The Cherokees spent the long, hot summer of 1838 in concentration camps. Starting that fall and lasting throughout the winter of 1839, thousands of Cherokee men, women, and children were marched more than twelve hundred miles to Indian Territory. Along the way many succumbed to whooping cough, typhus, dysentery, and cholera—all of which spread rapidly in such close quarters. All told, more than a thousand Cherokees died on their march.

The Indian diaspora ended in the wilderness. Oklahoma was where the problem was buried, but it would not stay that way for long. The nation's lust for land would not allow it.

• • •

Legend has it that when the Creeks arrived in their new home in Indian Territory, a young brave marched to the top of a hill overlooking the Arkansas River. On top of the hill was a great oak, where the young brave was said to have placed the ashes of the council fire. The ashes had been carried more than seven hundred miles from Alabama. The brave set them ablaze with only a single flint. The blaze was not an act of destruction but of creation, kindling a hope, however faint, for the rebirth of a people. The Council Oak Tree symbolized the new roots these people yearned to establish.

Tulsa was established in Indian Territory in 1836 by the Muscogee-Creeks and the Lochapokas, a branch of the Creeks named after their home in Alabama. The settlement was named Tallasi, meaning "old town" in the Muscogee language. The term "Tallasi" also inspired the name Tallahassee, the state capital of Florida, where the Muscogee originated.

The Five Civilized Tribes settled into their respective parts of the territory, living in accord, if not harmony, with their neighbors. The tribes adapted to their new lands and lives and over the next two decades built homes, established businesses and farms, founded towns, and tried to revive the lives they had lost. Isolated in Indian Territory, the early settlers were mostly unaware of the budding conflict that threatened to tear America apart. Ignorance was not bliss. The Five Civilized Tribes were soon dragged into America's Civil War. Being Southern slaveholders themselves and feeling no fidelity to the U.S.

federal government, the tribes mostly supported the Confederacy, with many Native people enlisting in the Confederate States Army. The complex, fratricidal dynamics of the conflict extended to Indian country, as many Creeks also joined the Union army.

The Battle of Round Mountain occurred in 1861 west of Tulsa when a force of Creeks in the Union army fought against the Texas cavalry and Confederate Native Americans. When the U.S. forces withdrew from Indian Territory, the tribes that did not have treaties with the Confederacy faced destruction. Despite the bayonets at their throats, many Cherokees and Creeks remained loyal to the Union. In February 1863 following the return of U.S. troops to Indian Territory, the Cherokee Nation terminated its treaty with the Confederacy, removed officials who were traitors to the Union, and abolished slavery.

The Creek Nation was not so fortunate. By 1864 raiding guerrillas and thieves from both sides of the conflict had pillaged the Creek Nation, leaving behind nothing but overgrown weeds. Homes were robbed and destroyed, livestock was stolen, and all progress from the past two decades was erased as if it had never happened. The Creek's fragile society perished, plunging the landscape back into wilderness. Once again, they had nothing; once again they rebuilt Tulsa.

Tulsa's first post office was established on March 25, 1879. A Creek Nation school and general store followed. Cattle ranching bustled as the grassy plains fattened the cattle en route to Kansas from Texas. Cattle begat railroads and railroads begat cities. On August 21, 1882, the first passenger train arrived in Tulsa. Stores, businesses, and professional services owned by whites and Creeks alike soon followed, as railroad workers and their families settled in the town. Cattle became the currency of success. By 1884 Tulsa had its first newspaper, *Indian Chief*. More newspapers, churches, and schools sprang up throughout the small city in the final decades of the nineteenth century.

While the seeds of civilization had been planted, Tulsa remained far from civilized. Tulsa was the mythic cow town of the Wild West. Famed outlaws and fugitives from the Dalton Gang, to the Bill Doolin Gang, to Crawford "Cherokee Bill" Goldsby and others found refuge from the noose in Tulsa. Creek hospitality was ingrained here, and in gratitude to the people's kindness, the city was spared the robbery, rape, murder, and raids that were common throughout the territory.

Some of the Wild West's most notorious villains behaved as upstanding citizens when they visited. U.S. Marshals on manhunts through Indian Territory found the trail went cold in Tulsa.

Tulsa was the stage where the human story played at an accelerated pace. In less than a century the hunting and gathering society of the Plains Indians had given way to the commercial culture of the Five Civilized Tribes, and it was soon replaced by the railroads and cattle ranches of the Wild West. They were also swiftly supplanted when ambitious settlers from the East, once hungry for Indian land, now lusted for the oil that flowed beneath it.

• • •

"I came out to the promised land," said one early Tulsa resident. His sentiment wasn't unique. America was open for business, and Oklahoma was for sale.

Veterans from the Civil War wanted a new start and the land to pursue it. Meanwhile, business leaders in St. Louis, Kansas City, Topeka, and Wichita used their considerable pull to open up Indian lands for sale. Their eyes were cast westward to the virgin plains and valleys of the twin territories—Oklahoma Territory in the west and Indian Territory to the east. In 1889 the federal government finally relented.

At noon on April 22, 1889, a U.S. Army cavalryman blew his bugle and dropped his flag, inaugurating the first Oklahoma Land Run. More than fifty thousand settlers swarmed the land like a prairie fire. Two more land runs followed in 1891 and 1893, with settlers claiming nearly the entire western half of Indian Territory. Yet this was only the beginning. Before it even had a name, Oklahoma had five land runs, one land lottery, and one land auction. In the end more than 15 million acres of Indian country, or greater than the total area of nine states, had been swallowed whole.

In 1895 federal judges ruled that the towns in the territory could incorporate as cities. Wealthy locals feared that land in Tulsa was going to be purchased from the Muscogee-Creek Indians and sold at outrageous prices. A town meeting was called to discuss incorporation, but the peaceful talks soon dissolved into a brawl. Fists were thrown and shots were fired, but nothing was settled, for the Creeks refused to give up their land. After three more years of tense debate,

Tulsa was officially incorporated as a city on January 18, 1898. On November 16, 1907, Oklahoma became America's forty-sixth state.

Hunger for land had defined the state's history, but as insatiable as it was, it would soon be eclipsed by a love of oil. On April 15, 1897, sixty miles north of Tulsa, outside of present-day Bartlesville, the Nellie Johnstone No. 1 struck oil, becoming the first commercial oil well in Oklahoma. Tulsa's first oil well was established in June 1901. It was named Sue Bland No. 1 by J. C. W. Bland, a physician and oilman, after his half-blood Muscogee-Creek wife who owned the homestead. Dr. Bland and fellow physician Dr. Fred S. Clinton had persuaded Pennsylvania producers to drill a test on Mrs. Bland's land. The resulting well produced around 10 barrels a day at a depth of only six hundred feet, proving the land was pregnant with crude.

On November 22, 1905, Robert Galbreath and Frank Chelsey brought in the Ida Glenn No. 1 fifteen miles southwest of Tulsa. Glenn Pool, as the area soon became known, had five hundred producing wells within two years, with some producing as much as 2,000 barrels a day. Glenn Pool was the largest oil field discovered at the time and the richest in the world, fueling a black gold rush of would-be wildcatters from coast to coast.

In 1907, the year of its birth, the state of Oklahoma led the nation in oil production. By 1913 the young state produced a quarter of all the oil in the country. By 1915 it was up to 300,000 barrels per day.

The dawn of the twentieth century was a boom period for much of the United States, as thirteen states more than doubled their populations. Oklahoma's growth was by far the greatest, as the population grew more than seven and a half times between 1890 and 1920. Migrators propelled Tulsa's population to more than eighteen thousand people by 1910. By 1920 the population was seventy-two thousand, according to the census bureau, while city directory estimates recorded the number was just shy of a hundred thousand. By the 1950s, in less than half a century, oil had turned this prairie town into the "Oil Capital of the World," making many men fabulously wealthy in the process.

With their newfound riches, these men signed the checks that built the city that *Reader's Digest* magazine hailed as "America's Most Beautiful City" in 1957. Tulsa's natural beauty was soon adorned with museums, universities, and majestic art deco architecture, with the nation's third-largest collection behind only New York City and Miami.

But it wasn't just the oil supply that made Tulsa the oil capital; many cities in Oklahoma and elsewhere had plenty of oil. Tulsa had to earn the title. When would-be wildcatters moved to Tulsa, restaurants did not raise prices and boardinghouses did not hike rents, as might have happened elsewhere. Hotels were built en masse, and there was even a bridge built across the Arkansas River, providing easier access between western oil fields and downtown Tulsa. Citizens made every effort to make oilmen feel comfortable and welcome. This wasn't the result of a long-term strategic initiative. It just reflected the Creek hospitality that had been bred into the city's character.

Tulsa became a prairie oasis for migrants from across the country. Rich or poor, black or white, from the East Coast or the West Coast, people made their home in the heartland and were restrained only by their own ambition. The promise of oil brought them here, but their love of the land and its potential kept them here.

Tulsa was "Magic City." More than an ordinary boomtown, Tulsa had grown into one of the Southwest's largest cities and one of the nation's most vital economic centers. It wasn't magic that fueled the rise; it was oil. "The story of Tulsa is the story of oil," a writer in 1920 said plainly. Tulsa provided the petroleum that powered the twentieth century. But the moniker "Magic City" hid an uncomfortable truth: Tulsa was not one city but two. But for one bright, brief, shining moment, the magic extended to both cities.

• • •

"Black Wall Street" is how history remembers the Greenwood District just east of downtown Tulsa. For nearly thirty years, Tulsa's promise and prosperity extended to the city's vibrant and thriving black community. At a time when African Americans were treated as second-class citizens or worse across the nation, these ten city blocks in the middle of the country were an anomaly.

African Americans had been in Tulsa for decades. Many were brought as Cherokee and Creek slaves, and they remained in the land as freedmen. Others had ancestors in the South who fled slavery to the Indian Territory. Many had been adopted into the Muscogee-speaking tribes, such as the Creeks, the Seminoles, and the Yuchis. In the 1880s there was even an effort to make the Indian Territory into an all-black state. In this new land African Americans had the opportunity to escape the fate that had befallen others of their race in America. They had the chance to make something else. Something better.

In 1905 a group of black Tulsans were sold a strip of land in the northeastern tip of downtown Tulsa, north of the Frisco railroad tracks. Dismissed as "Little Africa," the Greenwood District soon became the centerpiece of black life not just in the city but in the nation as well. Tulsa's African American attorneys, physicians, business owners, and other professionals were some of the most prominent in America. They made this place their home. Some even made themselves rich. While they were still denied service in restaurants and businesses in south Tulsa, this mile-long stretch in north Tulsa stood for hope, triumph, and validation. It became nationally known then as "Negro Wall Street."

The Oil Capital of the World, or Magic City, stood beside Negro Wall Street. Tulsa was two cities, and both of them were booming. By 1921 the black community had reached nearly eleven thousand people and had two schools, Dunbar and Booker T. Washington; a hospital; two newspapers, the *Tulsa Star* and the *Oklahoma Sun*; thirteen churches; three fraternal lodges; two black theaters; and a library.

The two cities lived in accord but not in peace. Perhaps some white Tulsans were threatened by the success of black Tulsa; maybe they were disturbed that a race they had viewed as inferior for so long was flourishing when left on its own. Tensions simmered between white and black Tulsa like water about to boil. On May 31, 1921, these tensions exploded.

It was the Friday afternoon before Memorial Day weekend. The *Tulsa Tribune* reported the alleged assault of a white elevator operator, seventeen-year-old Sarah Page, by a black shoe shiner, nineteen-year-old Dick Rowland, at the Drexel Building in downtown Tulsa. Rowland was arrested and held in the courthouse. While police investigated, the *Tulsa Tribune* wasted no time condemning the young man. With eight startling words, one newspaper lit the spark that ignited the flames: "Nab Negro for Attacking Girl in an Elevator."

Just forty-five minutes after the *Tulsa Tribune*'s headline hit the streets, there was talk of a lynching. Three hours later a mob assembled outside the courthouse. The crowd swelled to three hundred people by 7:30 p.m. and four hundred by 9:00 p.m. By 10:30 p.m. somewhere between fifteen hundred and two thousand people stood on the front steps of the courthouse. "Innocent until proven guilty" was not on anybody's minds. They had come for blood. The mass of humanity now included nearly a hundred black men who had offered their services to the police but were rebuffed and asked to leave. The story goes that a white man approached a black veteran, who was carrying an army issue .45-caliber sidearm.

"N——, what are you doing with that pistol?"

"I'm going to use it if I need to."

"No, you give it to me."

"Like hell I will."

As the white man tried to take the gun away, shots were fired, and several more followed. A dozen people dropped. They would be the first casualties of what would become America's bloodiest race war. At daybreak the next day, June 1, 1921, an army of enraged whites rushed past the police and the armed black citizens and invaded the Greenwood District.

Churches, homes, and businesses burned. Innocent bystanders, from an elderly black couple to the man the Mayo brothers called "the most able Negro surgeon in America," were killed. Police, National Guardsmen, special "deputies," and even unauthorized whites removed black people from their homes and arrested them. They survived the riots but sat imprisoned in makeshift internment camps, powerless to stop the destruction of their homes.

Negro Wall Street burned down in two days during the summer of 1921. The Tulsa Race Massacre, as history would remember it, remains the worst of its kind in America's history. While thirty-nine people were officially reported to have lost their lives, estimates range to as high as three hundred. Anywhere from eight thousand to ten thousand people lost their homes, while thirty-five city blocks were destroyed in the carnage.

Fact and fiction went down in flames, leaving only ashes to assemble the truth of what happened and why. Yet no one dares deny the role that one of the city's most authoritative institutions played in instigating the massacre. "The *Tribune*, through its May 31 issue, was the single most important force in the creation of the lynch mob outside of the courthouse; anything Dick Rowland might have done was secondary," wrote Scott Ellsworth in *Death in a Promised Land*.

"Nab Negro for Attacking Girl in an Elevator." In eight words a single newspaper established final say over truth and justice, law and order, life and death. The mob acted of its own volition, but the trusted voice of the daily paper incited the violence. No retraction could clear away the spilled blood. No editorial could change the fact that black America's lone refuge, the Greenwood District, was now ash and dust.

For the city this was a horror, a national embarrassment. Magic City was supposed to be immune from this violence and terror. State history books largely ignored the events of those two days, and for decades Tulsa schoolchildren grew up without ever hearing about them. Tulsa Public Schools only started teaching about the Tulsa Race Massacre in 2012, ninety-one years later. When the fires died and the ashes blew away, the truth was buried for the sake of progress.

• • •

Tulsa moved on. Oil companies continued to pour in, and the skyline began to take shape. Oilmen the likes of Waite Phillips, Frank Phillips, William G. Skelly, Thomas Gilcrease, J. Paul Getty, and more made their names and established much of their empires in Tulsa. Many used their fabulous fortunes to build the city of their dreams.

In 1923, or only two years removed from the riots, Tulsa hosted the first International Petroleum Exposition (IPE). Oil barons from across the nation and around the world converged on Tulsa to buy and sell the most state-of-the-art production equipment. It was only natural the Oil Capital of the World would be the IPE's home. The world needed oil, and Tulsa had it in abundance.

Except for 1926, the IPE was held annually between 1923 and 1930. In its first few years, the event grew from a few thousand attendees to more than 120,000. It even welcomed a U.S. president. In 1927 President Calvin Coolidge opened the IPE from the White House, pulling a lever that simulated a gusher on the IPE grounds.

Thanks to the Great Depression and the Dust Bowl, the IPE was only held sporadically in the 1930s and was suspended indefinitely for eight years when the United States entered World War II. When the IPE returned in 1948, it attracted more than 300,000 visitors. America was eager to put the past twenty years of war and strife behind it. The IPE, with its celebration of progress and the energy that powered it, was the perfect event.

However, skyrocketing logistical and financial demands forced organizers to adopt a new strategy. With competition from similar tradeshows increasing, it was essential the IPE retained its marquee as the world's premier oil industry event. To provide ample time to prepare, the exposition's board of directors voted to hold the IPE only once every five years. It decided the next showcase would be held in May 1953. Billed as the "world's fair of the oil industry" and the "world's largest single industry show," the 1953 IPE was expected to attract more than 300,000 people and generate more than $100 million in potential economic impact. The world's eyes would be on Tulsa in what promised to be one of the biggest events in the city's history. This exposition was Tulsa's opportunity to show the world what a great American city—the Oil Capital of the World—looked like.

Tulsa was a great American city in all its glory and contradictions. But as with other great American cities from coast to coast, Tulsa was still two cities. One city championed the enormous, unprecedented wealth of the twentieth century and the beauty and majesty it had brought; the other city hid those people left behind in the unstoppable march toward progress. Tulsa was both the shining city on the hill and the dilapidated shanty town on the other side of the tracks.

Those who built this city, whose names still christen the landmarks, found their fortune buried under the plains. They dedicated their lives and wealth to transforming Tulsa into America's most beautiful city. By many measures they succeeded.

None of those men lived here, at Sixteen Hundred North Yale Avenue.

3

Little Girl Lost

Josie Warren woke up on Friday, March 13, to find Phyllis's bed empty, just as she had left it. It hadn't even been slept in, as if the little girl had just vanished into the night. Josie was scared now. Robert was not. Annoyed maybe but not scared. He told Josie he would go and look for Phyllis, but he took his time, helped himself to a little breakfast, and let his wife suffer in silence. Once he was good and ready, Robert went looking for his daughter. He told his wife that Phyllis was probably at Jimmy's house. Jimmy was the Warrens' second-eldest child and Buster's stepdad. Phyllis would oftentimes spend weekends there. It seemed to be the only place she could get her clothes cleaned and have a good meal. Robert said he would start there.

Robert was a simple man. Quiet, reserved. He kept to himself mostly. Even the few people he kept around he did not keep close. Nobody knew a whole lot about him, maybe because there wasn't a whole lot to know. Robert didn't seem to ask much of life and didn't get much out of it either. It was an arrangement he was comfortable with; it was all he'd ever known. Robert did well, too well to keep his family in such a place. Nobody knew what Warren did with his money, but he wasn't wearing it, eating it, or living in it. And except for buying them new clothes now and then, he certainly wasn't sharing it with his family members. Robert made good money at the steel mill and even better money running moonshine on the side. Prohibition had been a dear friend to Old Man Warren. Oklahoma had been dry since statehood in 1907. Will Rogers once quipped, "Okla-homans will vote dry as long as they can stagger to the polls." Not a small amount of them staggered away from Robert's place.

Bootlegging was a pretty lucrative business in those days. Some bootleggers even had business cards with their names and numbers on one side, and their current prices for half-pints, pints, fifths, and jugs on the other. There were plenty of beer bars in town, but if you were looking for something with a little more kick, you could join a private club with membership dues that were only a dollar.

Given his circumstances, one imagines Robert had a much simpler operation. Not that this was a bad thing. In fact, it probably worked to his advantage. Robert sold his moonshine in a part of town nobody ever bothered with much. It was a pretty nice setup for both buyer and seller. One could visit him on the outskirts of society, pick a poi-son, and be on his or her way with nobody being any wiser.

When Robert arrived at his son Jimmy's home, just a few doors down, Jimmy said he had not seen his sister since nine o'clock the night before. He said he figured she went home but mentioned to his dad that Phyllis sometimes stayed the night with Gertrude Young, a friend of hers from school. Gertrude didn't live too far away, and chances were she was over there.

Robert said he didn't have time to go looking for her. He said he had to get to work and was running late already. Phyllis could be any-where. This was nothing new. She ran off all the time. Robert wasn't worried. Phyllis would turn up. She always did.

Robert got home around five o'clock in the evening, same as he always did. He probably expected to find a warm meal waiting for him after a hard day's work; instead, he found his wife at the table, her eyes stained red with tears. Phyllis wasn't home, Josie said. It had been hours. Even if Phyllis had spent the night somewhere else, Josie said, she would have been home from school.

The Warrens didn't have a telephone. None of their neighbors did either, so Robert walked several blocks to the corner store where the family did their shopping and trading. Robert telephoned Phyllis's elementary school, William Cullen Bryant, named after the Amer-ican poet and journalist. Her teacher had already left for the night, but Robert was given her home phone number. It was another dead end. Phyllis wasn't at school that day, her teacher told Robert. She said she figured the little girl was sick.

Nobody had seen Phyllis for nearly twenty-four hours. She didn't tell anyone where she was going, what she was doing, or who she was with. She had just vanished. It wasn't strange for her to disappear, sometimes for days at a time—everybody knew that—but not like this. This felt different.

Robert took the downtown bus to the sheriff's office, which was located in the county courthouse. Robert told his story to the officer at the front desk, who called for Deputy J. B. Manley. Robert told his story again to Deputy Manley, who called in another officer, Deputy Houston Johnson, and Robert repeated his story for the third time. He told the deputies that nobody had seen or heard from his daughter for nearly a day. She wasn't at any of the places she usually went. And she had last been seen playing the night before with the strange Indian fellow Buster Youngwolfe.

Deputies Manley and Johnson listened patiently to Robert's story, keeping their ears and eyes open for inconsistencies or clues. Deputy Manley said he and Deputy Johnson would take Robert home and have a look around. Despite being a moonshiner, Warren thought nothing of going directly to law enforcement or of bringing them to his neighborhood.

The deputies searched the area. All they found were Phyllis's tiny, barefoot tracks beside the creek. She had been alone, as there was just one set of prints skipping carelessly along the stream. Her tracks were winding and whimsical. You could almost hear her little voice humming the tune in her head. The deputies lost her tracks about two blocks from her home. The footprints didn't prove anything, however. Phyllis could have made them at any time. She played without shoes often, for she was happiest in her bare feet. They found no other clues.

The sun was starting to set. Deputies Manley and Johnson made their rounds through the neighborhood, speaking to friends, family, and neighbors. Nobody recalled seeing Phyllis past 9:00 to 9:30 the night before. Some people did remember that she was wearing blue jeans, a shirtwaist blouse, and a yellow sweater but nothing else. When the deputies got to the Warrens' house, they asked her mother,

Josie, point-blank: Did she run away? Josie said she couldn't imagine such a thing, Phyllis's running away.

If Phyllis did run away, she didn't make preparations. She didn't even pack a comb or any clothes, according to her parents. Phyllis's school friends said she cared about her looks. Even though she was a tomboy who loved playing outside, Phyllis would never leave home without her vanity items.

Deputies Manley and Johnson returned to the sheriff's office with nothing to show for their search. Deputy Johnson telephoned the girl's description to the Missing Person's Bureau of the Tulsa Metropolitan Police Department and the Oklahoma Highway Patrol. Phyllis's description would be broadcast on the radio. It was all they could do at this point.

The deputies noticed that not only did nobody in the neighborhood know where Phyllis was but also nobody seemed to care. She had been gone for more than a day and left behind almost no trace. It was as though the Earth had just opened up and swallowed her whole. In the critical first hours after the child disappeared, her parents had not contacted the authorities. The deputies were competing with time and losing.

• • •

The authorities got their first lead the next morning, Saturday, March 14. The owner of a diner in Bartlesville heard Phyllis's description on the radio and contacted the sheriff's office, saying a girl matching her description had eaten at his place the night before. Bartlesville was about sixty miles north of town. Did she get that far on her own feet? There was no way. Somebody must have taken her.

Undersheriff Gene Maxey ordered Deputies Manley and George Mallard to investigate. Undersheriff Maxey maintained a stern, authoritarian air that even his superiors must have found intimidating. With a long, slender face leathered from years on the hunt and a cold stare that betrayed no emotion save determination, Undersheriff Maxey looked every bit the bird of prey he was.

Before they left, Deputies Manley and Mallard stopped by the Warren home to grab a photo of Phyllis. The Warrens probably didn't have many photos of their daughter, but they were able to find one to hand over.

The deputies arrived at the Bartlesville diner later that morning. The owner said a girl had stopped by the night before and ordered a plate of french fried potatoes. She'd been by herself, which the restaurant owner thought was odd, but he didn't give it a further thought until he heard the missing person's report. The deputies showed Phyllis's picture to the owner, who gave it a quick glance and shook his head. No, that wasn't the girl, he said. A dead end.

The deputies thanked the man for his time and made their way back to the car for the journey home. They'd driven an hour but were empty-handed and no closer to finding the girl than when they started. Deputy Mallard asked what they should do next. Deputy Manley said he wanted to go back to where they started, back to the neighborhood. He had a feeling.

The deputies returned to north Tulsa, photo in hand, and went door-to-door, questioning every household in the neighborhood. They searched the creek. They searched the fields. They searched every blade of dead, brown grass to find any sign of Phyllis. But there was none. However, the deputies weren't going to leave empty-handed. Not again.

Buster Youngwolfe had raised the deputies' suspicions from the start. It was nothing he said or did; they just had a gut feeling about him more than anything else. There was just something off about him. Buster was nervous and jittery the entire time they talked to him. It was a warm spring day, but he was shaking like a puppy. While he strained to appear calm, he only managed to look as if he was hiding something. With his darting eyes on a cherubic face, Buster resembled a little boy who had told a big lie.

A feeling wasn't much to go on, but it was more than the deputies had so far. Phyllis was still lost without a trace, and opportunity was vanishing by the hour; the deputies had no room for error. Buster knew something, and they were going to find out what it was. They brought him in for questioning.

Back at the sheriff's office, Buster didn't give them anything new, just the same story as everybody else's: He hadn't seen the girl since the night she disappeared, around 9:00 p.m. It was hard to believe that in a neighborhood full of people packed together more tightly than meat in a can, none of them remembered seeing Phyllis. Buster said the last time he had seen Phyllis, he had been smoking a cigarette on her parents' front porch. When they asked him where he was the night the girl disappeared, he said he'd gone to the picture show in Dawson.

Buster wasn't telling the truth—the deputies were sure of it—but they needed evidence to corroborate their instincts. They tried to get Buster to take a lie detector test. He refused, so they jailed him overnight and kept him for twenty-four hours, the longest they could without formally charging him. When twenty-four hours had passed and they were no closer than when they started, they had to let him go. The deputies didn't have the girl and didn't have any evidence, but they knew they had something with Buster Youngwolfe.

• • •

The streams left behind by the coal companies' strip-mining process were deep and wide. In some places, they were as wide as ten feet and as deep as thirty to forty feet. Years of rain and mud had made the water as thick and as black as the bottom of a gas station coffeepot. You could lose anything down there and never find it. Even a body.

Deputies Manley and Mallard came to Undersheriff Maxey with a suggestion: drag the strip pits. If Phyllis was down there, they would find her. Undersheriff Maxey agreed. The authorities called in Assistant Fire Chief Charles Conger to spearhead the mission and Police Officers Jim Starts, Johnny Cole, and Ray Williams to handle the assignment.

For three days, the men floated the fetid black waters. They dragged ten-foot-long poles with sharp iron hooks on the end to grab whatever they could. Wading through this wide and winding urban swamp was a slow, tedious process, but the waters had nothing to hide. Phyllis wasn't there.

On March 15, 1953, three days after Phyllis's disappearance, *Tulsa World* subscribers opened their Sunday newspapers to read the first print accounts of this strange story. The headline read "Tulsa Girl Is Still Missing: No Progress Is Made in Search by Deputies." This short account described the fruitless investigation and included this troubling, but perhaps unsurprising, admission: "DEPUTY STATEMENT. The deputy (Houston Johnson) added that the child's parents, nor any

Little Girl Lost

of the relatives living in the squalid district, seemed very concerned over the girl's disappearance. 'But none of them have offered any suggestions of what might have happened to her,' he said."

While the statement seems garbled, perhaps this was intentional. The deputies had not found the girl after three days of searching, so if they could emphasize that nobody in the neighborhood cared, it removed the sense of urgency surrounding their own failure. Yet that does not change the troubling reality that nobody—not even her family and especially not her father, Robert—really seemed to care.

Phyllis Jean was gone, having vanished like a sprite into the night. The sheriff's office and the police were not any closer to finding Phyllis than when they had first started, only now the public was aware of their failure.

• • •

On Monday, March 16, the *Tulsa World* published a story with the headline "Missing Girl Believed Seen: Reported Near Dewey; Left Home Thursday." Dewey resident George Taylor had reported seeing a girl matching Phyllis's description and drove fifty miles south to Tulsa to make his report. Taylor said he saw her around 5:00 p.m. Saturday, just north of Dewey, "looking back all the time like she was scared." She was walking along U.S. Highway 75, the route into Caney, Kansas, but this road led nowhere for the authorities. While Deputy Johnson believed that Taylor was "thoroughly convinced" he saw Phyllis, he didn't. Whoever this other girl was, she wasn't Phyllis.

On Tuesday, March 17, St. Patrick's Day, the *Tulsa Tribune* published its first report on the search. Beside the headline "Officers Drag Pits for Girl" was a haunting silhouette of the three police officers coursing through the murky strip pits. The stream was wider than the boat and stretched beyond the photographer's lens into an endless void. Brush shadowed the searchers from both sides, making the image look as if it had been taken in some faraway jungle, a place people could only read about in *National Geographic*. Yet these foreign-looking swamplands were just a few miles to the north in the slums of this serene American city.

The girl hadn't even been found, but the narrative surrounding Buster was already being formed. "A young Indian character who lives in the neighborhood was jailed over the week-end [sic] by sheriffs' deputies for questioning about the disappearance. Although he refused to take a police lie detector test, he was freed after 24 hours in the county jail."

The "Indian character" was Buster. While *Tulsa Tribune* readers would not hear about the case again for two more weeks, the paper had planted the bitter seed of suspicion.

When dragging the pits failed to find Phyllis, the authorities began to grow desperate. By now both major local newspapers had covered the story, and the public was now very aware of it. The authorities decided to take drastic measures and brought in pumps to drain the swamps. If she was down there, then this way they would find her. They found nothing. Just junk. Years and years of rotting wood and garbage had gathered at the bottom of the stream, which served as a time capsule to an era that had left nothing behind but trash.

"She could be anywhere," Deputy Johnson said to the *Tulsa World*, a startling admission of failure from the deputy who had by now become the public face of the search. The sheriff's office, sworn to serve and protect the citizens—all citizens—could not find a missing child in this forgotten area in north Tulsa. As the days turned into weeks with no sign of Phyllis Jean Warren, the grim reality emerged: The little girl was probably never coming home, at least not alive.

Bitter frustration faded quickly into acceptance, as Phyllis's file was consigned to the missing person's cabinet in police headquarters. Phyllis's file was cast aside, much as she had been all her life. It had now been two weeks since Phyllis disappeared. At least one member of the Warren family still clung to hope. Man's methods had failed; now it was time to consult the dead.

• • •

"The law can't seem to help us. We can't help ourselves," said Mae Ellen Warren, who was married to Phyllis's older brother Kenneth.

The Reverend Leontine Bryant listened to the younger woman's words and nodded. Barely. Reverend Bryant wasted no motion. At her age, she couldn't afford to. The elderly matron and minister knew the girl was lost and no doubt anticipated her family would come looking for help.

Mae Ellen arrived at Reverend Bryant's home in a state of desperation. Even more than the other people in the neighborhood, Mae Ellen had been influenced by the Universal Church of the Master and was spellbound by the quiet charisma of its local practitioner.

Reverend Bryant had been the wife of the late Delmar DeForest Bryant, a respected figure in his faith who was known worldwide as an author and alchemist. As a writer, the late Bryant was prolific, having penned such provocative works as *The Divine Symbols*, *The Light of Life or The Mastery of Death*, and *Art of Alchemy or the Generation of Gold*. The late Bryant had been the son of a prominent Kansas City family. For years, he had taught math, music, languages, and philosophy before changing course to follow his true passion—the occult.

Bryant's work brought him comfort, if not fortune, though it did encourage the generosity of others—namely, O. J. Lea. The wealthy Norwegian industrialist claimed Bryant's books comforted him in times of need, so he sent the Bryant family $100 a month, or more than $1,500 today. Bryant's focus was on spiritual concerns, not material ones. He lived in a tar paper shack, just as his neighbors did, and next to the home shared by his wife, Leontine, and the couple's adopted son, Oliver Mueler. Delmar Bryant died in 1939 at age eighty, leaving behind $14,850, or the equivalent of almost $250,000 today. His modest fortune was enough that his widow didn't have to live in this neighborhood anymore.

Yet she stayed. The shepherd does not abandon her flock. Rev. Leontine Bryant carried on her late husband's work, serving as a liaison between the living and the dead. At a time long before new age spiritualism would be sold at bookstores, coffee shops, and shopping malls, Reverend Bryant was an iconoclast. As a minister in the Universal Church of the Master, she preached about the Divine Father-Mother God. She taught that individual existence, identity, and memory carry on after the transitional state, death. The residents who lived here on the residue of society came to Reverend Bryant when all hope was lost, just as Mae Ellen had tonight, Sunday, March 29, more than two weeks after Phyllis had disappeared.

In the dark living room where she'd spent so many sessions seeking out spiritual guidance, Mae Ellen now pleaded for Reverend Bryant to help find Phyllis. While the specific details of this encounter were never recorded, it may have played out this way: After patiently listening to the Mae Ellen's story, Reverend Bryant paused and stared intently into the young woman's tired, frightened eyes. The spiritualist's face, which had seen much in her many years, was likely weathered by time, though her eyes remained wide and vibrant, deep vessels brimming with the secrets she'd brought with her from beyond.

Reverend Bryant didn't say anything; she didn't even move. She just sat there and stared. Deeper, deeper, and deeper, past Mae Ellen's eyes and into the void. Did she see something? What?

The ticking of the clock broke the silence. It was a monotonous, morbid sound that shook the home to its foundation and echoed through Mae Ellen's skull.

Tick. Tick. Tick.

Seconds passed, now minutes. Time was relative in this congested space, for mere moments lasted forever. Mae Ellen's fingers clawed the table.

Where was Phyllis?

The ticking taunted her.

Where was Phyllis?

The old woman stared into the void like a wraith.

Where was Phyllis?

Mae Ellen wanted to scream, but her vocal cords were frozen.

Where was Phyllis?

The old woman's eyes widened, and she cried out, "It's come to me like a thunderclap!" She returned from wherever she had been and looked down at Mae Ellen.

"Quick, give me a pencil and paper!" Reverend Bryant spoke with an urgency the younger woman had never seen from her before. Mae Ellen did as she was told, fumbling through her purse and finding a pencil and paper. With withered flesh that clung to bony fingers, the spiritualist meticulously sketched a map. When she finished, she drew a waving line down the middle.

"This is Dawson Road, the path Phyllis followed," she said, scratching in harsh lines for the woods and a box for Phyllis's home. She drew ovals and a large X at the edge of the trail to represent the end of Phyllis's journey. "I have never been to this place before, but I found another missing child several years ago," said Reverend Bryant. Phyllis didn't disappear from her home. She had never left.

"She will be found in a crevice in the dumping ground, not far from her home," Reverend Bryant said, her weathered lips trembling as she spoke the words. "Phyllis will not be alive when she is found. She will be buried in a crevice. She has been murdered. Her body will be lying face up."

Mae Ellen's heart collapsed in her chest. Before finishing her revelation, Reverend Bryant added one more detail: The person who had killed Phyllis wore dirty overalls.

Dirty overalls. That detail meant nothing. Everybody wore dirty overalls here. Rev. Leontine Bryant, though, had confirmed what Mae Ellen and the family had feared most: Phyllis had been murdered. But if someone had taken Phyllis, if someone had killed her, then that meant the person must have been close to her, either a friend or a family member. Otherwise, he or she never would have gotten near her, for Smokey would not have allowed a stranger near his girl.

Mae Ellen raced home. Armed with Reverend Bryant's map, members of the Warren family searched the dumping grounds where the spiritualist said Phyllis would be found. Dead tree roots rose from the ground like skeletal fingers clawing through the earth, as if they belonged to bodies that refused to stay buried. The family had searched this place many times, and so had the police, to no avail. But they tried again, tearing through the thorns and clinging desperately to hope yet terrified of what they would find.

Nothing. They found nothing. Phyllis wasn't there.

The next morning, Monday, March 30, the family telephoned the *Tulsa Tribune*, detailing this latest development. A reporter and the police arrived on the scene and interviewed Reverend Bryant. She had nothing more to say.

"I can't make heads or tails out of the darn thing," said County Investigator William A. "Ace" Lang, holding the map. The map was all they had, but as with everything else, it led nowhere.

• • •

Robert Warren stumbled out of his home on the morning of Thursday, April 2, 1953. It was easy to get a bit stir crazy in this place, especially now. Phyllis had been gone three weeks, and Old Man Warren probably didn't see much use hoping anymore. He was never close to his daughter, or any of his kids for that matter, but he couldn't help but notice how it affected Josie.

"Reckon I'll look for salad greens," he said. With food being scarce, Robert would hunt for the poke greens that grew in a ravine down by the creek. Robert called Smokey, and the two went scrounging just before noon.

He wasn't gone long. While hunting for the greens, Robert Warren found something else. He burst onto the porch and ran through the door.

"Smokey found her," Robert said. "Smokey found Phyllis."

4

Manhunt

It made no sense.

Robert Warren had out been hunting greens near the ravine around 11:40 a.m., just as he'd done hundreds of mornings before. But this morning was different. Robert said Smokey had started barking and kept barking. Robert had never seen the dog more agitated. The calm, docile shepherd was suddenly as wild as a mad dog, nearly pulling Robert's arm off his shoulder as he dragged him across the field. The dog acted as though he was responding to a command, as if he was answering the voice of someone calling for him.

Robert told the authorities that he followed Smokey across the field and toward the brush pile. As soon as they arrived at the spot, Smokey's back hair stiffened. The dog sniffed the ground and began digging furiously at the roots of the upturned tree. The dog shot gobs of dirt onto Robert with every thrust of his paws. What was Smokey after? He did not dig for long before Robert saw Phyllis's blue jeans.

There she was, right where Reverend Bryant said she'd be. Right where family, friends, and the authorities had already looked so many times before. After weeks of waiting and wishing, clinging to hope and then succumbing to reality, Robert found his daughter's small, broken body buried just a few blocks from her home, beneath a pile of weeds and limbs, in dirt so shallow that even a dog could dig her out.

No, it didn't make any sense at all.

Robert Warren raced home to tell his wife that he'd found their daughter's dead body buried in the dirt. In this heart-wrenching moment, Josie confronted the callous reality that a mother's ever-hopeful heart could never prepare itself for: Her child was dead.

Whatever Josie's reaction, Robert didn't stay. He immediately ran to the grocery store and called the police. A police sergeant named Jimmy Jackson answered the phone and told Warren to stay calm and wait there. Sergeant Jackson ordered the dispatcher to rush the nearest cars to the scene. Field Sgt. Burg Hughes and Det. Ray Jones heard the report and sped to the store in separate cars, their screaming sirens piercing through the calm spring morning like a blade.

The police met Warren at the grocery store and drove him to the brush pile. Borrowing a spade from a neighbor, they began digging. They didn't dig for long. Blue jeans. A red checkered shirt. The legs and arms of a little girl. Finally, her face.

"It's Phyllis," Warren said.

It was Phyllis once. Now? Now she was something else entirely. What was left of her freckled, fair skin would have faded to a ghostly white, turning her once-rosy hue into a pale-blue and placid mask. Etched onto her vacant stare was the realization that she was going to die and that the last thing she would ever see was the face of her killer.

Detective Jones radioed police headquarters and was ordered to stop digging. Det. Chief Harold Haus, Commissioner Jay L. Jones, and County Investigator Ace Lang would lead the removal of Phyllis's body.

As moths are drawn to a flame, curiosity seekers followed the sirens to their source. They arrived by the hundreds, turning the slums into a circus. Police at the scene were ordered to hold back the spectators, but the mob continued to expand. The mass of humanity and their hastily parked cars caused a traffic jam, preventing the police from accessing the area. By the time the other authorities had arrived, the crowd had swelled to nearly a thousand people.

Under the command of Detective Chief Haus, Commissioner Jones, and Investigator Lang, the police began digging, carefully excavating the dirt surrounding the body. The curious onlookers watched in tense anticipation. If they came for a morbid spectacle, then they got one, though it took an hour before the police finally unearthed Phyllis.

Phyllis's body was now fully exposed. Lt. Harry L. Stege ordered that the body be removed, and *Tulsa World* photographer Jack Moncrief documented the gruesome sight. Phyllis was buried in her blue jeans and blouse, the same ones she had been wearing the night she had disappeared on March 13. Phyllis was buried in a perversion of the fetal position, on her back, with her knees drawn up to her stomach and with her left arm folded across her chest. All the playfulness she had displayed in life had been drained from her body like air from a balloon, leaving behind only a broken lump of flesh and bones.

She looked as if she'd been dead for months. Her body was caked head to toe in mud, making her look like a mummy. She was badly decomposed, and much of her face had rotted away from exposure. Only her eyes were spared. Her blue plastic belt was tied tightly around her neck, and her panties were stuffed into her hip pocket. They were stained with blood.

The police held back the anxious mob, which grew restless knowing the girl had been found. They'd come to see a body, the body of that missing girl they had been reading about in the papers. All they could see were the backs of the police officers who pulled her from her makeshift grave.

Phyllis's body was not all that the police found. Three beer cans were buried beside her body, each opened in a brutish manner, as somebody had clumsily poked three slits into each with a knife. Despite what her parents had said, Phyllis had taken a pocket comb with her after all, and it was in a case buried next to her. There was also a green rubber frog, the kind with a voice box that croaked when squeezed. It was just a silly little toy, the kind meant for a child even younger than Phyllis.

Phyllis's body was sent to Whisenhunt Funeral Home so the police physician, Dr. Lee Gentry, could examine her. Dr. Gentry did not perform a full autopsy, as was standard procedure, but did a cursory examination to determine the cause of death. His professional conclusion was obvious to plain sight: The eleven-year-old girl had been strangled to death with her blue plastic belt. Given the signs of genital injury, Dr. Gentry added, "there is not much doubt she had been raped." However, if any semen samples were collected or observed, they were not reported.

Phyllis Jean Warren was lost and now had been found but not in the way anybody had wanted or expected. It was a horror for the citizens of Tulsa and an embarrassment for the authorities sworn to protect them. How could the authorities let this happen? How had this child been missing for three weeks, only to be found buried in a brush pile just a few blocks from her home? None of it made sense.

The discovery of Phyllis's corpse set off one of the biggest manhunts in Tulsa history. The authorities had finally found the girl, but her secrets were lost with her. Who killed her and why were still mysteries, and the authorities had no more time to lose.

It was April 2, 1953, Holy Thursday. Phyllis would never see another Easter Sunday. After twenty-one days of fruitless searching for the girl, finding her killer would take a minor miracle.

• • •

The authorities had a body, a smattering of evidence—three cans, a comb, and a toy found at the burial site—and the unusual, some may even say improbable, circumstances of Phyllis's discovery. Troubling questions remained. How did Robert or, as he put it, the dog find the body in a place where many people had already looked? How did so many others miss it? Nobody had any answers. Almost nobody.

As soon as the body was removed, Undersheriff Maxey personally visited the one person who seemed to have any idea about what was going on. The person who knew where to find the body—Rev. Leontine Bryant.

One imagines Reverend Bryant's home was nothing like her neighbors'. While their shacks lacked even the basic necessities, her home was probably cluttered with eclectic books and trinkets she and her late husband had collected over a lifetime. Though dead for more than a decade, Delmar Bryant's apparition would have hung over the house like a morning fog. This would not have been the sort of place the buttoned-up and by-the-book Undersheriff Maxey, a man who looked as if he had been born in his Sunday suit, would expect to find himself nor where he hoped to stay long.

Undersheriff Maxey didn't know much about Reverend Bryant's abilities and almost certainly didn't care. What interested him was what else the spiritualist knew. Whatever power she possessed, be it earthly or otherworldly, the fact remained that she had been right, while everyone else had been so lost they had all but abandoned hope.

Now he wanted to know, could she provide a description of the killer?

Reverend Bryant didn't even pause. She matter-of-factly told Undersheriff Maxey that Phyllis's killer was a relative. She had nothing more to offer him. No height, weight, distinguishing marks, relation, or even gender—just that the killer was related to Phyllis. "Related" does not necessarily mean by blood. It was more than Undersheriff Maxey had otherwise, so he ran with it.

The sheriff's office and Tulsa Police Department took statements from forty different people that day. Some people the authorities sought out and questioned, while others came to them. Much of the information contained details they had already heard numerous times before, and some statements were so fantastic they weren't of any use. However, there were some interesting leads.

One came from a man named George Potts, a taxi driver. Potts walked into police headquarters that evening, about eight hours after Phyllis's body was found, and asked to see Det. Chief Harold Haus. Potts said that he had been out of town for about three weeks and therefore didn't know that a girl had gone missing. An unlikely story but at this point the police had little else to go on, so they entertained Mr. Potts's account.

Potts claimed that at 9:20 p.m. on March 12, the night Phyllis disappeared, he dropped a customer off at the airport and was cutting back on North Yale Avenue around where the Warrens lived. He said he saw a parked car, with a man leaning out of the right side and talking to a girl. Potts thought it was funny, given the man was talking to the girl on a lonely stretch of road where there were no houses—the perfect place if you're doing something you don't want anybody to see.

Potts said he stopped a hundred yards away from the scene and watched it unfold. Potts claimed that when he started to turn his car around the man pulled the girl into the car, slammed on the gas, and shot past him. Potts said he knew he should have reported it, but he immediately got a radio call to pick up a passenger, and then he left town the next morning. Now, three weeks later, he was here in Haus's office and apologizing for not reporting what appeared to be a kidnapping, one that might have led to the murder of a child.

Detective Chief Haus wasn't interested in hearing the man's contrition. He wanted to know if Potts had the make of the car or the license plate number. Potts said it was a 1952 Buick, dark blue or maybe green, though it was hard to tell at nighttime. It had a Tulsa County tag, but Potts said all he caught was the first number on the plate. It wasn't much, but it was something. Detective Chief Haus began firing questions at him. How old was the girl? What did she look like? What was she wearing? Potts said she was just a kid and couldn't have been more than thirteen or fourteen. She wasn't facing him, so that was all he knew.

Haus called Det. Jack Purdie and Det. Lozier Brown into his office. He gave them Potts's report and sent them to the neighborhood to see if anyone had seen a green or dark blue car or, better yet, if anyone owned one.

One person had seen the car many times—Phyllis's school friend Gertrude Young. Young told the detectives that a man with a green car had tried to pick her and Phyllis up the day that Phyllis had disappeared. All she could remember about him was that the man had a limp. In short order, the police tracked down and questioned two men with green cars matching Potts's description.

One man, a pale and slender bachelor, admitted that he talked to the girls but said he was just being friendly. The man was so nervous talking to the police that he was near tears. He claimed he couldn't have taken Phyllis, as he was at church choir practice that night with his mother. His pastor confirmed his story.

The other man was a traveling wholesale grocery salesman. Young said she had seen him many times. According to her, the salesman hung out at a drugstore near their school and bought the girls treats. In exchange for little gifts of candy, he asked the girls to go on rides with him. Phyllis was his favorite.

The police found out the salesman's name (the police never released his real name but gave the fake name "Jack Summers" to the press) and that he was out of town that day but due back the next morning. The next day the salesman was brought in to police headquarters for questioning. The man was so frightened he was shaking. He claimed he had no idea what the detectives were talking about and that there had been a mix-up.

Detective Chief Haus was patient, even accommodating, and apologized to the man if there had been a mistake. He asked the salesman if he would be willing to go with Detectives Purdie and Brown to the school and let the children identify him. The man never expected to be caught, much less to be responding to accusations of predatory behavior. He reached for a cigarette across the cold metal table, shaking so violently he could barely light it. The man inhaled a lungful of smoke to soothe his nerves.

"Look, Chief, I may have done some things wrong, but you can't hang a killing on me," he said. "Yes, I have gotten some of the girls to play hooky, but I had nothing to do with that girl's death."

The salesman was shaking, as the cigarette dangled perilously from his lips. The police could see he wasn't telling everything he knew. Detective Chief Haus asked him where he was that night, what he was doing, and who he was with.

"If I tell you all about it," said the salesman, "can you protect me and the other person?"

"Tell your story," said Detective Chief Haus.

The salesman had been meeting with a young girl. She was sixteen years old. The night George Potts spotted him was not the first time he had picked her up, and it was not the last.

"For heaven's sake, talk to her," the salesman said, stammering out his words in a stream of spit and tears. "But don't get her in a jam or me either."

The police did talk to her. The salesman's story held up, as the girl admitted she had secretly been seeing him. The night of March 12 they had been at a drive-in, and a witness corroborated their story. Whatever was happening between the grown man and the teenage girl didn't concern the police; they only wanted to confirm the fact that she wasn't Phyllis. The police department's best lead, their only lead, crumbled into dust.

A day had passed and despite talking to several people, the police department was no closer to finding Phyllis's killer than when they started. It was as if they were searching for her body all over again. Frustrated to the point of desperation, Detective Chief Haus called the sheriff's office to relay the story. Haus probably expected that the sheriff's office was no further along than the police department in the investigation.

He was mistaken. The authorities at the sheriff's office believed they had found their man.

5

Killer

The authorities were having a busy day. The courthouse had been a madhouse ever since noon, as county officials had to handle both the fallout from finding the missing girl's body and the media circus that followed. The afternoon *Tulsa Tribune* would be out in hours, detailing the bungled investigation that had failed to find the girl until she was already dead and then only thanks to the help of a curious dog and her poke green–hunting father. The *Tulsa World* would be on Tulsans' doorsteps the first thing the next morning with a similar account. The authorities couldn't afford another front-page embarrassment, so their every waking moment was now consumed with finding the girl's killer.

All hands were on deck. County Investigators Ace Lang and Forrest Castle, Deputies Lewis Downing and George Mallard, and Assistant County Attorneys Robert B. Simms, Dorothy Young, Ed Parks, and J. Howard Edmondson took statements "from quite a few persons," totaling forty in all. It was a grueling gauntlet, made even more stressful by the knowledge that likely one among the forty interviewees either killed Phyllis or knew who did. Yet despite everybody they talked to, every story they heard, and the fact that the girl's father had found her in a place they had already looked, the authorities had one lead that they just couldn't—or wouldn't—let go. It was the one they had circled since before Phyllis was even found.

Jimmy Warren, Phyllis's twenty-eight-year-old brother, was living about an hour and a half south of Tulsa in McAlester as a new resident of the Oklahoma State Penitentiary. Jimmy was sent there about a week after Phyllis disappeared because his probation on child abandonment charges had been revoked. Deputy Downing went to McAlester to bring Jimmy back for questioning, making the nearly hundred-mile journey around midnight, April 2. He was bringing Jimmy in for questioning ostensibly as a potential suspect—he was still at home when Phyllis vanished—but, more important, as a witness. Jimmy had said something weeks ago that still stuck with officials.

"Buster and Phyllis were playing in the yard," Jimmy had said in mid-March, when Phyllis went missing. "They played together a lot. He was sort of a big brother to her. That was the last time I saw her."

Buster Youngwolfe, Phyllis's twenty-one-year-old stepnephew, was a strange character. He had been acting suspiciously all along, as if even he didn't believe the story he was telling. His alibi was that he had gone to the movies the night Phyllis vanished. When the authorities locked him up for twenty-four hours the weekend after Phyllis went missing, they reported his temporary incarceration to the paper, which had published his picture on the front page. Now that Phyllis had been found dead, Buster was back on their radar.

Jimmy wasn't the only Warren who was suspicious of Buster. Old man Robert Warren, Buster's grandfather by marriage, told Det. Ray Jones something chilling. "A long time ago Jimmy warned us about his stepson Buster," said Warren. "He said, 'Watch out for Phyllis when she's around Buster.' And, you know, Buster didn't even help us look for Phyllis when she was missing."

These two Warrens had nothing nice to say about Buster, even the one who knew him best—his roommate and stepfather, Jimmy. There could've been any number of personal factors at play. Maybe Robert was prejudiced against the Cherokees, which seems odd given Jimmy was married to Buster's mother, but it wasn't beyond the realm of possibility. Or maybe they just didn't trust the quiet, taciturn Buster. Buster didn't talk much, but they could tell he had a million thoughts running behind his big brown eyes. What was he thinking about anyway? Phyllis? No, the two Warren men didn't trust Buster one bit. Their undisguised hostility filtered over to the authorities as well.

Buster had acted suspiciously when he was questioned and jailed three weeks earlier. For one thing, he refused to take a lie detector test. The authorities wondered, Why would a man who was telling the truth, a man who had nothing to hide, refuse to take a lie detector test? He also didn't help look for Phyllis, even while the rest of the family turned the neighborhood upside down. Buster's story about being at the movies didn't sound right either. The family never trusted him with Phyllis, and now she was dead. As far as anyone remembered, Buster was the last person to see her alive.

Also earlier that day, April 2, authorities learned that around noon, as soon as Buster heard that Phyllis's body had been found, he told his brother, Clarence, and his mother, Bessie, "Well, guess I had better get cleaned up because they'll be looking for me." Buster went to the hand pump to wash the dirt off his hands and face and then to the Dawson post office to mail a letter. Deputies Manley and R. B. Jones met him on his way back home and arrested him.

The deputies first took him to the burial site—before taking him downtown, before making any charges, and even before asking him any questions. Thus, Buster's picture was one of the many that photographer Jack Moncrief took at the scene. In the photo Buster is standing over the ravine, looking into the mangled, dismembered timber where Phyllis's body was found. He looks nonchalant, with his hands on his hips, almost as if he had been expecting all of this. Depending on one's point of view, he looked as though either he had done something wrong and been caught, or he was so used to being blamed that he was taking it in stride.

The front-page headline for that afternoon's *Tulsa Tribune* was blunt: "Body of Missing Girl, 11, Found Strangled." On the left side of the headline was a picture of the crowd gathered around the burial site. Beneath the headline was a picture of Phyllis, one of the last ever taken. She looks sad, as if the child did not know whether she was allowed to smile. The account by *Tulsa Tribune* reporter Roy Hanna briefly covered the investigation and how Phyllis's father had found the body. The reporter made sure to include another piece of information: "An Indian, 21 years old, who Deputy Sheriff Lloyd Miller said was the last person to see Phyllis Jean Warren alive, was held for questioning early this afternoon about her murder."

Tulsa Tribune readers who were horrified that a girl in their town had been kidnapped and murdered could rest easy that night; a suspect was in custody. The narrative was forming: A child had been murdered, and the villain, a twenty-one-year-old Indian, had been found.

Buster was taken to the county jail and questioned again about where he was March 12, the night Phyllis disappeared.

"We went downtown and drank beer, got home about midnight," Buster said, his recalcitrant tone no more convincing than before. His twenty-first birthday was the next day, March 13, and he was celebrating with a few people close to him. Why had he lied about going to the movies? Buster said that he lied because he was on probation for breaking into a couple of grocery stores, and he wasn't supposed to be out drinking. If he were caught, then he would have been sent to prison. Yet here he was, facing accusations for a far more serious crime.

County Investigator Ace Lang wrote down the names of Buster's reported drinking companions: Ellis Youngwolfe, his father; Clarence Youngwolfe, his brother; and Milford Williams, a friend and neighbor.

"Ask them, they'll tell you," said Buster.

The officers did just that. None of Buster's drinking companions remembered his going out with them that night. Each said they'd been drinking since noon that day, with Buster in tow. But as far as Buster's going out with them later that night, the last night Phyllis was seen alive, nobody could remember for certain. Maybe he was there, maybe he wasn't. Each had been drinking heavily, but it was three weeks ago, so it was hard to remember. A lot had happened since then, to put it mildly.

Though the three men said they could not remember if Buster was there, the county officials recorded statements from each saying definitively that Buster was not with them. Williams's recollection about that night was especially hazy, as he had been quite drunk. The authorities helped him with his story, filling in his memory gaps with details from Ellis's and Clarence's accounts. Foggy memories were recorded as definitive fact: Buster was not drinking with them the night that Phyllis disappeared.

The authorities told Buster that each of his supposed drinking companions said Buster wasn't there. After hearing that his father, his brother, and his friend all denied drinking with him that night,

Buster became frightened. He finally did what the authorities wanted him to do all along; he agreed to take a lie detector test.

But Lt. Harry Stege refused to administer the test "due to the subject's condition." Buster was "scared and tired and generally unfit to be given any kind of test without rest." If Buster was expecting to rest, though, he was sorely mistaken. His interrogation wasn't over. It was just getting started.

• • •

Midnight, Friday, April 3. It was a little more than twelve hours since Robert had found Phyllis's body. Now Buster sat in the dimly lit interrogation room, the only light coming from a single bulb in the ceiling. It could have been day or night, as far as Buster knew. County officials had been questioning him nonstop for hours. Now he existed in the dream state between asleep and awake. He was tired, he was hungry, and he was flailing. "He's told seven different stories," one of his interrogators told reporters while taking a break.

Buster got no breaks. He was forced to stay in the room and withstand the onslaught of questions, one by one by one.

"I don't know anything about the girl," he told Det. Ray Jones. "I was downtown having a few beers when she disappeared."

"Why didn't you help look for her?"

"She'd stayed out all night before," said Buster. "I thought the Warrens were just on another goose chase."

The officers never bothered checking with any of the taverns Buster claimed to have visited. They already had statements from Buster's father, brother, and neighbor saying he wasn't drinking with them. Buster also had lied once before about going to the movies. Buster's wife, Betty, didn't help his case, and all she did was tell the truth. "He was gone from home from about eight to ten that night," Betty told Undersheriff Maxey. She mentioned that when he came home, he had mud on his pants, both on the knees and the rear.

"Buster, your wife said you came in the house that night with your pants muddy on the knees," said Investigator Lang.

"The boys let me out of the car on Tecumseh Street," said Buster. "I walked across a field and fell down in the mud."

When Investigator Lang asked how he got mud on the rear of his pants, Buster said he'd had too much to drink. When he slipped and fell, he had landed on his backside.

The interrogation lasted for hours, all through the night and well into the next morning, not that Buster could tell what time it was. The names, the faces, and the voices of his interrogators were blurring as well. There was no good cop, bad cop routine. They were all the same. It was a blur of authority figures, each asking questions Buster had answered a thousand times before. One interrogator would leave the room, and another one would enter, a revolving door designed to give the authorities a breather while Buster sat there gasping.

Still Buster wouldn't budge. From the authorities' perspective, he was just a stubborn kid. Stupid, really, to stick to his story, even though with each passing hour it became more obvious that he had nothing to offer but a pack of lies. And they kept going back to the same demand.

"We want to give you a lie detector test before you go," said one of his interrogators.

"Not tonight, I'm tired and scared. I don't know what kind of answers would turn up," said Buster, pleading. "Please don't hold me. My wife and baby, they have no food."

But the authorities had no intention of stopping, especially not now that Buster was starting to break.

James Howard Edmondson took over the interrogation that Friday morning. Edmondson was the chief prosecutor in the office of County Attorney Robert L. Wheeler. Born and raised less than an hour away in Muskogee, Edmondson had the restless energy of a small-town boy whose surroundings were too meek for his ambitions. After a stint in the U.S. Army Air Forces from 1942 to 1945, he completed his law degree from the University of Oklahoma and briefly practiced law in his hometown. But being a country lawyer was never in the cards. Edmondson moved with his wife and kids up to Tulsa to work in criminal prosecution—being a defender of the people was a nice narrative—and at just twenty-seven years old was the heir apparent to the county attorney.

With his slicked-back black hair, sharp, pointed features, and wide, narrow eyes, Edmonson resembled a bird of prey. Edmondson smiled with the cool self-assurance of a man with a date with destiny. Edmondson was ambitious, more ambitious than his present position could satisfy. His appetite for acclaim was ravenous, and right now he had the main suspect for the highest-profile murder case in Tulsa sitting right in front of him, dangling like a worm.

"You think you've got me, don't you?" Buster said.

Edmondson did. Buster's vaguely threatening, bellicose tone didn't scare Edmonson. In fact, he probably liked it. He had a reputation as a bare-knuckle boxer when facing down defendants on the witness stand. This was no different. Edmondson had stared enough guilty men in the eyes to know that an animal always bites back hardest when it's in a corner. He had Buster in a corner right now.

"Buster, would you be willing to take a lie detector test?" said Edmondson. Buster refused, so the interrogation continued.

The authorities believed they had good reason to distrust Buster. Truth was, Buster had been getting into trouble since the beginning. His police record started when he just twelve years old. Police found the preteen sleeping in a doorway in west Tulsa, having run away from home, and trespassing on someone's property. Buster was arrested and sent to a boys' home as punishment. His mother, Bessie, took him home a week later, no doubt hoping the experience would scare him away from any future misdeeds. She would be mistaken.

On Monday, September 25, 1944, the thirteen-year-old Buster and some other boys were arrested for breaking into a school and vandalizing the place. This time they sent Buster to the Chilocco Indian School, about seven miles north of Newkirk, Oklahoma, on the Oklahoma-Kansas border. Not every student at Chilocco was as rebellious as Buster was. Most had no marks against them, save the fact they were born Native American in a society that didn't know what to do with them.

Founded in 1884 in then Oklahoma Territory, the Chilocco Indian School was a prominent part of the larger progressive social movement aimed at "civilizing" Native American children. By the 1940s when Buster was sent there, thousands of children had been through Chilocco's doors. Its focus was on vocational training, which both activists and social scientists saw as a way to direct the course of society by fashioning the worker's skills to meet the needs of industry.

Native American children were not trained for the needs of urban, factory-style, industrialized society but for small-scale, rural crafts-manship: masonry, blacksmithing, carpentry, and other individual-ized trades. Native American schools across the nation focused on developing skills suitable for rural farm life. The educational estab-lishment believed the Native Americans' proper place in society was in providing manual labor in rural areas to support America's agrar-ian economy.

Training Native American children in a trade wasn't the school's sole aim. After centuries of killing and exiling Native peoples, the goal of schools such as Chilocco was comparably tame—to rid Native American children of their Native tendencies. The so-called pas-sionate vision of the social reformers was to send children to these Indian schools, where they'd shed their respective tribal identities, learn a skill, and become valuable, if not valued, members of soci-ety. But grand visions tend to crumble when faced with the realities of human nature. Chilocco and other Indian schools unintention-ally deepened the children's tribal affiliations and even helped them develop a pan-Indian identity. The reformers' social experiment didn't work on Buster either, though not necessarily for the same reason.

Buster never celebrated his Cherokee heritage, but he never tried to hide it either. With his black, velvet hair and copper-colored eyes, he couldn't even if he wanted to. To Buster being Cherokee was an identifier, not an identity. If his time at Chilocco unintentionally culti-vated his Cherokee or Native identification as it did for so many other children, then he didn't show it. He was too independent, too indi-vidualistic to celebrate any affiliation, tribal or otherwise. Any system as regimented and as rigid as Chilocco's was never going to work for Buster. He ran away on Tuesday, April 10, 1945, the earliest he could make a getaway, but was quickly caught and sent back. Buster never talked much about his time at the Chilocco Indian School. The teen-ager who emerged from the school was not as outwardly rebellious as he had been, but he was no less stubbornly independent.

Perhaps even Buster was naive about his nature. At seventeen years old he lied about his age on his admissions form and joined the U.S. Army. Patriotism may have played a part, though most likely Buster just wanted the life of adventure he thought the army promised. Buster trained as a medic, but his military service was destined to be short lived given his hatred of the rigor and routine. Buster had his mother bail him out, saying he was too young to serve. He could have been prosecuted, but the army didn't file charges.

Buster came home, met and married a local girl named Betty, and started a family. He found work here and there, mostly as a roofer, though it was never steady and hardly enough to feed three mouths. Flying right and living responsibly proved a challenge, and Buster began reverting to his boyhood ways.

In the fall of 1952, about six months before Phyllis was killed, Buster was arrested for robbing two grocery stores. Buster pleaded guilty to two charges of second-degree burglary and was sentenced to two, one-year concurrent terms for each charge. Because he had two dependents, instead of serving time in prison, Buster was placed on probation on September 20, 1952. Under his probation, he was forbidden from drinking and had to find work.

While his record suggested otherwise, Buster was never a trouble-maker, not in his heart. Buster hated authority, but autonomy never came naturally to him either. This conflict was written into his character and drove his decision-making all of his life, oftentimes for the worst.

From boyhood until the day he died, Buster feared being considered a "dumb Indian." It said as much about the cultural attitudes at the time as it did about him. Buster was never given much of a chance because he had had been born poor and Native American. Indian schools such as Chilocco didn't cultivate doctors, lawyers, business-people, or teachers; instead, they trained farmers, bricklayers, maids, and other low-skilled labor positions, jobs that society needed to fill and for which social experts deemed Native Americans well suited. A trade wasn't the only thing Indian schools taught. Generations of Native American kids such as Buster were also taught that there was something fundamentally wrong with them. To be acceptable to society, they had to abandon their respective cultures even if, as in Buster's case, they had never really adopted them in the first place. Once they adopted white ways, their worth as human beings would be limited to serving at the bottom and living on the fringes.

Buster was smart, certainly too smart for the life he was living and the choices he had made. But as with most Native American men of his time, Buster's potential was never considered. He was placed in a narrow box and never allowed to escape. The more he resisted and rebelled the smaller the box became. Buster's Cherokee identity was more important to the society he lived in than it ever was to him. To society it was a marker; to him it became a burden. Other men make mistakes, but Buster was a "dumb Indian." His shy demeanor only validated the fears of those who never trusted him from the start. Life on the fringes was all Buster ever knew, and even there he was viewed with suspicion.

Watch out for Buster, Jimmy Warren had said. Stay away from him, Robert Warren had warned. Phyllis Jean Warren didn't listen, and now she was dead. It was enough to convince Buster's captors that he couldn't be trusted—and that maybe he was even a killer.

The authorities told the press they were also checking into Robert Warren, since he had found Phyllis's body buried in the same spot where the police and family had already checked several times. This peculiar fact will "certainly will bear looking into," Undersheriff Maxey assured reporters. Det. Ray Jones, however, only spoke to Warren once.

The county also claimed to be checking the story of Rev. Leontine Bryant. It was hard to believe this septuagenarian could have killed Phyllis, but her knowledge of the girl's burial spot might have suggested collusion. Reverend Bryant told a *Tulsa Tribune* reporter that she had a "vision" and could "probably name a suspect." She refused to tell the reporter who it was, and reporters never questioned her again.

Authorities knew that at least four other potential suspects lived in Phyllis's neighborhood, including one who had previously been accused of rape. All were significant leads, but authorities did not actively pursue them. It had been three weeks since Phyllis had been killed and more than a day since her body had been found. The authorities were not interested in chasing down dead ends, even if the leads were noteworthy. As far as they were concerned, the most obvious culprit was staring them right in the face.

"Let's take the lie detector test, Buster."

"No," said Buster. "I know I don't have to take the test."

The authorities were becoming increasingly frustrated. Their hopes for a quick solution were fading fast. The authorities knew Buster was their man, and they were determined to break him.

The interrogation continued throughout Friday night. The authorities were not obligated to release Buster within twenty-four hours now that he was a suspect of a serious crime. Buster barely slept and hardly ate while the parade of interrogators took turns questioning him. He was offered a meal at one point, but he was so anxious all he asked for was a glass of milk. Otherwise, he just sat there for hours on end, reciting the same story, the one nobody seemed—or wanted—to believe.

Buster had been out drinking and not at the movies, as he had originally told the police. Yes, he had lied but only because, ironically, he didn't want to break his parole and go to prison. Now he found himself facing the possibility of a life behind bars or, more likely, the electric chair. No, he didn't know why his father, his brother, and his friend said he wasn't with them. Sure, he knew Phyllis—she was sort of a younger sister—but he had no idea who killed her. The police were pressuring Buster to confess and made it clear that a confession was the only way to end the interrogation.

Buster finally acquiesced to the authorities' demands and agreed to take the lie detector test. But first Buster asked to speak to his wife, Betty, and to his mother, Bessie. After meeting separately with them, he was taken to police headquarters. Assistant County Attorney Edmondson, Investigator Lang, and Deputy Mallard surrounded Buster as Lieutenant Stege conducted the test.

While commonly called a lie detector, the actual name for the machine was the polygraph, meaning "many writings." The polygraph was invented in 1921 by John Augustus Larson, a Canadian-born medical student at the University of California who was also a police officer at the Berkeley Police Department. In addition to his polygraph machine, Dr. Larson incorporated lie detection methods that Dr. William Moulton Marston developed in the Harvard Psychological Laboratory in 1915. Dr. Larson took Dr. Marston's applied methods from World War I and adapted them for police procedure. Dr. Marston's fascination with the truth also extended far beyond the academic. In 1941 he created the comic book character Wonder Woman, whose "Lasso of Truth" compelled those who were bound by it to tell the truth.

Dr. Larson's polygraph machine and lie detection methods were considered authoritative in police stations across the nation. One of the most prominent practitioners was Capt. Phil Hoyt with the Kansas City Police Department, who was himself an innovator in the field of forensic science. Despite its purported reliability, the lie detector test was only admissible as evidence if both sides agreed to it. Given that Buster accepted the county's demands to submit to a test, this was not a problem.

While Lieutenant Stege had been commended in 1951 by Director J. Edgar Hoover of the Federal Bureau of Investigation (FBI) for his work on a Tulsa murder case, he was not as skilled at administering the test as Captain Hoyt was. Even so, Lieutenant Stege had twenty years of experience on the Tulsa police force and had conducted the lie detector test numerous times.

Stege would have begun the test by asking Buster to purposely make a false statement; this "stim test" would determine how Buster's charts would appear when he lied. The lieutenant next would have asked Buster a series of questions, mixing questions about the case with others that were irrelevant. When Buster answered each question, the polygraph machine would measure and record his blood pressure, pulse, respiration rate, and skin conductivity based on the theory that people are physiologically more anxious when telling a lie. Lieutenant Stege would interpret the charts, known as polygrams, to determine if Buster was telling the truth. If Buster's physiological responses were higher when answering the relevant questions, he failed.

The test took an hour. Buster was much calmer than he had been the night before, perhaps too tired to even be afraid. After the session concluded, Assistant County Attorney Edmondson approached Lieutenant Stege.

"What's the answer?" he said.

"He has knowledge of this crime," said Lieutenant Stege. "It doesn't exonerate him." Innocent until proven guilty or guilty until proven innocent? The lines blurred in the case of Buster Youngwolfe.

"The test didn't establish his innocence," Lieutenant Stege told the press. "His story doesn't check out." Stege didn't elaborate; he didn't need to. The county attorney's office received a more detailed report than what Lieutenant Stege told the newspapers. Whatever the results were, they weren't enough to convict Buster, but they weren't enough to release him either. Buster was returned to the county jail.

"I'm going to stick with my story and take my chances," said Buster, at least according to Assistant County Attorney Edmondson in a quote to the *Tulsa World*. "I'm not going to cop out." The purpose of Edmondson's quote was clear—to establish Buster as a defiant thug.

On Saturday morning, April 4, *Tulsa World* readers awoke to the front-page headline "Suspect 'All but Confesses' Slaying of 11-Year Old Girl, County Criminal Aide Says." Edmondson went so far as to boast to the paper, "I was never fully convinced of his guilt until now." It was a premature declaration of victory, but Buster's situation looked grim.

Buster asked to see his mother, Bessie. "She may be able to help me make up my mind," he told the authorities. Buster's relationship with his mother was loving but formal. Buster was probably closer to her than anyone else, but even so he kept a respectful distance, treating his mother more as if she were a respected adviser. When the press asked to take a picture of Buster giving his mother a hug, he demurred, saying, "We've never done anything but shake hands." Buster and his mother were not demonstrative people, and Buster refused to pose for the media circus that followed him.

Since his arrest, Buster's story had appeared in the *Tulsa World* and *Tulsa Tribune* every day. He was just a suspect but was portrayed as the culprit. The press was following the authorities' lead: The daily coverage was not about Phyllis's murder or the investigation but about the number one suspect—the only suspect—Buster Youngwolfe. Whether he confessed or not, he was now the public face of Phyllis's murder. He became a symbol for the danger that threatened the fragile safety of this fair city.

Bessie Warren was brought to the county attorney's office by Assistant County Attorney Edmondson, Undersheriff Maxey, Investigators Lang and Forrest Castle, and Deputy George Mallard. Before Bessie was allowed to see her son, she was interrogated by Assistant County Attorney Edmondson and Investigator Lang. If they couldn't talk any sense into Buster, then maybe his mother could. After an hour of questioning, the authorities brought Buster over from the county jail and allowed him to see his mother.

Buster and his mother spoke for the better part of an hour. Unbeknownst to either of them, their conversation was recorded. Thankfully for Buster and his mother, they said nothing incriminating. Bessie opened the door at 12:30 p.m. and summoned the officers, who were convinced that a confession was near.

"Well, Buster? Have something to tell us?"

"I have told you my story," said Buster. "I don't think you can convict me. You have evidence that tends to prove me guilty, but I don't think you have enough."

Buster was right, and the authorities knew it. In his statement to the press, Assistant County Attorney Edmondson quoted Buster as saying, "I am either going to fall all the way or not at all."

If Buster actually said that, whatever he meant wasn't clear. He may not have known himself. Buster had been interrogated since early Thursday afternoon, and it was now Saturday. He had had little sleep and practically nothing to eat. The few times the authorities offered to take Buster to a nearby restaurant under custody, he refused, lest it appear he was in any way complying with his interrogation. Hour after hour, day after day, time creeped slowly by as one person after another told Buster his story didn't add up, that he had killed that girl, and that all he had to do was confess and this would all be over. Maybe, just maybe, Buster started to believe them. "At one point during the questioning," Assistant County Attorney Edmondson told the *Tulsa World*, "he suddenly said: 'I can't stand confinement.'"

While the authorities wanted a confession, they weren't taking any chances. Lieutenant Stege's forensic office was investigating the lid on a five-gallon can found by Phyllis's grave for fingerprints. Officials believed Buster used the can to dig the hole in which Phyllis was found. The authorities next focused their attention on what they hoped was a damning piece of evidence—the toy frog. A deputy had found the frog just a few feet away from where Phyllis had been buried. Several witnesses said the toy frog was a gift to Phyllis from Buster. Though this didn't prove anything, by Saturday night county officials were going on three days of interrogating Buster, with nothing to show. They had hoped the marathon interrogation sessions would break him, but they hadn't. Even with heavy eyes and an empty stomach, Buster refused to confess. The authorities needed a killer, and they needed it to be Buster.

Buster wasn't playing his part, but the press was playing theirs. The toy frog story was on the front page of the Sunday *Tulsa World*. "Youngwolfe reportedly gave it to Phyllis shortly before she disappeared," said County Attorney Edmondson. However, he admitted, "we received conflicting testimony when it was shown to witnesses." Officials still had a long way to go to convict Buster in a court of law, but in the court of public opinion, he was already guilty. Only one question remained: What would it take for him to confess?

• • •

Phyllis Jean Warren's funeral was held at the Dawson Assembly of God Church, Saturday, April 4, at 2:00 p.m. She would forever be eleven years old. Her extended family attended, including her older brother Jimmy Warren, who was allowed to attend with permission from the state prison. Her tragic end was more significant than her short life had been. The Warren family didn't just bury Phyllis's body that day; they also buried her memory. The family never spoke of her again. If anybody tried, even decades later, her brothers would change the subject. Phyllis was gone. End of story.

One member of Phyllis's family was not in attendance—her nephew, Buster Youngwolfe. While Buster sat in jail, Probation Officer Chauncey O. Moore requested that the county attorney's office revoke Buster's parole because he had admitted to drinking. One way or the other, the authorities were going to get him.

Since the primary suspect was still uncooperative, the authorities made a cursory investigation into a few alternatives. The same Saturday as his sister's funeral Jimmy Warren was also subjected to a lie detector test. Lieutenant Stege said the results absolved him. "[Jimmy Warren] doesn't know a thing about the disappearance or murder—he's clean as a whistle," Stege told the press. His enthusiastic exoneration was a far cry from his misleading report about Buster's results.

Another pseudo-suspect was an unnamed city street department employee who'd served in the army and roomed with the Warrens. He'd been questioned at length—though not for days on end as Buster was—and was denied a lie detector test even though he asked for one. "We don't want to pass up anything," Assistant County Attorney Edmondson assured the press. Even so, the army veteran's questioning was a formality.

When the authorities received the lab report on the oil can lid found near Phyllis's body, Undersheriff Maxey told the *Tulsa World*, "There's no doubt but that lid was used to shovel dirt onto the girl's body." His statement neglected to mention that the oil can lid didn't show Buster's fingerprints. Whatever evidence they found on the can, if anything, it wasn't enough to convict Buster. The *Tulsa World* article ended with Undersheriff Maxey making a plea to the public to contact county officials with any information. Meanwhile, he said, the sheriff's office would begin "retrenching," making as close to an admission of defeat as he would offer. The authorities were getting desperate, and the entire city was watching.

On Sunday, April 6, County Attorney Robert Wheeler and Sheriff W. W. "Bill" Field returned to Tulsa from Los Angeles, California, where they had returned a man charged with child abandonment. This morning saw both men's first involvement in the case since Phyllis's body had been found and Buster had been arrested. The bosses arrived home at 3:00 a.m. and wasted no time entering the investigation, getting to work at 7:00 a.m. "We're going to do everything that law officers can do to break this case," said Sheriff Field.

Dogged and determined, Sheriff Field wasn't going to lose a public battle to a twenty-one-year-old Cherokee Indian like Buster. Heavy-set and thick-skinned, Sheriff Field was as blunt as a bully club. A veteran of the Tulsa Police Department for several years, Field had served in World War II as a flight officer and glider pilot in Europe and had fought in the invasions of Normandy and southern France. Field had also served as a warrant officer in the Korean War, fighting in the Thunderbird division. While serving overseas in Korea, he still managed to campaign for Tulsa County sheriff. Field won his race and returned home to serve. Sheriff Field didn't like losing, and he wasn't going to start now. If Buster had killed Phyllis—and by now Sheriff Field's colleagues had convinced him he had—Sheriff Field would get him.

County Attorney Wheeler was neither as headstrong and as tenacious as Sheriff Field nor as aggressively ambitious as his assistant, J.

Howard Edmondson. Folks who knew him said the county attorney was a solid lawyer, though one who thought highly of himself, and was maybe even a bit pompous. With his slicked-back hair and honest face, punctuated by a pair of soft, bird-dog eyes, County Attorney Wheeler looked every bit the local politician he was. He liked seeing his name in the paper as much as Assistant County Attorney Edmondson did, and he liked to win as much as Sheriff Field did. Based on what he'd heard, Buster Youngwolfe offered an opportunity for both.

County Attorney Wheeler and Sheriff Field questioned Buster in Field's office, telling him that his story held no water. Why not just give up? Stop this silliness. Confess. But Buster wouldn't budge.

Sheriff Field enlisted the aid of the FBI and the State Crime Bureau to dig up whatever they could find to put Buster away. Field also assigned two of his best men to the investigation—Criminal Deputies Houston Johnson and Lewis Downing. The deputies removed dirt from Buster's fingernails and hair from his head and sent them along with matching evidence from the brush pile to the FBI laboratory in Washington DC.

For Buster, Sunday was another full day of little sleep, little food, and lots of questioning. By now he had been in custody for more than seventy-two hours. Even as a primary suspect in a murder case, the authorities were running out of time to hold Buster, not that the press or the public was clamoring for his release. He was alone.

Buster asked to see his wife, Betty, and spoke to her from 11:00 p.m. until midnight in what were reported as closed-door discussions. They weren't. The authorities had once again wired the room. Maybe Buster knew, for both he and his wife spoke in hushed tones that made the recording barely audible.

Betty was stronger than her delicate frame would suggest. But four days of this were starting to wear on her.

"If you'd helped the family search for her, maybe we wouldn't be in this jam," she said.

"It wouldn't have helped," said Buster.

When his wife left the room, the officials entered. "Well, are you ready to confess?"

"I'm innocent," said Buster. "I didn't kill her."

Deputies Johnson and Downing had enough. They worked on Buster in relays. They read him the statements from his father, his brother, and his friend saying he wasn't with them the night Phyllis disappeared. They told him his fingerprints were on Phyllis's belt. They said his footprints and elbow prints were found near the grave. They told him they had evidence against him, so why not confess?

Buster knew it wasn't true. How could they have his prints? He wasn't there! But he'd gone four days with barely any sleep and practically nothing to eat. Four days in jail without being charged with a crime. Did he even know what was true anymore? If they said they had prints, then maybe, somehow, they did.

Deputies Johnson and Downing told Buster that confessing was the only way to save his life. He was still young, just twenty-one. They promised him life in prison, and with good behavior, he might be out by the time he was thirty-six. Buster could help finish raising his baby boy; Buster Jr. would be fifteen if his father was released early. Besides, his probation officer had already revoked his parole for drinking and idleness, so he was going to prison anyway.

Confess and you get to live. Keep lying and you will get the chair. You will die. Never see your wife, your mother, your boy again.

It didn't work. Buster would not confess.

Deputies Johnson and Downing had to get creative, so they threatened Buster's mother. Bessie was sure to testify on her son's behalf. If she did, they told Buster, and she said just one lie in her testimony, then they'd charge her with perjury. She'd go to prison too. Buster would be dead, and his mother would be behind bars, an old woman spending her remaining days knowing that she couldn't save her own son from the chair.

On Monday morning, April 6, before the crack of dawn, Buster asked to see his mother again.

"I no more than get upstairs and get my shoes off than they bring me back down," Buster told his mother. Maybe he was hoping his mother could fix this, make it all go away so his life could go back to normal. She couldn't. Buster knew only one thing could.

"Shorty, I guess this is what they want," said Buster, resigned. Shorty was his nickname for his mother. "I'm not going to tell you I did it,

Killer

because I didn't. But I'm going to say I did it. It's my only chance to get out of this."

After Buster had finished speaking to his mother, Sheriff Field took over questioning. It was still early, before 5:00 a.m. The sheriff played the recording of Buster's private conversations. Buster words echoed through the tiny room. The disembodied, scratchy white noise was like the voice of a ghost.

Buster said nothing incriminating on the tape, but Sheriff Field pointed out the inconsistencies in Buster's story. Buster listened quietly, as though he were a child being reprimanded. It was all he could do. Finally, he asked for his wife and mother. Deputies were sent to get them.

"You've told several different stories to different persons, Buster," Sheriff Field said.

Buster looked up at him. His face was flat and empty. His brown skin was pale. Any emotion, any fight had drained away. Five days in this place had done that to him. Buster didn't even resemble a human being anymore. He was but a wax figure.

"Why didn't you help the Warrens look for Phyllis?" said Sheriff Field.

Buster stared at Sheriff Field and shrugged. "I didn't need to. I already knew where she was," Buster said. "I killed her."

6

Confession

"Yes, I killed her."

Buster's words spread through the room like a wraith. His mother and his wife gasped. Buster had told them he would confess, but hearing him say "I killed her" was chilling. The cold, cruel reality of what was happening to them cut like a knife. Their circumstances were wrenching, and they were powerless to stop it.

For his part, Buster was calm. Exhausted, yes. Hungry, yes. So cold he was shaking from the inside out but calm. With four words, Buster ended five days of incarceration and interrogation. His suffering was over, or so he hoped. Buster had confessed to killing the girl. Now they wanted to know how. Buster told his story.

• • •

County Attorney Robert Wheeler gathered a large audience: Buster's mother and his wife; Deputies John Harlan, Walter W. Whisenhunt, Houston Johnson, R. B. Jones, Lewis Downing, and Lloyd Miller; and Sheriff Field.

Buster started his story by saying that for years Phyllis would come over to the house and get in bed with him. Every time he'd have to run her off to avoid trouble. Phyllis was frisky around him and had been for a while. But he never had sex with her. Not until that night.

It was late in the evening, Thursday, March 12, about 7:30 or 8:00 p.m. Buster had just finished supper after a full day of drinking with his father, his brother, and a friend. He was on the front porch smoking a cigarette, while Betty cleaned the dishes.

After finishing his cigarette, Buster went to visit his sister. He was crossing the field when Phyllis spotted him. Phyllis had been playing at his house and was in no mood to end the evening so early. Nighttime was the same as daytime to her, and her parents didn't care where she was most of the time anyway. Nothing could stop the fun-loving, carefree Phyllis. She caught up with Buster and asked him to take her for a walk. Maybe he was still a bit tipsy from drinking all day or maybe he was just bored. Whatever the reason, he did.

After walking for about three hundred yards, Phyllis stopped Buster by the brush pile beside the uprooted tree. "I want to wash my feet," she said. Buster and Phyllis climbed through the barbwire fence and slid down the hill to the grassy bank beside the creek. Phyllis slipped off her shoes and put her tiny feet into the cold, muddy water.

"We got into an argument about something, I don't remember what," Buster told the authorities. "But, anyway, I hit her. I knocked her down." The authorities didn't ask what the fight was about. It didn't matter.

Buster said he apologized when Phyllis said she'd tell her dad. The two then sat down on a log, and Buster gave her a cigarette. They sat beside the stream in silence, smoking and listening to the water flow past.

"Then she began teasing me about my wife, telling me that I didn't love Betty," said Buster. "Saying that she'd make a lot better wife than Betty if I'd wait for her to grow up." This wasn't the first time she'd made such a claim, Buster said. Phyllis had been pestering him for two years to get rid of Betty.

"I told her she was crazy," said Buster. "But Phyllis is from a family, well, you know, where she'd learned things a lot faster than she would if she was just a regular kind of a girl."

Phyllis took one last drag on her cigarette, threw the ash to the ground, and pulled off her clothes. Buster then described the rape, though he never called it such, insisting in this account that the sex was consensual. "And I wasn't the first man, either," Buster alleged in his confession.

When they finished, Phyllis put her panties back on and nothing else. She said she was going back home just like that, so Buster said he grabbed her. "I'm going to tell Daddy and my brothers," she said. "I'm going home to your wife and tell her."

Buster hit her hard, so hard he knocked her to the ground. Somehow he didn't knock her out, and she got up to run but not fast enough. Buster grabbed Phyllis tightly around her tiny arms, a grip she could never break. She only had one way out.

"She started hollering, and I put my hand over her mouth and held for a while." His hands were rough and strong from a lifetime spent working with them. "She went limp."

Buster held her tiny body in his arms, he said. Like a doll, she folded lifelessly over his forearm, her piercing blue eyes staring vacantly through drooping eyelids.

"I was afraid she was dead, but then I didn't know," said Buster. "I was afraid she might wake up and go and tell her folks about what we had done."

Buster thought about running away. He was scared and wasn't thinking straight. No, running was a bad idea. She could wake up any minute, and then what?

Buster dropped Phyllis on the ground and pulled the plastic belt from her blue jeans. He wrapped the blue belt around her throat and strangled her. His fears were well founded, for Phyllis was still alive. But not for long.

"She kicked around a little, but not very much," said Buster. "I looked to see if she was dead. She was."

Buster wasted no time. He put her clothes back on piece by piece. But once she was dressed, he saw that he forgot to put on her panties. Buster said he stuffed the panties in the rear pocket of her jeans as "a sort of afterthought." None of the authorities asked why Phyllis didn't have her panties on anymore. It didn't matter. Buster was confessing; that's what they wanted.

Buster said he took Phyllis's body up the steep bank of the ravine, lifting her back up and over the barbwire fence. After he "looked around for a place to hide the body," he settled on a spot near the brush pile, under the massive uprooted tree they had visited minutes before. The tree's roots jutted out like arms, as if it were a demon ready to drag a body down into hell. Buster dropped to his knees and dug out a burial plot with his bare hands. Once it was as deep as he could make it, Buster dropped Phyllis into the hole. He buried her hastily, covering her lifeless little body with the surrounding dead wood and dirt. He was cold and careless. He treated her as though she had never been alive in the first place. As if they had never talked, never played, never even cared for each other. She was nothing, nothing but a nuisance to be thrown away like trash.

"I put her in that place on her back, her knees doubled up over her stomach and then went home," said Buster. It took him about an hour, all told. Strangling and burying the girl had made quite the mess, and his khaki pants were covered in mud. Buster gave his clothes to his wife. Betty, unaware of what her husband had done, scrubbed the mud from the murderer's clothes, baptismal waters washing away the gravest of all sins.

Buster said he returned to the murder scene only once, about three days later. He had no reason to return more than that. Besides, it would be too suspicious. He passed about eight or nine feet from the spot, and that was it.

Buster told his grisly tale of raping and murdering a child to the rapt audience of ten people, including the two people closest to him— his wife and his mother.

"Why did you kill the girl?" someone asked Buster point-blank.

"I didn't do it because I was afraid I'd get in trouble," said Buster, "but because she just made me mad, teasing me about my wife like that all the time."

Wheeler sent for a secretary, Mrs. Freda Melton, who took a seven-page statement detailing Buster's confession. Buster then signed the statement, confessing to the rape and murder of Phyllis Jean Warren.

Later that morning *Tulsa Tribune* reporter Roy Hanna asked Buster what he thought would happen to him. Puzzled, with the face a child who hadn't considered the consequences of his actions, Buster looked at the reporter. "Gosh, I really don't know," said Buster. "Those guys talked like they might be able to get me life because I had a good reason to do what happened."

Buster's statement is telling. He said he had a good reason "to do what happened," not that he had a good reason "to do what I did." The reporter didn't pick up on the discrepancy. Buster was already divorcing himself from the murder, perhaps without even being aware of it. Even after signing the confession, even after detailing the gruesome act, Buster couldn't bring himself to say to the reporter, "I did it."

Five days of being questioned in that cold, dark room had taken their toll. Buster began to shake uncontrollably from a chill. "But I guess it's just as well like this," Buster told the reporter. "They'd drag this thing on forever and ever. Now I think it's about over."

Buster was wrong.

• • •

"Youngwolfe Confesses Killing, Burying Young Warren Girl," the *Tulsa Tribune* heralded triumphantly. The front-page story had all of the flourish and fanfare one would expect from a declaration of victory in war. The subhead read "'She Was Always Pestering Me about My Wife,' Indian Tells Sheriff, Deputies." Readers were not spared any of the grisly details of Buster's confession.

Buster, Bessie, and Betty Youngwolfe each signed statements saying that Buster had not been threatened, coerced, or promised anything. This part had to be done by the book; the authorities made sure of that. They wanted to make clear that Buster had confessed to the crime of his own accord, with no extraordinary measures taken by the authorities.

At 11:00 a.m., Monday, April 6, Buster was taken to the common pleas court before Judge Stanley Edmister. In Oklahoma in the 1950s, arraignments and preliminary hearings were held in common pleas court, while trials were set in district court. Buster entered a plea of guilty, hoping his confession would prompt the court's mercy. It did not. Judge Edmister refused Buster's plea, entered a plea of not guilty, and set Buster's preliminary hearing for that Friday, April 10.

Buster was assigned a public defender, Quinn Dickason, a clean-cut, stone-faced man with the dispassionate demeanor of a university administrator. Whether motivated by stubborn defiance or fatalistic acceptance, Buster rejected Dickason, saying he didn't want a defense attorney. Buster thought his ordeal was over, and that now, finally, he could get some rest. Sheriff Field had other plans.

Since he had already given the story of Buster's confession to the *Tulsa Tribune*, the afternoon paper, Sheriff Field made an arrange-

Confession

ment with the morning daily, the *Tulsa World*. After the *Tulsa Tribune* went to press, around 2:00 p.m., the *Tulsa World* would get an exclusive story: Buster was going to show the authorities how he killed the girl at the actual scene of the crime.

That afternoon Buster was taken from his jail cell and escorted to his neighborhood on North Yale. In violation of his constitutional rights, the authorities forced Buster to re-create the murder for *Tulsa World's* cameras.

It was a surreal experience for everyone involved, especially for Buster. His behavior was strange. He laughed easily while Undersheriff Maxey and Deputy Mallard joked with each other, as if he was just one of the guys. Perhaps after four sleepless nights with these men, he figured he was. The group arrived at the neighborhood and waited for Investigator Tom Collins, a surveyor who was going to make detailed diagrams of Buster's re-creation. While they waited, Buster saw Josie Warren drive by and remarked sarcastically, "There goes the heartbroken mother to get the Old Man some beer."

When Investigator Collins arrived, the entire group went to work. Buster's audience included six law enforcement officials—Undersheriff Maxey, Deputies Mallard and Manley, and Investigators Lang, Collins, and Castle—*Tulsa World* reporter Troy Gordon and photographer Jack Moncrief; and even his own wife, Betty. Before this rapt audience, he re-created the murder of Phyllis Jean Warren.

It was a lovely, sunny spring day, with perfect lighting for the cameras documenting Buster's morbid tour. With his hands cuffed in front of him, Buster started on his front porch and led the group across the field. Next they went down the ravine to the creek where the murder took place and finally to the upturned tree where Phyllis's body was found. All throughout the act, Buster was strangely serene, as if he were no longer in possession of his own body, as if he were just a dancing marionette being held by his strings.

When Moncrief asked Buster to hold his son and kiss his wife goodbye for the camera, he obliged. Gordon noticed Buster was shivering. "I'm cold, not nervous," he said.

A big group had come to see the spectacle, but a key figure was missing—Buster's new attorney, Elliott Howe.

7

The Believer

Elliott Howe's salary as a Tulsa County public defender wasn't worth it. For $250 a month, Howe handled some fifty cases a month, with no office, no staff, and no expense money. It was only Howe, working part time to help those who couldn't afford to help themselves. Back then, public defense work was treated as a training ground for young lawyers, just as residency is for new physicians. They did their time and got out. Howe was one of only eighty-four public defenders in the entire country. Only sixty-four were full time. There was also a discrepancy between cities. Big cities such as Los Angeles had sixteen public defenders, while many cities had none. Tulsa had Elliott Howe working part time.

The value the county placed on Howe's services—defending people who couldn't afford an attorney—wasn't enough to feed a family. It was the right thing for him to do, sure, but doing the right thing didn't put much food on the table. But with a wife and a five-month-old baby daughter at home, Howe couldn't afford to be greedy.

After Buster rejected Quinn Dickason, he was assigned Elliott Howe. Many of those closest to him called him Bill, a childhood nickname, though Howe always introduced himself as Elliott.

Though only a few years out of law school at the University of Tulsa, Howe looked much older than his thirty-three years. Part Native American himself, Howe and Buster looked as though they could have been related, though Howe was Creek, not Cherokee, and had fairer skin.

Howe was the strong, silent type, with a wide, contemplative forehead and deep-set blue eyes that spoke more loudly than he ever did. Yet hidden beneath his deep stare was the mirthful, almost childlike glint of the ornery little boy he had once been.

People would say he was "always the same"—always polite, always pleasant—so they never knew how much of himself he kept hidden. Howe maintained a healthy distrust of the human race. People had to earn his confidence, for it wasn't given freely. After everything Howe had lived through, everything he'd lost, he wasn't completely corroded by cynicism, but he wasn't quick to trust people either.

Howe had been on the job since January 1, roughly three months. In his previous job he had been on the other side of the criminal justice system as a prosecutor. Howe had done well, had a bright future, and was going places—all those things established men tell young men on their way up.

A few years before, Howe's older sister Virginia, a nurse at St. John Hospital in Tulsa, had introduced him to a young nurse named Imelda Jane McNamara. Howe had all but sworn off serious romance years before. While he was stationed on a destroyer in the South Pacific, his then fiancée had broken off their engagement in a letter. Howe didn't expect much from this date with Imelda, but he figured he'd throw his older sister a bone. Turned out there was something special about this fiery Irish Catholic farm girl from Wagoner, Oklahoma, forty miles outside of Tulsa. She was every bit as sharp as he was and even more stubborn. They were married on June 10, 1950. Two years later, the couple was expecting a baby. Life was good for Bill Howe.

Then November 4, 1952, happened. Election day seemed like a great night for Howe and his fellow Republicans. World War II hero and general Dwight David Eisenhower had routed Adlai Stevenson II, the governor of Illinois, winning 442 electoral votes to Stevenson's 89 to become the thirty-fourth president of the United States. Howe never fought for Eisenhower, but he liked Ike all the same and loved a winner.

Howe celebrated the returns at a watch party downtown, beaming as the results came in, showing one Republican victory after another—except for one race. Howe suspected something was wrong when he saw the look on Imelda's face. She was crying. She had spent her childhood with five siblings on a small farm during the Dust Bowl. She didn't cry easily.

"What's the matter, Mac?" Bill said, calling her by her nickname. "We're winning!"

"Yes," she said, "but you're out of a job!"

Republicans were winning that night, yes, but not Howe's boss, Lewis J. Bicking, the county attorney. The news brought Howe's celebration to a close. The newly elected county attorney, Robert L. Wheeler, was a Democrat and would bring in his own staff. Howe would not be one of them. It was November, Imelda was due in December, and Howe was out of work.

Private practice plus $250 a month as a public defender paid the mortgage. Time with Howe's young family was stretched, but they got by. Howe lost his first case as a public defender but won his next two. Most public defense cases were pretty cut and dry. None was more so than the Buster Youngwolfe case.

Howe had read the papers, saw the reports, and knew how the twenty-one-year-old had confessed to murdering eleven-year-old Phyllis Jean Warren. Based on what he knew, Howe believed Buster was a monster of the worst kind, but he deserved a defense just the same.

Howe first met Buster's mother, Bessie, in the courthouse on April 6. She told him the county was trying to "railroad" her son. Howe had heard it all before. Nobody behind bars was ever guilty, certainly not in a mother's eyes. Howe had a job to do and was going to do it well, but he took Bessie's conviction for what it was—a heartbroken mother's plea to save her son's life.

Howe met Buster at noon downstairs at the Tulsa County Jail. What must have been going through Howe's mind? Howe was the new father of a girl, and Buster had admitted just a few hours before to killing one. Still, Howe had a job to do.

Buster was several inches shorter than Howe and looked as if he could have been Howe's kid brother. Buster was gaunt and tired, and didn't talk much. The case didn't even come up. The two young fathers shared a few cigarettes and not much else.

Buster had done nothing but talk for five days now. He was probably convinced his new lawyer was irrelevant at best and untrustworthy at worst. His experience with county employees so far had been less than inspiring. Nobody was interested in what he had to say, only in telling him what to say. He must have thought Howe was probably no different; that his representing Buster was just a formality, same as with the last guy, Quinn Dickason; and that he wasn't even a public defender but a part-time government hack charged with delivering the dead. Buster figured he wouldn't see Howe again before the arraignment. Howe figured the same. Just as well.

That afternoon Howe started to have different ideas. First, Buster was taken in handcuffs to reenact the crime before county officials, and a reporter and a photographer from the *Tulsa World* were brought along to document the spectacle. Howe wasn't invited. He wasn't even told. Now he was livid.

"No one is to talk to him except in my presence," Howe told the county attorney and the sheriff later that afternoon. Howe's political experience was limited to his time serving as an assistant county attorney. Yet in that short time, he'd learned that suspects are tried in the court of public opinion as much as they are in a court of law. Howe spoke to the *Tulsa World*, saying he was seeking an injunction in common pleas court. He also said that he was seeking to restrain county officials from talking to, communicating with, taking statements from, or "in any way further [violating] the constitutional rights of this defendant."

In his injunction, Howe noted he was also going to point out that Buster had been jailed for nearly five days without being charged with a crime. Furthermore, Buster had effectively been forced to perjure himself when he had been taken to the alleged scene of the crime and forced to reenact it, a violation of his Fifth Amendment rights. Howe left no room for interpretation: Buster was innocent until proven guilty.

Still, Howe figured Buster was guilty. After all, he had confessed.

Buster sat in his cell that night with nothing better to do but think. He was still suspicious about working with the county, even with a public defender, but there was something different about Howe. Howe was the first person who'd gone to bat for him. Howe could have just as easily let the sheriff's office conduct the reenactment and parade him in front of the cameras without saying a word—just collected his check and gone home—but he didn't.

Howe didn't talk a lot, but he listened well. It was a far cry from Buster's experience so far. Maybe that's what Buster needed to hear—silence. For the first time a man wasn't pressuring him to confess or to say anything. Instead, Howe just waited patiently for him to talk, to tell him what happened, what really happened. If Buster wanted to live, then he had no choice but to tell him.

• • •

Despite Howe's objections, there was nothing he could do to stop the *Tulsa World*. On Tuesday morning, April 7, the newspaper published a photo of Buster, handcuffed and surrounded by the authorities, giving a guided tour of the crime scene. The headline read "Girl Slaying Is Re-enacted for Officers." Underneath the headline was another photo, this one of Buster kissing his wife, while his infant son, Buster Jr., stares off, unaware of the fate that awaited his father.

Tulsa World reporter Troy Gordon detailed Buster's confession and the reenactment, including Buster's chilling, strange statement to Undersheriff Gene Maxey: "I should have killed the whole Warren family and left the girl alive. It would have been good riddance." Perhaps Buster no longer cared about what he said or how it sounded. What did it matter either way?

Howe spent the day getting up to speed on the case and gathering evidence of his own. Even after the county's publicity stunt, Howe still assumed his client was guilty. It was hard not to. Yet the deeper he dug, the more Howe was appalled by everything that the authorities had done—and not done. They did not visit any of the bars where Buster said he went drinking. They did not talk to everyone in the neighborhood, which was home to not just four but six convicted sex criminals. They did not even find physical evidence that corroborated Buster's statement. All they had was a confession. In the five days following the discovery of Phyllis's body, they had not conducted a competent investigation, just an interrogation. To top it off, they paraded Buster around for the cameras in a media circus act of a re-creation. Maybe Buster's mother was right; maybe her son had been railroaded by the county—but, still, Buster had confessed.

Late in the evening as Howe was about to go home, he received a call from the county jail. Buster wanted to speak to him. He said it was urgent. Howe had no idea what it could be, but he packed up and headed there as fast as he could.

Howe walked up to Buster's cell in a darkened corner of the county jail. The timid, cowering young man he'd met only a day before was gone. Now Buster impatiently paced back and forth across his narrow cell like a trapped animal. When Buster saw Howe, he stuck his head against the cold, iron bars and looked up at him. Howe approached the dimly lit cell, the only thing standing between him and a confessed child murderer.

"You had something to tell me?" Howe said.

"Yeah," Buster said. His speech was heavy. His words taut. "I didn't do it."

Howe wasn't surprised. Nobody on the wrong side of iron bars is ever guilty.

"But you confessed," Howe said, incredulously.

"Sure, I confessed," Buster said, snapping back. "They worked on me for five days. I only had two meals. I only slept four hours. Every time I stretched out to sleep, they brought me back for more questioning. I tell you, they wouldn't let me alone. And they said if I kept on being smart, then they'd really work me."

Buster was out of breath. The quiet young man spoke with an unrestrained urgency, his speech tumbling out like waves bursting through a broken levee. In the one day that he'd known Buster, Howe never heard him talk this fast and didn't imagine that he even could.

"They said they had my knee prints and elbow prints near the buried body," said Buster, his words continuing to pour out. "I knew they didn't, because I didn't do it, but it's my word against theirs. Who's gonna believe an ex-convict? Besides, they promised to get me off with a light sentence if I confessed; otherwise, they send me to the chair. I knew they could do it, so I confessed."

Howe took it all in, but he was still skeptical. Buster had confessed only thirty-six hours before to raping and murdering an eleven-year-old. He had detailed and even re-created the crime step-by-step, showing exactly how he did it. Now in flash of energy he was denying everything he had said and everything he had done, even his own signed confession.

Yet Howe could tell a liar when he saw one; he had met plenty before. Howe had little reason to believe Buster, but there was something about the way he spoke, something honest. Howe had a gut feeling this frightened young man was telling the truth.

Howe called in the courthouse reporter Troy Gordon, who was also covering the story for the *Tulsa World* and had been at the reenactment the previous day. Born in Kansas, Gordon had started as a proofreader for the *Coffeyville (KS) Journal*, followed by stints at the *Kansas City (MO) Star* and the International News Service. He joined the *Tulsa World* in 1952 as a courthouse reporter and currently served in the position. Besides his folksy, gregarious personality, Gordon's most notable feature was his crippled right arm. A childhood fall rendered the appendage useless, though he never let his handicap slow him down. He not only taught himself to write and type with only his left hand, but he also was a tenacious tennis player.

Howe wasn't friends with Gordon, but Tulsa was still a small town in many ways, especially at the courthouse. In his dealings with Gordon, Howe knew him to be an honest man and a fair reporter. He also knew, the prior day's antics notwithstanding, that the *Tulsa World* had been less hostile to Buster than the *Tulsa Tribune* was.

Howe and Gordon grilled Buster for the rest of the night. Buster was being interrogated yet again, and his attorney wasn't any easier on him than his accusers had been. Buster took it in stride. He had no choice. Howe and Gordon took turns asking questions, each as piercing as the last.

Gordon challenged Buster's belief that the authorities could imprison his mother.

"Buster, if you are not guilty, why did you think that could be done?" asked Gordon.

"I figured if they were able to get enough to convict me, they could do the same to my mother," said Buster. "They have no money," Buster said about his family. He was in jail, and Jimmy Warren was back in prison as well. The county sent groceries on Monday, but that was all they had.

Howe hadn't been sure what to expect from this evening, but believing Buster was almost certainly not it. After three hours, Howe stared down at Buster with soft blue eyes that were now as cold as a grave. He was searching for the truth, searching for the human being behind the monster he had been led to believe Buster was. The law and the press had formed a narrative. Howe was starting to see it was all a lie.

"Buster, do you realize that if you're lying and you take the witness stand, you're going to be caught up in your lies, and you'll be sent to the electric chair?" said Howe.

Buster's eyes widened. He leaned forward and looked through the narrow bars, as if he was whispering a confession to a priest or a prayer to God. He looked up at Howe, a man he didn't know but who was his only hope, and spoke with a soft but defiant voice: "I didn't do it."

Howe believed him. Tulsa County didn't. The sheriff's office and the police department didn't. The press didn't. Even Howe's own wife didn't. But Howe did. The entire city had convicted Buster and would gladly watch him die, but Howe was different. Howe believed. Call it intuition, call it logic, or just call it a gut feeling. Howe's belief was bolstered by facts, but it went down deeper to the realm of faith.

Taking on this case was his job, but proving Buster's innocence was a choice. Howe would fight for Buster, risking the reputation that he valued as much as anything in the world and, moreover, risking the peace he'd spent his young life to attain.

Howe believed he had an innocent man. He wasn't going to let him die.

8

Boyhood

"I know Indians because I'm part Indian myself," Howe told the *Tulsa World* months later as he explained why he believed Buster was innocent. "My grandmother was a full-blooded Creek Indian. And I went to Indian school when I was a kid. Indians have a natural reticence, and if you don't know that, then you think they're hiding something."

Howe believed Buster for reasons even he didn't realize at the time. His reasons traced back before the two even met. Howe saw in Buster what he could have become himself. The trials of Howe's childhood nearly took him down a different path, a path not far removed from where Buster's had brought him.

Perhaps Buster could sense this too. After the misery Buster had endured over the past few days, he had no reason to trust anyone. But he trusted Howe. Each man was formed by similar journeys and had much in common, though their lives had taken dramatically different turns. Buster's life had brought him here, lost and alone in a Tulsa County Jail cell, behind bars and charged with the rape and murder of an eleven-year-old girl. Howe's life brought him to the other side of those bars, standing as Buster's only hope of survival.

"From the long talk I had with Buster—the way he answered all my questions, the way he looked at me—even though I hadn't been able to check the facts yet, and though I didn't even know what all the facts were," Howe said, "I still had a deep feeling that the boy was innocent."

To know why Elliott Howe believed in Buster Youngwolfe, you have to know him.

• • •

Eufaula was a small town, but to a boy like Elliott, it supplied endless possibilities for adventure. He could run for miles and never reach the end. The air was scented with the sweet fragrance of honeysuckle, while the fields were a lush green that splashed the earth as though it were painted from an impressionists' brush. For a brief moment, Howe's childhood was idyllic, like a dream. Maybe it was a dream, for it was all over in the blink of an eye.

A little more than two thousand people called Eufaula home in the early 1920s. Ten of them belonged to the household of Samuel Shepherd and Mattie Posey Howe. The Howes brought eight children into the world: Robert, Virginia, Elizabeth, Louise, Margaret, Elliott, John, and Sammye. The Howe clan lived in a modest home with Mattie's mother, Nancy Phillips, or Pohas Harjo, a full-blooded Creek woman who did not speak any English.

Nancy Phillips had been married to Lawrence Henderson ("Hence") Posey, an orphan of Scots-Irish ancestry. Posey was raised by a Creek family in the late 1800s and claimed to be a member of the tribe. Though not a member by blood, he was accepted by the tribe and became a respected leader among his adopted people. He rose to the rank of captain of the Lighthorsemen, the Creek tribe's mounted police force, and was charged with maintaining order and the Creek law. It was ironic, since some thought Posey was an outlaw himself due to his friendship with the James Gang and the Dalton brothers. Before statehood the law abiding often lived beside and even befriended the law breaking. Posey was no different. His outlaw status was only a myth, one he himself did not discourage, for it added to his aura.

Hence Posey was one of eleven cattlemen running his herd over what is now Oklahoma. His family's home was called Bald Hill, though his house was a home to all. Traveling cattlemen stayed with Posey on drives from Texas through Oklahoma to Kansas City and Fort Gibson. They were never charged for food or shelter on Bald Hill, for Creek hospitality forbade it.

Speaking English was strictly enforced among the twelve Posey children, once they reached their teen years. Hence Posey's eldest, his son Alexander, developed such a facility for the language that he became a journalist and poet. Alexander Posey was the editor of the *Muskogee (OK) Times* and the *Eufaula (OK) Indian Journal*, the first Indian-published daily newspaper, and he served in the Creek House of Kings, which represented half of the Creek Nation's bicameral legislature alongside the House of Warriors. Alexander Posey was something of a Native Thomas Jefferson, an American renaissance man with a gift for rhetoric that was greatly admired among the tribes in Indian Territory. He is perhaps best remembered for his satirical "Fus Fixico Letters." These editorial letters were published internationally and were told from the point of view of the fictional Fus Fixico. Fus Fixico (translated as "Heartless Bird") provided a wry commentary on the debate over statehood, the realities of reservation life at the turn of the century, and the government's Indian policy. Alexander and his way with words were so respected, he was elected at thirty-two years old to serve as the secretary for the Sequoyah Constitutional Convention, a vital but volatile position at the turn of the last century.

Pressure was mounting from the white settlers to open the territories for statehood; the Sequoyah Constitutional Convention was the Native American tribes' attempt to turn Indian Territory into the state of Sequoyah and gain admittance as a majority-Indian state. As secretary of the convention, held August 21, 1905, Alexander was charged with drafting the Constitution and is often credited with writing most of it. In addition to the Constitution, the convention prepared a plan for organizing the state's government, developed a map outlining counties, and elected delegates to petition the U.S. Congress for statehood. The dream of a majority–Native American state was not to be. The federal government rejected every proposal presented. On June 16, 1906, President Theodore Roosevelt signed the Oklahoma Enabling Act, declaring that the Oklahoma and Indian Territories could only be admitted to the union as a single state.

Under the Dawes Act of 1887, Indian tribal lands were carved into thousands of separate, 160-acre allotments and divvied among individual Native Americans. To receive an allotment, one had to accept registration and claim membership in only one tribe, though many

Fig. 1. Elliott Howe enlisted in the navy before the United States entered World War II. He hoped to serve on the USS *Oklahoma*, but before he could the ship was sunk during the Japanese attack on Pearl Harbor. COURTESY OF THE AUTHOR.

Fig. 2. Buster Youngwolfe lied about his age and joined the U.S. Army at seventeen. He trained as a medic, but his mother, Bessie, bailed him out. COURTESY OF THE AUTHOR.

Fig. 3. The Howe children were separated after their parents died, but many came together for Elliott's marriage to Imelda McNamara in 1950. COURTESY OF THE AUTHOR.

Fig. 4. Howe served on both sides of the courtroom—first as an assistant county attorney and later as a public defender. As the latter, he made only $250 a month. COURTESY OF THE AUTHOR.

Fig. 5. Howe served as an assistant county attorney for Lewis J. Bicking. When Bicking lost his seat to Robert Wheeler in 1952, Howe lost his job.
COURTESY OF THE AUTHOR.

Fig. 6. Phyllis Jean Warren outside her home. Phyllis was known for being fun loving and carefree. COURTESY OF THE AUTHOR.

Fig. 7. Phyllis with Buster in the background. Buster was Phyllis's stepnephew but was more like a big brother. COURTESY OF THE AUTHOR.

Fig. 8. Photo of Phyllis from the *Tulsa World*. COURTESY OF TULSA WORLD MEDIA CO.

Phyllis Warren, only eleven: She stayed out far too late

Fig. 9. The city had condemned the shacks at Fourth North Yale Avenue, but the people who lived there had nowhere else to go. COURTESY OF THE AUTHOR.

Fig. 10. Friends, family, and police officers scoured the neighborhood for three weeks but never found any sign of Phyllis. COURTESY OF THE AUTHOR.

Fig. 11. Several generations, including this unidentified woman, were the unfortunate few who called these slums home. COURTESY OF THE AUTHOR.

Fig. 12. Phyllis Warren's father, Robert, found her body buried near this upturned tree just a few blocks from their home. COURTESY OF THE AUTHOR.

Fig. 13. When Phyllis was found, Buster was arrested and brought to her burial site. COURTESY OF THE AUTHOR.

people had multiple bloodlines. Registration in the Dawes Rolls was mandatory. Those who refused were left with nothing.

Oklahoma became a state on November 16, 1907, and Alexander Posey died six months later on May 27, 1908. Only thirty-four years old, Posey drowned while trying to cross the flooded North Canadian River. His death was an apt metaphor for his life, as he swam mightily against the raging current before finally succumbing to tides far beyond his control.

Alexander was the eldest and most famous of Hence Posey's twelve children, but Hence's favorite, it was believed, was his daughter Mattie, born May 7, 1884. Her story was entwined with a man from the East named Howe.

• • •

Samuel Shepherd "Shep" Howe was born at Sunnyside, the Howe family estate in Virginia, on June 20, 1868. Shep was the second of twelve children to Capt. John Thomas Howe, an officer in the Confederacy, and his wife, Sallie Lewis DeJarnette. Shep's great-grandfather Joseph Howe had emigrated from England. According to George Washington's diary records, Joseph Howe helped him survey southwest Virginia. For his efforts to the English crown, Joseph was awarded a land grant and built Sunnyside in 1758. Four generations of Howes would be born and buried in the Old Dominion, yet Shep and his older brother, Robert, wanted nothing more than to leave this place. As soon as they were able, the eldest Howe sons left their homeland and headed west, Robert first and Shepherd next, just as their ancestor Joseph had done more than a century before.

Oil had been discovered in the Indian Territory. The land rush had just begun, and the new frontier was open for settlement. The Howe brothers journeyed to what is now Oklahoma, the land of cowboys and Indians, for word had spread out east that this vast land was fertile for farming and bountiful with black gold. The brothers arrived and immediately formed an oil company to buy and sell leases, establishing their headquarters in Muskogee, Oklahoma, fifty miles south of Tulsa.

Tall and trim, with sharp blue eyes and thick blonde hair, Shep Howe cut a dashing figure. He wore elegant attire from back east in even the warmest weather, making him look quite strange among the dirt- and dust-stained cowboys and wildcatters. He and his business partners—now including his younger brother Elliott, after whom Shep would name a son—traveled to Stidham, Oklahoma, then an oil boom town, and met with Hence Posey, one of the largest landowners in the territory.

While stopping in town, the Howe brothers met the shy but admiring gaze of a slender, raven-haired, young Native American woman.

"Pardon me, Miss," said Shep. "Would you be so kind as to direct us to Captain Posey's Bald Hill ranch?" Hence Posey had served in the Confederate Creek regiment under Col. D. N. McIntosh, so decorum dictated he be referred to by his rank.

"Why do you wish to see him?" the young woman asked.

"We have oil leases requiring his signature and have ridden from Muskogee this morning to discuss them with him," said Shep.

"Oh, yes," she said, "Pa said someone would be coming today. Follow me. I will take you to him. Hence Posey is my father."

Unbeknownst to Shep Howe, he had just met Mattie Posey, the woman who would change his life.

The Howe brothers spent several days on Bald Hill, concluding their business but staying to conduct more. Posey knew several Creeks who were interested in selling leases, and the Howe brothers were interested in buying them. Besides business, they enjoyed Posey's company. A gifted raconteur, Posey loved regaling the three sons of a Confederate captain with his own tales of lost causes and bitter defeats, an old man's memories from another life.

Shep's other life weighed heavily on his mind as well. Back home in Virginia he was betrothed to Jennie, the daughter of a wealthy Richmond family, who was as lovely and as delicate as a flower. Shep knew the Wild West was no place for Jennie. She was accustomed to comfort and luxury, while the frontier promised none. These plains offered opportunity—nothing more—and did not give it freely. Besides Jennie's well-being, Shep had another concern; his heart was falling for another.

One night Shep sat smoking a pipe on the front porch, staring into a sky as populated with stars as his mind was with thoughts. The black prairie sky was like the future, endless with possibilities but selfish with its secrets. Shep was shaken by uncertainty, an unfamiliar and uncomfortable feeling for such a naturally confident man. His peaceful meditation was broken by the sounds of a woman crying. He followed them to their source. Young Mattie sat sobbing outside her house, too ashamed to show herself but too consumed by emotion not to cry. Mattie was always so happy, so kind. Who could have made her cry and why? Shep was furious.

"Darwin sold my horse," Mattie said. Darwin Posey was her brother, the prodigal son. Darwin had racked up gambling debts to a man named V. E. Hill and paid them off with his sister's horse. Hill was sure to turn her riding horse into a racing horse. "Ma won't let me tell Pa because he'll know Darwin has been gambling again!" said Mattie. "Hill will race him to death." Shep promised he'd settle the matter.

The next morning Shep invited Mattie to join him in the corral, where her beloved horse greeted her. Shep had bought back the horse after coaxing Hill to sell it, lest Shep expose his and Darwin's improper transaction. As Shep spoke, Darwin emerged from the shadows. A giant at six foot four and almost as wide across the shoulders, Darwin assumed his mere presence would frighten Shep. It did not. Unfazed and unintimidated, Shep shamed Darwin for how he had treated his sister, to the point the much larger man backed down. Mattie was smitten, but her mother, Nancy, would never forgive this cocksure man from the South for humiliating her son.

His business concluded, Shep still found excuses to visit Bald Hill time and again. Ostensibly he came to visit the patriarch; in truth he came to visit the daughter. Fate intervened when one day Shep received a letter from Jennie, informing him that a young Norfolk doctor had asked for her hand in marriage. Shep did not object. He was now free of guilt and obligation, free to follow his heart and marry the love of his life.

• • •

Following Hence Posey's death, Bald Hill was divided among his survivors. Mattie and Shep inherited the ranch house and turned it into a hotel to accommodate the constant stream of fortune seekers. Shep planted apple and peach orchards, as well as a grape vineyard. The first four of Shepherd and Mattie Howe's eight children were born on

Bald Hill. When his children were old enough to go to school, Shep decided it was time to leave their isolated surroundings. The family turned over the ranch to the care of a tenant farmer and moved to Eufaula, where Shep's brother Robert Howe, Uncle Bob to the kids, was practicing law.

Shep quickly established himself in Eufaula and was elected justice of the peace for McIntosh County. Folks called him Judge Howe. This land had been lawless within living memory, so Judge Howe's sworn duty to secure the peace made him no friends among those who preferred the past. When a local trader hired men to slit the throats of a competing homesteader's mules, Judge Howe helped the victim press charges. For Shep's temerity, the trader hired two men on a three-hundred-dollar bounty to kill him. Their incompetence was his salvation, but they accidentally killed his best friend in his place. Shep dodged death this time, but in the Wild West death would not be cheated for long.

Neither life nor the law was precious here. If either got in the way of greedy men, it would be sacrificed on the blood-stained altar of ambition without a moment's hesitation.

R. J. Mullins was both the mayor and the superintendent of Eufaula, and he grasped power with little thought for the duties of public service. Judge Shep Howe denounced Mullins and his friend Tom Young in Shep's office one night, much as he had done to Darwin Posey years before. When Shep turned his back and headed to the door to leave, the mayor hurled a glass paperweight across the room. It buried into the back of Shep's head, sending him to the floor with a sickening thud.

The men left Shep to bleed out as if he were a slaughtered hog. Several hours later they returned to flip him over and clean up the blood. They didn't know that a Creek couple who owned a restaurant next door saw everything. Thinking Shep was dead, Young ran to the law office of Shep's brother Robert in hysterics.

"Where is he?" Robert screamed. "What did you do with him?"

Robert knew Young was a liar and didn't wait for an answer. He ran to Shep's office to find his younger brother surrounded by a pool of his own blood, but he wasn't dead.

"What happened?" Shep said. The last thing he remembered was having his hand on the doorknob when he was struck in the back of the head. Robert got medical care for his little brother, who clung to life for a few days, but it was too late. Samuel Shepherd Howe died January 20, 1924. His oldest child was sixteen. His youngest hadn't even been born.

The night he died two men arrived at his widow's doorstep. One was John Pemberton, Shep's friend; the other was Roman Beaver, a Creek Indian there on behalf of Mattie's family. The men arrived through the back door into the kitchen, each holding a loaded pistol. "It will be tonight." That was all they said. Eye for an eye, life for a life.

Mattie said no. "Even though Pa would have expected it, I forbid you to kill them." Her voice was firm, even as her eyes were filled with tears. "Both have families, as you all do. Their deaths will not bring Shepherd back." The men left. Shepherd Howe's murderers would live. It was up to the law to see justice was served.

Mullins was tried for first-degree murder, but the McIntosh County Courthouse burned to the ground soon after Shep's death, taking with it any evidence of a motive for his murder. Throughout the trial, the defense had eight men guarding Shep's widow, Mattie, out of fear that a Creek woman and the daughter of the Lighthorsemen chief would murder both men if given the chance. In the court's eyes she was the cold-blooded savage and not the defendant, whose hands were stained with Shepherd Howe's blood.

Fearing for their lives, the Creek couple who had witnessed the murder refused to testify. The trial ended with a hung jury. One must be proven guilty beyond a shadow of a doubt, so Mullins was set free. He was ruined politically and driven out of town, but he was still alive. Samuel Shepherd Howe—father to eight, husband to one, friend to all—was dead.

• • •

While Shep was alive, his family lived comfortably. They owned an entire block, with livestock, orchards, gardens, and even a gas station. After Shep was killed, the family's income dried up. Mattie's heart was broken, and as the years went by, her health began fading. Four years of widowhood took their toll. The slender figure of her youth had changed after eight children and several illnesses. She had gained weight and frequently had agonizing pains in her chest. While getting dressed to go to church one evening, she suddenly took violently ill.

It was hard to tell what was wrong, but even in the warmth of the spring night, her skin was cold to the touch as if she were already dead. The family doctor visited her bedside but was unable to help. Surgery was the only option, but the physician refused to treat her because she owed him money. Early the next morning, on May 1, 1928, Mattie Posey, the favorite daughter of Hence Posey's, died at the age of forty-three.

Mattie Posey was loved and respected by both of her peoples. She was mourned with two funerals—one in the Creek language, the other with a Christian minister. Out of respect for her mother, Nancy, Mattie was buried according to the Creek burial ritual. Fistfuls of dirt were thrown one by one onto her casket by those who wished to offer a "farewell handshake." By the time the ritual concluded, her casket was covered.

Mattie Posey left behind eight children. Her youngest, daughter Sammye, was only three, while her eldest, Robert, was twenty. A custody battle ensued between Shep's older brother, Uncle Bob, and Mattie's mother, Nancy, for the six underage Howe children.

Elizabeth, at sixteen the third eldest, was sent to speak to her grandmother Nancy. She wasted no time on delicacy or decorum. "What will you do with us, Grandma?" Elizabeth said bluntly to her elderly Creek grandmother. Nancy called for her daughter Melissa to translate and said in Creek she would keep the toddler Sammye but would have to send the rest of the children to the Chilocco Indian School.

While the custody battle played out, Uncle Bob took the situation into his own hands and sent the children to live with his mother, Sallie DeJarnette Howe, in Virginia. Their grandmother Nancy Posey had no income and couldn't speak English, so he believed this was best for the children.

The Howe children idolized their grandmother from a thousand miles away. While Grandma Posey was a source of stability and familiarity, their grandmother Sallie DeJarnette Howe was a figure of adoration, a beautiful queen in a faraway castle. But most important to the Howe children, staying with her meant they would be together. In four short years, they had lost both parents. They could not bear to lose each other.

Their grandmother Posey was heartbroken, yet she hid her hurt

behind her thick veil of stoicism. Her long life had been one tragedy after the next. She was scarred by life and was made stronger for
it, but scars can still bleed when cut. She did the only thing that she
could do as her grandchildren left for Virginia—accept it.

The cemetery was on the left side of the train tracks leaving Eufaula.
The last thing the sons and daughters of Mattie and Shepherd Howe
saw were their parents' headstones. As the train traveled on its cross-
country journey to Virginia, the headstones become distant specks
on the horizon, painful relics of a past that was now gone but would
never be forgotten.

• • •

The Howe children could see their new home long before they reached
it. Sunnyside, the former Howe family estate, was long gone and had
been replaced by Clifton, in Radford, Virginia. Clifton sat on the highest bluff in Virginia. The hillside was covered by a field of lilies that
were as wide and as white as clouds and that perfumed the spring air
with their gentle, inviting scent. The home was not stately or grand,
but to the Howe children it was like a castle in the sky.

Grandmother Howe beamed at the sight of her eight grandchildren, who belonged to the son whom she adored most. With skin
as white as the lilies surrounding her home, Sallie must have looked
so different from her own grandchildren, especially to those of old
wealth in Virginia. Each of the Howe children had the raven hair
and brown skin of their mother, save little Elliott, with the fair hair
and skin of his father.

Yet these differences were merely superficial. They were "Shepherd's children." Sallie could sense her beloved son's presence in each.
It was all she had left of him, and she lavished each with the affection
she could no longer give to her own murdered son.

Sallie DeJarnette Howe lived in mourning. She had been widowed
since 1909 and had lost four of her children: Her daughter Ellen died
in infancy to pneumonia, her daughter Bessie at three years of age fell
into a hog boiling pit and died in agony an hour later, her son Elliott
was killed in 1918 in the Great War, and in 1924 Shep was murdered
in the Wild West. She wore a black dress all of her days, even under
the most sweltering southern sun. Its material changed—cotton for

summer, wool for winter, silk for special occasions—but it was always black. She was raised to adhere to this ritual and even in the 1920s remained devoted to the traditions of her youth. Yet wearing black was more than an arbitrary custom, for hidden behind her warm smile was a broken heart she could never mend.

Grandmother Howe cultivated a blissful idyll for her grandchildren, an escape from reality for her as much as it was for them. Conversation flourished at every meal, and a constant stream of aunts, uncles, and cousins visited the home. It was a gentle reminder for her orphaned grandchildren that they were not alone. At night Elliott and John would fall asleep in her lap, while she stroked their heads, saying, "Shep's boys."

While the hills and valleys of Virginia were different from the Oklahoma plains back home, adventure could be found for any child eager to seek it. The grounds of the estate were on the New River and its adjoining valley. It was a storybook setting for the rambunctious Elliott most of all, who would spend hours exploring the area's caves, woods, and valleys. His uncle George Howe tended a large garden and taught the children how to farm tomatoes, squash, green beans, potatoes, and cabbage. Radford was a brief respite from reality. Yet this dream, as with every one in the Howe children's experience, was short lived.

Grandmother Howe was in her eighties, and Aunt Minnie, the daughter who lived with her, was in failing health. Caring for her grandchildren was a heavy burden for the senior woman, so tending to the little ones fell often on the older children. Yet like all young people, they had ambitions of their own. Robert was going to the United States Indian Industrial Training School, now Haskell Indian Nations University, in Lawrence, Kansas; Virginia enrolled in nursing school in Richmond, Virginia; and while Elizabeth stayed nearby at the State Teachers College in Radford, her days were consumed with studying.

Grandmother Howe's other children were uninterested in raising their late brother's children. Shepherd's having brought Native Americans into the family bloodline had long been a source of tension with his siblings partially due to their own prejudice but also because they knew how the brown-skinned children would be treated. Eighteen-year-old Virginia was even told to claim she was of Spanish heritage.

Uncle Bob didn't share his sibling's prejudice. After winning custody of the underage children, he sent word that they all could return to their homeland, to Oklahoma—except for one. With the bright blonde hair and blue eyes of his father, Elliott looked nothing like his black-haired, brown-eyed brothers and sisters. He was all boy, stubborn and ornery, with a seemingly endless supply of enthusiasm for a world that had taken so much from him. One of Shepherd's brothers wished to take in Elliott and only Elliott. He wanted to care for one of his late brother's children, and Elliott was his favorite. Wild, yes, and spirited, but with his white skin, Elliott appeared as though he could belong to him. Elliott was a fine boy, and his uncle believed he could make him a good man. To prepare Elliott for his new life, the family purchased a dozen pairs of white linen knickers and shirts to help him dress the part of a young gentleman. Elliott's future was a far cry from that of his little brother, five-year-old John, who would go back west to attend the Chilocco Indian School.

Robert arrived at the family home behind the wheel of an Oldsmobile, a gift from an uncle. The eight-year-old Elliott stood on the porch in his new clothes and watched as his only remaining brother prepared to leave for the journey back to Oklahoma. The thought of being separated was too much to bear. He politely returned his new clothes, saying they were unfit for western wear. "Where John goes, I go," he said.

Elliott climbed into the car and refused to get out. Even when his relatives successfully got him out, he ran right back in. They tried to talk sense into him and explain that he had a bright future in Virginia with his uncle. It was useless. Elliott was stubborn and would not leave his little brother, John. So the family finally gave up and allowed Elliott to join his brothers on the journey to Oklahoma.

The night before the boys left for home, they sat with their sister Elizabeth on a bluff overlooking the New River. She told them to study hard and to remember their Ten Commandments. She also told them how much their parents loved them. She said how their mother and father had high hopes for both of them and prayed that both of them would live honorable lives. The three of them cried as their memories came flooding back. They could not have known then, but the brothers would only see their sister Elizabeth twice in the next ten years. The orphaned children's one desire was for all of them to stay together. Now the family was being pulled apart.

• • •

"Indians, having land in abundance, needed civilization; whites possessed civilization, but needed land," writes historian David Wallace Adams, summing up the unwritten social contract—a perverted quid pro quo—upon which federal Indian policy had been built. Among the many justifications behind manifest destiny, perhaps none was more pernicious or delusional than this—the cult of social progress. According to this principle, removing the Natives from their homes and lands was a good thing. Even while they clung bitterly to their customs, their culture was unsustainable in the face of civilization's advance. This principle espoused that it was in the Native people's own self-interest to surrender their lands and adopt a sedentary agricultural life. This was progress. To resist was to stand on the wrong side of history.

"Put into the hands of their children the primer and the hoe, and they will naturally, in time, take hold of the plough," the House Committee on Indian Affairs informed Congress in 1818. "And as their minds become enlightened and expand, the Bible will be their book, and they will grow up in habits of morality and industry, leave the chase to those whose minds are less cultivated, and become useful members of society."

However, educating Native Americans was not the story of the nineteenth century; exiling and executing them was. Any efforts to educate the millions of Native peoples who lived in the diaspora were minimal, and those that were implemented were insufficient to the challenge. The self-proclaimed enlightened minds of the time began to conclude that perhaps the Indian was incapable of civilization. Perhaps the Indian was doomed to extinction.

In the late 1800s, a new generation of social reformers took up the cause of civilizing Native Americans. The American Indian was fully capable of assimilating into American life, these reformers believed; the sustained political will to encourage and enforce it simply had been lacking.

The social reformer's ideas gained legitimacy among academic and intellectual circles with the publication in 1877 of Lewis Henry Morgan's *Ancient Society: Or Researches in the Lines of Human Progress from Savagery through Barbarism to Civilization.* An anthropologist and social theorist, Morgan was the only American social theorist to be cited by Karl Marx, Charles Darwin, and Sigmund Freud.

Morgan determined there were seven "ethical periods" to which all peoples around the world and throughout history belonged: lower savagery, middle savagery, upper savagery, lower barbarism, middle barbarism, upper barbarism, and civilization. No Native American tribe had ever reached the pinnacle of civilization, but Morgan believed that by the universal law of social progress, every society had the "germ" of progressive evolution.

"Civilizing" Native Americans was not simply a matter of solving the Indian problem for white society. This issue was about progress, social justice, and standing on the right side of history. Native Americans needed to civilize to survive, and they had the potential to do so. They only needed the light to show them the way. Civilization could be theirs, thanks to the influence of open-minded, enlightened, and educated people working through the compassionate hand of government. It made good economic sense as well. Educating a Native American for eight years was estimated to cost twelve hundred dollars, or a mere fraction of the price it cost for killing one in war.

For more than a hundred years, the Native Americans' land and laws had been taken from them. Now the federal government was coming for the Indian family. The pull of reservation life and the "savagery" it cultivated was too much for any child to resist. To be effectively assimilated into white civilization, the Native American child had to be separated from the reservation.

"The United States government established off-reservation boarding schools in the late 1800s as part of its grand civilizing plan to transform Native American people," writes Adams. "Federal policymakers and administrators cooperated to remove thousands of Native American children and young adults from their families, homes and tribes in order to educate them in a new way of life."

On May 17, 1882, Congress authorized the construction of one such Indian boarding school in Oklahoma. It was south of the Kansas state line, adjacent to the Ponca and Pawnee Reservations, and along the banks of the Chilocco Creek. Its name was Chilocco Indian School. The name most likely came from the Creek phrase *tci lako*, meaning "big deer" (referring to a horse); though another explanation is that it was a combination of the Choctaw *Chilukki* and the Cherokee *Tsalagi*, both meaning "cave people."

The first graduating class in 1894 consisted of six boys and nine girls who had completed the eighth grade. By 1906 the number of students had grown to seven hundred from forty tribes. By the 1920s, the student population had swelled to eight hundred and went as high as twelve hundred throughout its final decades of operation.

An agriculture teacher named L. E. Correll arrived at Chilocco in 1918 and served as superintendent from 1926 until he retired in 1952. During his tenure, Correll developed and implemented a comprehensive agriculture training program. His Boy Farm Plan gave male students direct supervision over an acre of land in the hopes of instilling an appreciation for hard work and responsibility. In turn, they would be allowed to share in the fruits of their labor.

The Great Depression brought many children through Chilocco's doors. Work and food were often scarce back home, and in many ways education was even rarer, especially for juniors and seniors in high school. Many rural communities had no public schools, and those that did exist were unwelcoming to Native Americans. Chilocco became something of a refuge for many students.

Despite the desires of the Bureau of Indian Affairs in Washington, Chilocco continued to enroll mixed-blood students. In the 1920s the number of full-blooded students barely exceeded 50 percent and declined to 31 percent by 1940. Also in the 1920s enrollment shifted to focus on older students, as it was believed that small children's needs were better met at home. As the decade ended, the Chilocco Indian School no longer accepted orphans. One of them arrived just in time.

• • •

The bugle sounded twenty-two times a day at Chilocco. Before the sun rose, students practiced close-order drills. Boys as young as nine years old wore old World War I uniforms, with wrap leggings and high-button collars, and carried Enfield rifles on their shoulders. Older students served as officers and company commanders, leading the younger students in marching. As drill sergeants, they would call out disobedient students with cuss words and nicknames. One especially ornery student earned his nickname that way. "You dizzy bastard, get in step!"

Dizzy was Elliott Howe.

After spending his last Christmas with his family, Elliott arrived at Chilocco with his sister Margaret before the new year in 1929. John would arrive a short time later. Elliott was only ten years old. Even with his sister and some distant blood relatives there, Chilocco was not a warm and welcoming place for Elliott. As he walked up the steps to Home 2, the dormitory for young boys, an old Otoe Indian man who was big and broad enough to earn the nickname "Hippo" looked down at him and grunted, "Hmm, white boy. You got no business here." Hippo thought nothing of striking students for no other reason than he wanted to.

Violence was part of the student experience. Kids called Elliott *stahitkey*, or "white man." As far as Elliott was concerned, that was the worst thing anyone could call him. "We looked down on white people. I mean, I did," Elliott would say years later. "There was a pride, or whatever it was, that we had in being an Indian. If you weren't an Indian, [we] just felt sorry for you."

Elliott had two fist fights on his first day. He was afraid but knew if he didn't fight—and didn't win—then he would be bullied for the rest of his days. By fighting back, he earned some measure of respect, though he went to bed with dried blood in his nose and tears in his eyes. There would be many more fist fights to come, but the one saving grace was that all of them were fair. No knives, no clubs, no stomping—just closed fists into the soft flesh of another kid's face.

The Indian boarding school experiment sought to detribalize children into the obedient model of successful citizens. However, when naive, self-serving ideals confront the ambivalent reality of human nature, unintended consequences result. Homogenizing Native American children was the goal, but the exact opposite occurred. Pan-Indian and tribal identity only grew stronger among the students, even those with mixed blood and fair skin like Elliott. Yet despite his pride in his Creek ancestry, Elliott's white skin made him an outsider. His place in the Native social realm wasn't a given; he had to earn it.

At Chilocco the boys followed a strict code of honor that applied to everyone, one that valued bravery and loyalty above all. Honesty was the highest virtue and snitching the gravest sin. For every child, respect was earned, mostly at the wrong end of a fist. Boys from the same tribe would form gangs to defend their own. Elliott had no such protection. Fighting became his daily ritual, as much as marching and going to class.

Chilocco was where Elliott formed his lifelong hatred of bullies, people who used their power or position to pick on those who could not defend themselves. One day Elliott and a group of boys were playing marbles with Willy. Willy was three years older and thirty pounds heavier, all of it muscle. He did not like to lose, and Elliott made the mistake of winning. When Willy smacked him in the mouth, he said, "Willy, you can't do that." Then he stood up and took off his jacket. Willy stared at him in shock, a look that morphed into the wicked snarl of a hungry wolf baring its fangs.

"Well, by God, you're not going to fight me, are you?"

"I'll fight you," Elliott said, knowing full well he was going to get killed doing it.

At the top of the stairs watching this was a boy named JM. Tall and lanky, about Willy's age, JM was quiet and unassuming. He wasn't Elliott's enemy, but he wasn't his friend either. Just another kid with nowhere else to go.

"Hell, Dizzy, you ain't got no business fighting. I'll fight him," said JM.

There was no reason to think JM could fight anyone, let alone fight a boy as big and strong as Willy was. But JM walked calmly down the steps and made quick work of Willy. Violence begets violence, but on this occasion, it put a stop to it. Willy never bothered Elliott, or anybody else for that matter, ever again. In that moment, Elliott learned to stand up not only for himself but also for others.

• • •

Elliott wasn't a model student by any means. Chilocco issued demerits, which they called red cards. If a student got caught stealing from the commissary, poultry yard, or bakery, he or she got a red card and spent the weekend working in the rock pile. While the kids at Chilocco were luckier than many during the Great Depression, their three square meals a day provided meager portions. Stealing food was the only way Elliott kept from going hungry. Justified or not, stealing began to come just as naturally to Elliott as breathing. So while other kids spent their weekends playing, Elliott spent his smashing big rocks into small ones.

Discipline and defiance rise as one, and a school as structured as Chilocco was always going to be difficult for a boy such as Elliott Howe. He successfully ran away from Chilocco when he was eleven years old, hiding on a train and making it all the way to Tulsa, more than a hundred miles away. However, his adventure was short lived. He was no more off the tracks than he ran into his older brother, Robert, who took him back the next day. As much as he rebelled against the rules, the rules would always win.

Chilocco wasn't a prison by any means. Will Rogers, one of the most famous men alive at the time, had nephews there. Jim Thorpe, among the greatest athletes in history, sent his daughters there. Thorpe would visit from time to time and showed the boys how to play football. Elliott even got to see him kick a pigskin from goal to goal.

Every other Saturday there'd be a dance in the gymnasium, and the other Saturdays there'd be a picture show. There were sports too. Native American schools were barred from playing other high schools, so they had to play football, baseball, and basketball against college teams. When the school got rid of football, it took up boxing. It was a good fit, and *The Ring* magazine named Chilocco's boxing team one of the best amateur programs in the nation. Elliott fought for the team. After all of the experience he'd had in the schoolyard, he'd become a pretty good fighter. Technique and finesse, however, were never his strong suit. He knew how to hit hard and, even more important, how to get hit without falling down.

Boxing was a good outlet for the angry young man, but even the discipline of the ring couldn't temper his defiant character. His nature made him a rebel, while his white skin made him an outsider. He had friends, but he was always a stranger. School administrators didn't expect much out of him, nothing good anyway. Elliott earned a reputation. He broke into the commissary and bakery so many times that he was blamed for theft even on the rare occasions that he didn't do it.

As a Boy Scout, Elliott was sent to his scoutmaster every time he was caught stealing, and every time he recited his scout's oath and was given another chance. On one occasion after burglarizing the commissary, Elliott entered his scoutmaster's office. He straightened his back, took a breath, and prepared to recite his scout's oath just as he'd done dozens of times before. "Elliott, you're a Boy Scout," his scoutmaster said. "Well, you're not anymore. You're not anymore." There was no hesitation; he had given up on Elliott. And he was not the only one.

Elliott's headmaster L. E. Correll went so far as to say, "Howe, you'll be in the penitentiary before you're twenty-one." It wasn't a warning; it was a prediction. He had no hope of saving Elliott, no hope for his being anything other than just another young man headed for prison. Chilocco had lost faith in Elliott Howe. Almost everybody had.

Chilocco allowed a Baptist missionary from the small town of Arkansas City, Kansas, right on the border of Kansas and Oklahoma, to minister to the students. (While her name has been forgotten, her actions never will be.) Every Wednesday and Friday night, she'd drive down and lead the Baptist Young Person's Union. Elliott didn't have a close relationship with God or any faith. At his age, after his life, he didn't have reason to believe there was a God looking out for him. Take care of yourself because nobody else was going to do it—that was Elliott's faith.

Preachers would visit Chilocco, thump their Bibles, and say their prayers, but they never changed anything. Elliott called them Ether because they put everyone to sleep. While they droned on, he'd stare up at the ceiling and count the rafters.

The Baptist missionary was different. The first thing he noticed about her was her age. She was an old maid who showed up in a rickety old car. She didn't boast about her faith, because she was too busy living it. Unlike just about everybody else in his life, she saw something redeemable in Elliott. She saw that he was adrift and could be so much more if only he would let go of his anger.

She told him to quit stealing because it was wrong. He had already heard it a hundred times from just as many people, but from her it meant something. She wasn't punishing him; instead, she was telling him to quit stealing for his sake because he was better than that. Elliott didn't have any reason to believe that he was, other than the fact that she did.

Elliott began to change his ways, much to the surprise of his teachers, friends, and administrators. He served on the Student Council, played the lead in the school plays, and escorted the Arkalala Queen at the main function of the year at Chilocco. He was even selected to represent Chilocco on a radio program in Kansas City.

Elliott wasn't the only one whose life the missionary touched. She continued to serve the young people at Chilocco the next few years after Elliott graduated. But as times changed, resentment and envy for her influence grew. She never took a nickel from anyone, but her mere presence was a threat. Around 1941 while Elliott was fighting in the Pacific, she was asked to never come back to Chilocco. Her life lost its purpose, so she ended it.

Perhaps it was just as well Elliott was out to sea, thousands of miles away. He'd already lost so many loved ones to tragedy. He wouldn't find out until much later that the old Baptist missionary who had saved his life had taken her own.

• • •

After graduating from Chilocco, Howe moved in with Uncle Bob and retook his senior year at Eufaula High School. He didn't think Chilocco had prepared him academically. His concerns were well founded. Chilocco trained him to work with his hands, not his mind, and he needed that extra year of school. Elliott had been an unremarkable student and a gifted troublemaker while at Chilocco, but he graduated at the top of his class at Eufaula and planned to go to college.

By now it was the middle of the Great Depression, which was even more miserable in Oklahoma, thanks to the Dust Bowl. While a successful attorney, Uncle Bob was not well-off because his clients weren't either. In lieu of payment, farmers would trade eggs with him, giving him more than he could ever eat. "What am I supposed to do with all of these damn eggs?" Elliott would recall his uncle saying. It was frustrating, but Uncle Bob's clients had no choice, so neither did he.

Elliott barely got to know his father, so in many ways his uncle Bob took his father's place. He trusted and admired him more than anyone and wanted to be an attorney because his uncle was. Trouble was, Elliott couldn't afford to go to a university. Uncle Bob didn't have much to give him, so he mortgaged his one cow for a hundred dollars so Elliott could go to Connors State College in Warner, Oklahoma.

It was there that he first saw Imelda Jane McNamara, a drum majorette from Wagoner High School. While he was struck by her beauty, he didn't speak to her and fully expected to never see her again. A little more than ten years later, his sister would formally introduce the two, and they would later marry.

While Elliott was in school, Uncle Bob passed away on January 24, 1941, leaving behind his wife, Bertha, and his late brother's mostly grown children. Elliott continued his schooling for a brief period, but the world had other plans.

Storm clouds were once again gathering over Europe, and Elliott anticipated the worst. Shortly after Uncle Bob died, Elliott dropped out of college and enlisted in the navy. Believing conflict across the pond was inevitable, Elliott hoped to avoid getting drafted to the infantry and being killed in the green fields of France, as his namesake, Uncle Elliott, had been in 1918. The navy would be much safer, he figured. While he had hoped to serve on the uss *Oklahoma*, his ambition was never realized. The ship was sunk by Japanese fighters in their surprise raid on Pearl Harbor. Instead of Europe, Howe spent the next three years fighting in the Pacific theater, rising to the rank of first class petty officer. While at sea, Howe had a portion of his paycheck sent to support his aunt Bertha back home, as she now had no one left.

After v-j Day on September 2, 1945, Elliott was honorably discharged from the navy, and he returned to Oklahoma to complete his schooling at the University of Tulsa on the GI Bill. He graduated with a bachelor of arts and enrolled in the University of Tulsa School of Law. He was one step closer to becoming a lawyer.

Now in his late twenties, Howe put himself through law school by painting houses and working as a minute clerk in the court clerk's office. This experience landed him his first job out of law school as an assistant in the county attorney's office.

Elliott Howe had come a long way from poor orphan, to lost cause, to public defender for Tulsa County. He knew the only reason was because somebody had believed in him when everybody else had given up. Howe never forgot that. He believed that without the intervention of that Baptist missionary, he would have wound up in jail just as Buster Youngwolfe had.

Now Howe was the only hope to save that young man's life.

9

A Line in the Sand

"Indian Shifts Stand, Denies Slaying Girl," the *Tulsa World* declared on Wednesday, April 8, 1953. Reporter Troy Gordon had rushed from the Tulsa County Jail, where he and Howe had interviewed Buster the night before, to write his story for the next morning's paper.

For the first time, *Tulsa World* readers were introduced to Buster's side of the story. In the article, Buster claimed he was "hungry and without sleep" during his five days of confinement and that county officials "threatened to put [his] mother in jail." He said the authorities "put words in my mouth" during his confession and that he made up his reenactment as he went along. He chose the spot by the creek for Phyllis's murder because "it was the first logical place I saw."

"I'll swear on the Bible I didn't kill her," Buster said bluntly.

"I categorically deny all these statements," said County Attorney Robert Wheeler, delivering the county's rebuttal to the paper. Wheeler insisted that Buster's confession was not given under pressure. He also asserted that he had made that clear to Buster at both the beginning and the end of the signed statement.

"He said in his statement he wasn't mistreated, threatened, or promised anything. And that is the truth," said Wheeler. Wheeler claimed that the authorities let Buster see his wife and mother whenever he asked, frequently asked him if he wanted anything, and made sure he didn't miss a meal. When asked if Buster was sleepy, Wheeler remarked, "So were we."

"No threats, no promises—just routine questioning," said Sheriff Bill Field. "If the guy's innocent, why did he try so hard to plead guilty when arraigned before Judge Stanley Edmister Monday?"

While the *Tulsa World* reported the defense's claims and the county's rebuttal, the *Tulsa Tribune* gave Buster no such opportunity. The *Tulsa Tribune* article that afternoon was essentially a question-and-answer session with the county attorney. One by one Wheeler savaged each of Buster's claims.

"He had to repudiate his confession," Wheeler said. "It was his only possible defense." Wheeler's observation was ironic, as Buster's confession was the only evidence the county had to prosecute him. According to Wheeler, Buster had asked Assistant County Attorney J. Howard Edmondson if he would get a life term if he confessed, but Edmondson refused. "I told him he would get the electric chair if I had anything to say about it," said Wheeler. "And I told him that before he confessed."

The *Tulsa Tribune* wasn't reporting a story; it was printing a response. Neither Buster nor Howe were quoted in the *Tribune*'s coverage, which was featured on the front page under the headline "Youngwolfe's Renege Follows Familiar Path." To further discredit Buster, the county attorney also recounted two similar events from Tulsa's recent past. Each time a young woman had been brutally murdered. Each time the suspect—a man of color as Buster was—had confessed to the crime only to recant it later, saying he had been pressured by authorities. And each time the confessor was convicted. The parallels Wheeler was making to Buster's own claims were loud and clear.

In May 1945 almost eight years before the Youngwolfe case, twenty-year-old Panta Lou Liles was raped and bludgeoned to death in her bedroom. Liles was an aircraft employee and the wife of a sailor stationed in the South Pacific. Tulsa police officers discovered her body after a friend telephoned her apartment bur received no answer. A fruitless investigation followed, with several weeks passing with no arrests. Even the FBI was called in, to no avail. For weeks frightened Tulsans were left to believe that a crazed murderer was on the loose. The press reports only heightened their sense of fear and urgency. Who would be the next victim?

Finally, a suspect was arrested—Leroy Benton, an African American man described as a "two-time loser" in the press. Tulsa County filed charges against Benton after he failed a lie detector test in Kansas City, Missouri. Benton confessed to the crime and even signed a statement, but he recanted on the witness stand during his trial, saying his confession was coerced. Benton claimed that he was interrogated without food or water. He even claimed his interrogators told him a lynch mob was trying to break into the jail and take justice into their own hands. Twenty-four years removed from the Tulsa Race Massacre, an event the thirty-five-year-old Benton surely remembered, this threat held incredible gravity.

Despite Benton's pleas, he was found guilty by a jury and sentenced to life in prison on November 17, 1945. Tulsans could sleep soundly at night once again, for a rapist-murderer was behind bars. Justice was served—except it wasn't. Benton spent nearly two years in prison for a crime he didn't commit and was lucky he wasn't put to death for it. During his appeal, it was determined that Benton was forced into confessing. Unless evidence was provided for a new trial, the criminal court of appeals ordered that Benton be released from prison. Benton was freed early in March 1947, an event that the press treated nonchalantly. Wheeler neglected to mention Benton's release in his statement to the *Tulsa Tribune*.

In the same article, Wheeler recounted another Tulsa County murder case with similar circumstances. The victim's name was Dorothy Waldrop. She was a twenty-two-year-old expectant mother who was raped and murdered in June 1951. Waldrop was found with a dirty handkerchief wrapped around her throat. A twenty-year-old African American suspect named Eugene Monroe was charged with the crime. Originally from California, where he was charged with armed robbery, Monroe had been paroled to an aunt in Tulsa. He was described as "slight" with "tortured eyes and a scarred face." After eleven hours of questioning, including a lie detector test conducted by Lt. Harry Stege, Monroe signed a confession. Stege received a commendation from FBI director J. Edgar Hoover for his work on the case. However, Monroe repudiated the confession at his trial, claiming that the officers told him his seventy-one-year-old grandmother was in jail and that they would only release her if he confessed. Monroe was found guilty of murder.

Wheeler's point to the *Tulsa Tribune* and its readership was clear: Tulsa County had a history of young men of color raping and murdering young white women, confessing to the crimes, and then recanting their confessions by claiming they were coerced by the authorities. Buster's claims were nothing new. The authorities had their man. Buster Youngwolfe had killed Phyllis Jean Warren.

Wheeler was crafting his narrative for the pliant press and appealing to a public that was looking for convenient truths. The prospect that the county had forced a confession out of an innocent man was troubling. The thought that a child rapist and murderer was still loose was even worse. And the idea that a man would confess to a crime—murder no less—that he didn't commit was unfathomable. However, assuring the public that this "21-year-old Indian" was guilty of the crime and was safely behind bars provided readers some semblance of solace—true or not.

Elliott Howe didn't draw a line in the sand; the line was already there, and he chose his side. By taking on the county and using a public forum such as the *Tulsa World* to stage his assault, the part-time public defender showed remarkable savvy—and maybe a little foolishness. As far as everyday Tulsans were concerned, Buster was a confessed child rapist and murderer, a monster. Now Howe was defending that same monster. Changing people's perceptions would not be easy. It would take a miracle.

• • •

Why would a man confess to a murder he didn't commit? The question was on everyone's minds, and many no doubt reached the same, unshakable conclusion: He wouldn't. The idea that someone would say he killed another person—a child, no less—when he didn't defied logic. Yet even before Buster Youngwolfe recanted his confession, as Wheeler's recollections to the *Tulsa Tribune* showed, there had been a history of suspects doing the same.

What the public didn't know was how startlingly common coerced confessions were, and they still are to this day. "[False confessions] are consistently one of the leading, yet most misunderstood, causes of error in the American legal system," Richard A. Leo, a professor of law and psychology and an expert on police interrogation tactics, said in his article "False Confessions: Causes, Consequences, and Implications" in the *Journal of the American Academy of Psychiatry and the Law.* "[False confessions] remain one of the most prejudicial sources of false evidence that lead to wrongful convictions."

Leo's article, published in 2009, shows little has changed in fifty-six years. His description of the scenario that often leads to false confessions could have been written about Buster: "Getting a confession becomes particularly important when there is no other evidence against the suspect, especially in high-profile cases in which there is great pressure on police detectives to solve the crime."

For decades, similar situations to Buster's have been a major cause of error in criminal justice and prosecution. Studies have shown that when people who falsely confess to a crime go to trial, anywhere from 73 to 81 percent of these innocent people are convicted. These percentages were based on cases from the 1990s and 2000s; one can only imagine they were even higher in the 1950s, illustrating just how dire Buster's situation was.

Not all false confessions are the same. In 1985 social psychologists Saul Kassin and Lawrence Wrightsman identified three different categories of false confession. Modern researchers have expanded on these terms and today recognize three types of false confessions: voluntary, persuaded, and coerced-compliant.

Voluntary false confessions are just that: A person voluntarily confesses to a crime he or she did not commit without police coercion. The individual's motivation may be self-punishment, attention seeking, threats from people other than police, or simply delusion. For instance, a voluntary false confessor may be trying to protect the real culprit. In other cases, a person may falsely confess to a crime based on what he or she has learned from media reports for no other reason than to get attention.

More troubling are persuaded false confessions. Originally known as internalized in Kassin and Wrightsman's terminology, persuaded false confessions occur when the innocent suspects actually believe that they committed the crime. The suspects become so damaged and confused by police interrogation that they begin to doubt their own memories. When their confidence is so shattered, they confess to a crime they come to believe they committed, even though they did not.

Buster's confession falls into the third category of coerced-compliant. "The pages of legal history are filled with stories of coerced-compliant confessions," said Kassin. The description for this type of false confession should sound familiar. "[Compliant false confessions] are coerced by police conduct, and are generally made in the hope of ending the coercion," according to Marc Bookman in his 2013 article "The Confessions of Innocent Men" published in *The Atlantic*. "Promises of food, a phone call, drugs to feed a habit—all of these led to compliant false confessions. The guarantee of sleep or simply being left alone has been enough to get an innocent person to admit to a horrendous crime." Put simply, when suspects fear they have no chance of ending their interrogation through continued denials, they may think their only hope of escape is telling their interrogators what they want to hear—a confession. Just as Buster did.

Also as in Buster's case, coerced-compliant false confessors will immediately recant their confessions, naively believing that in the end their innocence will exonerate them. The problem is that as Buster was learning, a confession becomes similar to a noose around the neck: It only gets tighter the more the accused struggles against it. According to Leo, as the case against an innocent false confessor moves through the criminal justice system, it "gathers more force, and the error becomes increasingly difficult to reverse."

As the U.S. Supreme Court stated in the 1991 case *Arizona v. Fulminate*, "A confession is like no other evidence." Confessions are powerful weapons, even when they are false. What was true in Buster Youngwolfe's case is just as true today. Jurors and the public have a hard time believing an innocent person would falsely confess to a crime he or she did not commit. Even mock jurors who acknowledge the power of coercion over the mind still feel that if they were in a similar situation, they would resist.

"Other than physical evidence such as DNA or fingerprints left at the scene of the crime—and in some documented cases even in spite of exculpatory DNA or other physical evidence—a confession is the most powerful proof of guilt," said Bookman. Indeed, DNA evidence has been the salvation for numerous individuals falsely charged with crimes they did not commit, including as many as 15–20 percent who were incarcerated as a result of police-induced false confessions.

But Buster's trial was in 1953. While the DNA double helix had been recently discovered by James Watson and Francis Crick, its potential for forensic science and criminology was still years away. Buster Youngwolfe didn't have such tests to save him. All he had was a public defender named Elliott Howe.

10

Changing the Conversation

Howe was alone. No one in the county government believed Buster was innocent. No one in the city government believed he was innocent. Most of the press and the majority of the public did not believe Buster was innocent. "Even I didn't believe in Buster's innocence," Howe's wife, Imelda, said to the *Tulsa World* months later. "But Bill was all alone and I couldn't let him know how I really felt."

Howe was a man alone against a city, a county, perhaps even common sense. As far as the public was concerned, he was a fool at best and a charlatan at worst. After the weeks-long nightmare that was Phyllis's disappearance and discovery, Tulsans wanted to put this tragedy behind them and Buster behind bars. Buster had confessed to killing the girl. Case closed. But now the story had flipped. Now Buster denied killing the girl and was even claiming the authorities had forced him to lie. The strange case of Buster Youngwolfe was not coming to a close anytime soon.

Following Buster's public denial, Howe's case got off to a rocky start. On Wednesday, April 8, Howe tried to prevent the county attorney and the sheriff from questioning his client any further. Howe claimed that the authorities had violated Buster's constitutional rights by holding him for four days without charge and by forcing him to reenact the crime. Wheeler fought back, claiming he had no idea Howe was Buster's attorney at the time of the reenactment. Perhaps displaying his sense of invulnerability, Wheeler said, "The most you can say was violated was some moral or ethical standards."

"I think Mr. Wheeler has very ably stated my case," said Howe.

Only one opinion mattered here, and unfortunately for Howe, Judge Elmer Adams did not agree with the public defender. According to Judge Adams, Wheeler had violated a "canon of the bar association" by communicating with Buster without Howe present but had not violated the Constitution. Howe's appeal to prevent the county from speaking to Buster was denied.

Howe asked for Wheeler's personal assurance that it would not happen again, but he was denied that as well. Wheeler said there was no reason for the court to forbid the county from unethical acts because "we have done nothing unethical." Wheeler was contradicting himself in the press, and only Howe was willing to call him on it. In any event, the county attorney had little incentive to cede any ground. He was winning. For added measure, Wheeler said that Howe's petition was "ridiculous."

"It is not ridiculous under what has transpired," said Howe.

Tensions between the two sides simmered from the start and for good reason. To prove Buster's innocence, Howe had to prove that the county attorney was incompetent at best and corrupt at worst. From the county attorney's vantage point, he was no longer fighting just to put a murderer behind bars but also to protect his reputation.

Tension spilled beyond the courtroom. Clifton Brooks, Buster's brother-in-law, arrived to work at a rendering plant and received a threatening note. Addressed to "C.B.," the note cryptically said, "Do not be here when B comes to trial. I mean it and you know that." Who wrote the note and what it meant were never determined. It would not be the last time a Youngwolfe was threatened.

Howe hit another snag that Friday, April 10. Judge Stanley C. Edminster, who had already refused Buster's guilty plea, now heard Howe's first choice for an investigator. The court had granted Howe permission to use county funds to hire a private investigator. He had selected Ray Graves, a former Tulsa policeman and county investigator. Wheeler opposed Ray Graves on account of his being a former member of a local law enforcement agency. Wheeler noted that he did not object to the county's paying for a private investigator but did not approve of the one Howe wanted. Wheeler's objection was enough to sink Ray Graves. Howe's request was denied.

The prosecution had county resources, public opinion, a confession, and seemingly the court's sympathies. The defense only had Bill Howe. With little in the way of resources, Howe's colorful personality would prove to be his most powerful weapon. If the county was going to have ample newspaper space in the *Tulsa Tribune* for dry, misleading question-and-answer sessions, Howe had to be more creative to earn his ink. In Judge Edminster's courtroom, Howe declared that "there are six sex maniacs running loose in the neighborhood where the girl was killed and I think we will find the killer among them." "Dizzy" had grown up but never lost his defiance. Howe still knew how to get attention.

"We have made a thorough investigation," said Wheeler, outraged at Howe's suggestion. "We are convinced we have the right man. We think our case is made."

By provoking the county, Howe carved a wound channel right through the heart of the existing narrative. The local authorities, symbols of law and order, were being demystified in the public's eyes. These guys knew how to punch someone in the face; they weren't expecting Howe to punch back.

Howe's ploy won him attention but few friends. Many of his colleagues wondered if this was all some publicity stunt. Gossipmongers accused him of defending a child rapist and murderer just to make a name for himself. If Buster had already been tried and hanged by the court of public opinion, then Howe swung right next to him. And the rope around his throat was getting tighter. Slowly but surely, though, Howe's brash brand of justice was making its mark.

On Sunday, April 12, the front page of the *Tulsa World* highlighted in hideous black and white the once-hidden slums of north Tulsa. This unimaginable poverty, camouflaged in plain sight from gentrified Tulsa, was the place Buster and Phyllis once called home. For the first time, everyday Tulsans got to see the depths of poverty that existed a few blocks from their own backyards. "America's most beautiful city" was home to a third world community, and most of the public had no idea. The tumble-down shacks didn't look as though they could withstand a stiff gust of wind, let alone the violent storms and tornadoes for which Oklahoma is famous. Yet many people lived in these shacks, for they had no place else to go.

Under the headline "Elimination of Crime-Breeding Slum Areas Essential, Authorities Agree," Troy Gordon wrote that "the insides of the houses are indescribable." Gordon attempted to do so nevertheless, detailing the "old, unsafe and sagging" shacks as best as he could. There weren't many details to provide. The homes were two or three rooms, Gordon wrote, with as many as two to six adults and four or more children living in the same space. They had no sewer, no water, and no heat, save a wood-burning stove. Nothing but walls. "If you've been there, you know what they're like," wrote Gordon. "If you haven't, the words won't mean anything."

In the same article, Gordon quoted city-county health director Dr. T. Paul Haney, who said, "As Tulsa grows, we will have to adopt a program of slum clearance." What would happen to the people who lived there? Nobody asked the question, because nobody had a good answer.

The people in this neighborhood held onto their dignity, if nothing else, for it was all that they had. Yet curiosity seekers even tried to take that away. Ever since Phyllis's body had been found, people had come to the neighborhood to take pictures and point at the residents, as if they were animals in the wild. The sightseers were motivated by morbid curiosity and were ambivalent to their fellow man. They came to see if this place was real, to see if people could actually live this way. When they saw that everything they had heard and read about was true, they pointed, they laughed, they snapped pictures, and then they left, tourists returning to their safe, comfortable worlds just a few miles away. The sightseers stared into the residents' faces, worn out, ragged, and aged beyond their years; the residents looked back and saw the real animals staring at them.

"Life isn't too good to them, probably in part through their own fault, but not completely," wrote Gordon. "They don't have much future and, consequently, no ambition. They live from day to day and are surprisingly cheerful. Actually, they feel just like you would if you lived here."

• • •

Gordon's coverage of the neighborhood in the *Tulsa World* was critical, but Howe knew it would not be enough. Even so, after being vilified from all corners, he appreciated the fair press.

It is hard to overstate the importance of the local newspaper, especially in 1953. Just as the media that would eventually take its place—television and the internet—the newspaper did more than just provide people information; it also actively directed the reader's sense of reality: This is what happened, this is who was involved, and, most important, this is what it means for you.

As the weeks passed, two distinct narratives began to form on the pages of Tulsa's morning and afternoon newspapers. In the morning, *Tulsa World* readers saw a passionate public defender with a combative personality fight the good fight against controversial Tulsa County officials. In the afternoon, *Tulsa Tribune* readers cheered on the vigilant prosecutors who fought to see that justice was served against a craven, attention-hungry attorney and his client, a confessed child rapist and murderer.

More than sixty years later, with the benefit of hindsight, the *Tulsa World*'s reporting now reads as firsthand coverage of an innocent man's long, grueling fight for justice. Conversely, the *Tulsa Tribune* paints Buster and Howe as villains who were foolishly delaying the prosecution's inevitable, rightful victory. The modern reader witnesses history unfolding in real time, involving people who did not know how the story would end. While both narratives could not be true, neither was false per se; such is the paradox of the press. Each newspaper's coverage was factual but distorted, reflecting the narrative that would appeal most to its respective readers. If you were to read both papers in 1953, as many Tulsans did, you would have no idea what—or whom—to believe.

The *Tulsa World* and the *Tulsa Tribune* weren't the only periodicals to cover the story. The case of Buster Youngwolfe received national coverage in two lurid but popular pulp detective magazines, *Official Detective Stories* and *Inside Detective*.

Published in the June 1953 edition of *Official Detective Stories*, "But She Teased Me about My Wife" by Steven Nolen is a seedy crime story. Creating melodramatic dialogue to fill in narrative gaps, Nolen's account stops just shy of the sensational as it details Phyllis's disappearance and the authorities' investigation. Nolen also goes to great lengths to portray Robert and Josie Warren as concerned, doting parents to their lost daughter Phyllis. Conversely, newspaper accounts from that same time depicted them as not particularly concerned about Phyllis, either before or after her disappearance. Following Buster's arrest, the Warrens practically vanish from every account.

The photo in Paul McClung's "Tease" from the July 1953 edition of *Inside Detective* makes the magazine's motives clear. It is a chilling picture of Buster staring at the reader with the cold, emotionless expression of a killer looking down on his dying victim. McClung covers much of the same territory as Nolen did, succinctly sketching the events and players involved in the investigation. Unlike Nolen, however, McClung includes the Rev. Leontine Bryant. Her inclusion is not surprising, as the septuagenarian spiritualist was quite a bewitching character for true crime readers in the 1950s.

Both accounts, published after the trial concluded, end with Howe's arrival in the story and Buster's subsequent recanting of his confession. In "Tease," McClung closes with a cryptic, ominous statement: "A jury will decide which of Buster Youngwolfe's stories to believe, his confession or denial; decide whether Buster did kill Phyllis—or whether another girl has been swallowed up in the darkness of unsolved cases in Tulsa."

While the war of words would play out in print, the case would be contested in the courtroom. The battle lines had been drawn, and Wheeler and Howe stood on opposing sides. One man was sworn to protect and the other to defend, with each staking his prized reputation on Buster's guilt or innocence. As the young man's life hung in the balance, only one could be right.

• • •

Howe didn't get his first choice for a special investigator, Ray Graves, but on Saturday, April 11, he successfully hired his second, Phil San Angelo. San Angelo was a former county deputy sheriff with a gentle, meek appearance that belied his years spent in law enforcement. Retired from the force, San Angelo now worked as a security officer for the Douglas Aircraft Company plant. Most of his face was covered by his thick, black-rimmed glasses, giving him a bookish, unassuming air. It was probably for the best that San Angelo looked more quiet and taciturn, for Howe more than made up the difference.

"We have some hot suspects," said Howe. He added a dig at the opposition: "I have given the county attorney's office and the sheriff a chance to get out of this gracefully, to get out and help find the killer. Now I predict there's going to be some red faces in the county attorney's office."

Wheeler insisted that the county had made a thorough investigation and that Buster was the culprit. "The case is solved and this is just a smoke screen."

Howe and San Angelo spent Sunday with Buster in the county jail, rehashing the details of Phyllis's disappearance for what must have felt like the millionth time. Following a three-hour marathon session, Howe said, "I do not stand alone now," and that San Angelo shared his belief in Buster's innocence. Howe even went so far as to say that after studying the evidence, "it hit me like a slap in the face who the real murderer was."

After San Angelo began investigating the case and canvassing the neighborhood, Howe's "hot suspects" soon became one "very, very hot suspect." Living within walking distance of Phyllis's home were six sex criminals, none of whom had been questioned by the authorities; however, San Angelo narrowed in on one suspect. Howe wanted the suspect to be arrested and given a lie detector test, just as Buster had been. But there was one significant problem: Who would make the arrest?

In his haste and inexperience, Howe had failed to request that San Angelo be granted all the rights of a law officer, including carrying a weapon and making arrests. Judge Edmister said that he saw no reason why San Angelo should not have the right to make an arrest; Wheeler wasn't having it.

"Phil San Angelo has no more right to make an arrest than any other private citizen, no matter what his background," said Wheeler. He added that he had opposed the court's appointing Ray Graves for that same reason. The one man who could grant San Angelo the authority to make an arrest, Wheeler, was the same person who had no incentive to do so. Thus, while Howe had his special investigator and even had his suspect, he simply could not do anything with either. While Howe and San Angelo were convinced they knew who really killed Phyllis, they never publicly named their suspect. The county never gave this deference to Buster.

Wheeler did grant Howe one caveat: If the public defender presented the county attorney's office with enough evidence to justify arresting his suspect, then a law officer would make the arrest. It was an empty public gesture. Wheeler was the opposition. The defense team's finding the real murderer would be a game changer that not only would kill the prosecution's case but also would humiliate and delegitimize the police, the sheriff's office, and the county in one fell swoop. Charging the wrong man based on a false confession was bad enough, but if the real murderer was discovered by a security guard turned special investigator within twenty-four hours of being hired? Wheeler couldn't have it.

"We believe him [Buster] guilty beyond any doubt," said Wheeler. "We have no intention of reopening the investigation because we are sure we have the guilty man."

Howe was sure they didn't. Even without an alternate suspect, Howe said that Buster's innocence "can be proved beyond the doubt of anyone." He noted in the *Tulsa World* that Buster drank at least fifteen beers the night the prosecution claimed he strangled Phyllis. Even if he could have killed the girl in his inebriated state, it was unlikely he would have been able to bury her "in such a neat fashion." Howe also raised the possibility that Phyllis wasn't killed that night at all. "We have good reason to believe that she was not buried immediately following her slaying, as the case against Buster says." If Phyllis was not even killed the night witnesses last saw her with Buster, then the county's case crumbled. Howe added another dig at Wheeler and Sheriff Field, saying Buster's signed confession sounded "fictitious."

Wheeler found his bully pulpit on the pages of the *Tulsa Tribune* and used every last line. With his front-page platform, Wheeler denied Buster's claims that he and his family members were threatened. In the same article, the county attorney then proceeded to threaten Buster and his family: "If any of Youngwolfe's relatives or friends decide to change their stories, perjury charges will be considered." The irony of the county attorney's publicly threatening people he claimed to have never threatened was lost on the complacent *Tulsa Tribune*. Wheeler's statement to the *Tulsa Tribune* appeared under the ominous headline "Perjury Looms in Death Case." Buster and his family were still cast as the villains.

In the same article, an unnamed county official was also quoted as saying there was "absolutely nothing legal" about San Angelo's appointment and that it was unlikely the county would approve any claims for his services. While the *Tulsa Tribune* did not cover any details about Howe's case, it did report Wheeler's refutation of Howe's unnamed suspect.

"I will be the first person to welcome the evidence and will take immediate steps to correct any wrong we have done," said Wheeler. "But I am still convinced Youngwolfe is the slayer."

• • •

Howe made an amended petition to the court. In a statement made to make headlines, Howe charged that county officials had used "agents and stool-pigeons" to pry information from Buster. With his daily barrage of provocative statements, Howe was stealing press from the prosecution and throwing Wheeler off message. Every day Wheeler was forced to defend the county from Howe's latest charge of corruption and incompetence.

The *Tulsa World* was proving to be a valuable platform for the public defender's attacks. While Howe and Gordon were not friends, they were forming an interdependent relationship, with Howe providing Gordon vibrant quotes and juicy details, and Gordon giving Howe precious coverage. Gordon was, if not Howe's ally, a megaphone for getting his message to the public and rattling the prosecution's cage.

The morning of Wednesday, April 15, proved to be a milestone moment in Buster's long march for freedom. That morning, *Tulsa World* readers opened their papers to see the front-page headline "Interviewers Find Youngwolfe's Alibi 'Convincing;' Key Witnesses Claimed." Gordon became more of an observer; he was now an advocate.

The day prior, Howe had arranged for Buster to undergo another round of questioning. For one uninterrupted, intense hour, Howe, Gordon, and a University of Tulsa journalism student named Jack

Brockman grilled Buster. Even though each interviewer tried to trip him up, Buster never waffled or wavered. While Gordon admitted that Buster "has had a long time to get a story together" and that he and Brockman were "amateur" suspect interrogators, the reporter now believed Buster was innocent.

"Buster Youngwolfe tells a pretty convincing story about where he was and what he was doing the night of March 12," Gordon wrote to the thousands of daily *Tulsa World* readers. "The story sounded plausible and if Howe can produce witnesses to support it, Youngwolfe should go free."

Howe was changing the conversation. But while Gordon's cautious endorsement of Buster's story—and the legitimacy the *Tulsa World* granted by printing it—was significant, it was not enough. As Gordon's caveat stated, Buster's alibi was only as good as Howe's ability to prove it. If he was going to help free Buster, then the public defender still had to produce witnesses.

11

The Strain

Special investigator San Angelo resigned only a few days after he was hired. He said he couldn't put in the time the job required but added that his resignation "ha[d] nothing to do with Youngwolfe's guilt or innocence." San Angelo turned over the information he had gathered to Howe and noted, "There are other good suspects who haven't been questioned." Stepping down wasn't an option for Howe. He was in too deep.

Every time the public defender started to gain momentum, a new barrier stood in his way. San Angelo's resignation was just the latest example and would not be the last. The defense got a bit of a break when Buster's preliminary hearing was postponed from that Friday, April 17, to the following Friday, April 24, due to the number of cases on the docket. A week wasn't much, but Howe needed all the time he could get. The preliminary hearing would determine whether this case would go to a jury trial. With the public's perception of Buster fueled by the *Tulsa Tribune*'s negative coverage, Howe hoped to avoid a trial, especially now that he was once again working by himself.

Howe wanted nothing more than to arrest his potential suspect. Not only would this move save his client, Buster, but it would potentially bring the girl's real murderer to justice. Perhaps he was also motivated by stubborn pride, or even a defiant desire to publicly humiliate the prosecution team, just as it had done to Buster and was trying to do to him. Even though Howe kept his suspect a secret to the outside world, deep down he was convinced this other person did it. But he was racing against time and fighting an opposition with more resources, more time, and more power. Howe wasn't on the case to arrest a guilty man; he was there to save an innocent one. Without the ability to make an arrest and with his special investigator now out of the picture, Howe stopped pursuing an alternate suspect and focused solely on defending Buster.

"I don't have the necessary equipment to bring in the guilty party," said Howe with a hint of resigned acceptance. "My job is to defend Buster Youngwolfe and to show he couldn't have committed this crime." This was exactly what Howe set out to do.

• • •

Howe's case relied on an alibi. He had to prove Buster Youngwolfe couldn't have murdered Phyllis on March 12 because he wasn't anywhere near her when she was kidnapped and killed. As noted, since noon that day, Buster had been celebrating his twenty-first birthday with family and friends at a series of bars. Because drinking would have violated his probation, Buster lied to investigators to stay out of jail; that proved the ultimate irony, as that mistake could now cost him his life.

The authorities never believed a word Buster said and consequently never bothered to check his story and visit the bars. Howe did. Several bartenders and patrons said they saw Buster at various points throughout the day and night in question. That alone would have been enough to validate Buster's alibi, except for one critical complication: Ellis Youngwolfe, Clarence Youngwolfe, and Milford Williams had each signed a statement saying Buster was not with them. However, their statements were manufactured, as each man told the authorities that they could not remember exactly when they went out drinking or who was with them. The authorities turned ambiguity into an absolute and made each man sign a statement claiming definitively that Buster was not with them. But again, this was a case of Buster and his family's word against the prosecution's word. It wasn't enough.

Howe also visited the brush pile where Phyllis's body was found. He discovered that the dirt was packed in tightly, even in relatively warm

April. It would have been all but impossible for Buster to dig into the dirt with his bare hands on that chilly March night. Even if Buster had used the can that was found at the scene of the crime, his prints were not on it anywhere. The authorities' claim was nothing but conjecture.

What the public had been led to believe was an open-and-shut murder case had a far more sinister underbelly. Not only did the authorities appear to have set up Buster but just as disturbingly they never bothered to investigate numerous other leads.

Howe did. He combed the neighborhood and discovered that the eleven-year-old Phyllis lived within walking distance of six convicted sex criminals. Among them was a man named Tom Bennett. Bennett wasn't home when Howe stopped by to ask questions, so Howe asked his wife where her husband had been the night of March 12. Mrs. Bennett said her husband had been out drinking and returned past midnight with mud all over his pants. He wouldn't tell her where he'd gone. Bennett was a major potential suspect, one the authorities never bothered to explore.

Howe also spoke to another man named Lester Goosby who worked at the nearby rendering plant. According to Goosby, a young man who had raped a baby had been staying with the Warrens on the night Phyllis disappeared. The next day the man had left without ever saying a word. Whether Goosby's story was true or just a wild claim was almost irrelevant as the authorities never even tried to find out.

Most troubling of all was this story: On the morning of April 2, the day Phyllis's body was found, Howe learned that Ellis Youngwolfe, Clarence Youngwolfe, and Milford Williams were out hunting scrap iron. Clifton Brooks, Buster's brother-in-law, was also in the field hitting golf balls. The four men were close to the brush pile where Phyllis's body was found. According to them, the girl's father, Robert Warren, appeared out of nowhere and walked over to the brush pile. Suddenly, faster than anybody had ever seen Warren move before, he bolted back to his house. According to Genevieve "Geneva" Williams, Milford's daughter, Warren called Joe Brown—a friend and neighbor who owned the nearby packing plant—and told his son Bobby to call the police. Warren found his daughter's body after he'd asked Bobby to call the police and was there when the police arrived. Nobody saw Warren hunting greens or remembered seeing any dog.

The sex criminal Tom Bennett, the child rapist who lived with the Warrens, and the murdered girl's own father, Robert Warren—each was a compelling lead. Each was at least as plausible a suspect as Buster was. Yet the authorities never seriously pursued any of them. Why? Suspects were staring the authorities right in the face, yet they had their sights set on Buster from the start. Their reasons could have been as pernicious as racism or as benign as sloth. They could have stemmed from corruption or incompetence, or from Jimmy Warren's warning to watch out for his stepson, or from Buster's reserved manner, criminal record, and proximity, all of which made the authorities suspicious. Most likely, they didn't target Buster for any one reason. Buster had been their man from the beginning, and all their "evidence" was used to support that outcome.

There was no turning back now for the authorities. It was too late. The county attorney, the sheriff, and the police had publicly declared that Buster was their only suspect, and nobody else was even being considered. Buster's life was on the line, but as far as the authorities were concerned, what mattered the most was securing their reputations.

Howe's reputation was on the line as well. By now complete strangers who recognized him from the newspapers would move to the other side of the street if they saw him walking their way. Even friends moved out of his way, or at least Howe had thought they were his friends. Maybe they were in better times, when there was nothing at stake and everything to gain by being friends with Bill Howe. Howe had been an up-and-comer. Knowing him was once beneficial to the fair-weather friends he had met on his way up. Now that Howe was a pariah, a leper, a man who had chosen to defend a confessed child murderer, those same people ostracized him.

The only supporter Howe had left was his wife, Imelda. She kept her concerns hidden and wouldn't dare tell her husband that she, too, had doubts about Buster's innocence. Imelda's head was in conflict with her heart, as the young wife and mother couldn't help but think that Buster might be a murderer. He had confessed to taking the young girl's life and had even described how he'd done it. Besides, the idea that the county had forced an innocent man to confess to a crime he didn't commit—that also meant a murderer was still on the loose—was just too fantastic, too horrible a thought for most people to consider. Though she had misgivings about Buster, Imelda believed in the man she trusted the most. If Bill believed in his innocence, then she had to try.

So she worked almost as hard as he did, answering the phone at all hours of the day and cataloging leads. Most of the calls were from crackpots or people who wanted nothing more than to condemn her husband, but some were good leads. So every time the phone rang, Imelda would drop whatever she was doing and hastily scribble notes, hoping it was something her husband could use. Hundreds of times it would ring, day and night, each time waking up the baby. Between the six-month-old's crying and the phone's constant ringing, Imelda's modest home in midtown Tulsa was a cacophony of noise. Though she'd been toughened by the Dust Bowl–era farm life she had shared with five siblings and by her career as a nurse, this life was exhausting for the twenty-seven-year-old wife and mother. But she would do anything she could to help Bill.

Imelda never knew when her husband was coming home, and when he did, it wasn't for long. Howe would arrive late at night, grab a sandwich from Imelda, and race out the door just as quickly as he came in, leaving behind his wife and child.

The strain was wearing on them both. The only thing they talked about was Buster, and their conversations were growing tense. As was her way, the headstrong Imelda would give advice to her husband, who'd bark at her, "You're no attorney. You let me figure this out my way!" Howe wasn't one to yell, but he was exhausted, tired to the bone. He was too tired to realize how much his wife was helping him and how much his family life was suffering.

It wasn't just the time and the pressure that were getting to him. Howe was spending money he couldn't spare to pursue this case and neglecting his private practice on top of it. Money was tight before Buster's case, but now stacks of bills began piling up on the Howe's tiny kitchen table. Babies were expensive. Homes were expensive. Yet Howe was being consumed by his low-paying, part-time job. Meanwhile, people he had thought were his friends were treating him like dirt.

It was enough to break a man, but life had prepared Howe for this trial. Howe was able to insulate himself from the insults because he was used to being alone. It was how he grew up: no mom or dad, his sisters and brothers spread across different corners of the country, his going to a boarding school where he was isolated and abused based on the color of his skin. Howe knew the bitter sting of solitude. Most of all, he knew about the casual cruelty of his fellow man. Howe didn't need people's approval, because he knew how fickle people could be.

The public's ignorance was inevitable. Nobody knew what Howe knew because he had to keep his cards close to his chest. It was the only way to save Buster.

12

A Fishing Expedition

Tulsans had been glued to their newspapers and radios to witness this strange, sordid story unfold; now they packed the courtroom of Judge Stanley Edmister on Friday morning, April 24, for the preliminary hearing of Buster Youngwolfe's case. By the end of the hearing, they'd know whether Buster would face trial or go free.

So many people had arrived anticipating a show that nearly twenty were left standing. Most of the crowd stayed the entire day, and two women even brought their infants. When one child began to cry, the woman left her baby with someone outside so she could race back into the courtroom. It was unusual for this many people to witness courtroom proceedings, especially a preliminary hearing. But there had been nothing usual about this case, which had become something of a spectacle.

Bill Howe's and Robert Wheeler's antipathy, which had been building on the pages of the city's newspapers, now spilled into the courtroom.

"The hearing won't take long as far as the state is concerned," said Wheeler, confident as ever. The state's only responsibility, he noted, was to show enough cause to justify a trial.

All day long Wheeler objected to Howe's cross-examinations of the state's witnesses, condemning the public defender's "attempts to explore the evidence we have" and ridiculing him for not asking "intelligible questions."

"I'm not treating this as lightly as the county attorney," Howe snapped back. "I have to ask about these things because I wasn't there."

The defendant, who by far had the most to lose, watched the hearing as silently as any spectator. Buster's calmness was a smokescreen. Beneath his solemn demeanor was a frightened man, who relieved his anxiety by methodically chewing gum all day long. And it was a long day, seven and a half hours, starting at 9:00 a.m. and lasting until 4:30 p.m. The state subpoenaed only six witnesses to make its case. Howe called in twenty.

Robert Warren was the state's first witness. Phyllis's father restated his story about finding her body while hunting greens. Howe's distrust of Warren was clear by his cross-examination, as he asked Warren if he had visited the brush pile multiple times before Phyllis was found. Warren denied it and said that he "had a feeling" the day he found the body there. Warren's stating that he "had a feeling" clearly contradicted his story that it wasn't him who found the body but Smokey the dog.

"Did you ever sell liquor out there?" Howe asked. Wheeler objected, but not before Warren answered, "I might have." Warren admitted to a federal liquor conviction, as well as convictions for public drunkenness and disturbing the peace. After he was dismissed, Warren didn't stay to watch the proceedings.

The state's next witness, Dr. Nevin Dodd, the county medical director who oversaw the examination of Phyllis's corpse, estimated that Phyllis had been dead for three weeks when she was found. Dr. Dodd said he "figured it was strangulation" because of the blue plastic belt tied around her neck, but Howe got him to admit that he did not discern from his "own knowledge" that she was strangled. Neither Dr. Dodd nor the police physician Dr. Lee Gentry ever performed a formal autopsy. Their respective professional diagnoses were based on observation and speculation.

The state next submitted a key piece of evidence—the twenty photographs taken by photographer Jack Moncrief. The photos documented Phyllis's mangled, mud-caked body being removed from the brush pile. It was a gruesome sight for those in the courtroom who had never seen these photos before. Most of Phyllis's facial features were gone, rotted away from exposure; her hair was a dirty, tangled mess of corn-colored weeds; and her body was as crumpled as a dead spider found on the ground. Howe objected to the photos' being admitted, but Judge Edmister overruled him.

Deputy Houston Johnson, the state's next witness, repeated the company line, testifying that Buster was informed of his constitutional rights when he was questioned and that no threats or promises were made. Deputy Johnson then described the long weekend of Buster's myriad denials before he finally confessed to the murder.

Following Deputy Johnson's testimony, Wheeler submitted the state's most critical piece of evidence—Buster's signed confession. Howe demanded that he be given time to study the confession. After all this time, the county had never given him a copy or had even allowed him to see it.

Howe took five minutes to read the confession and then objected to its being admitted. "It is incompetent, irrelevant and immaterial," said Howe. "No proper procedure has been laid out for it. And this was obtained by threats and promises."

Once again, Judge Edmister overruled him. This decision was a serious setback to the defense. Buster's signed confession was not only the state's deadliest weapon but its only weapon. Without it, the state had nothing. With it, the state had Buster's admission of murder. If Howe couldn't remove the confession, he now had no choice but to disprove it.

Next, Sheriff Bill Field testified that Buster was told his fingerprints were on the belt and that he would get the chair for lying. Howe got Sheriff Field to admit that he had recorded Buster and his mother's private conversations, setting off another shouting match between the prosecution and the defense. Wheeler and Howe fought over whether the tape should be presented. When it became clear the tape wasn't available anyway, Sheriff Field said most of it was inaudible.

Jimmy Warren testified that he last saw his sister when she was with Buster on the night she disappeared. During his cross-examination, Howe asked Warren if he thought he had heard Phyllis come into his house that night. Once again Wheeler objected, and Judge Edmister sustained it. Following Jimmy Warren's testimony, the state rested its case. Howe issued a demurrer, objecting that the prosecution's case was invalid and that the state "has only an uncorroborated confession." Once again the prosecution and the defense were at each other's throats until Judge Edmister overruled Howe's demurrer.

　　　　　　　　　　　　　　　　　　A Fishing Expedition

The spectators in the courtroom were on the edge of their seats, watching Howe and Wheeler fight it out. But the day was only getting started, as Howe began calling his witnesses. "I don't want to appear obnoxious," Howe said midway through his lengthy call sheet, "but I feel this case should be gone into."

Wheeler's skills as a courtroom combatant were on full display with Howe's first witness, Officer C. E. Tucker. Officer Tucker testified that Buster was present when he broke up a bar fight between Ellis Youngwolfe and another patron on the night Phyllis was killed. This would have been a coup for the defense, but Wheeler's cross-examination cast doubt on Officer Tucker's testimony, as the policeman couldn't actually remember the specific date.

For all of Howe's feistiness and fire, Wheeler had spent more time in courtroom battles than the young public defender had, and Howe's inexperience showed. Howe could be long winded and undisciplined in his cross-examinations, frequently inciting objections. Conversely, Wheeler was pointed and strategic in his questions, a gentleman sniper who took out his victims without getting any blood on himself. Yet for all his courtroom skills, even Wheeler had a difficult time disguising how sloppy the county's investigation had been.

During County Investigator Ace Lang's testimony, Howe and Wheeler clashed over Lang's qualifications as an expert. Lang finally acknowledged he was not an expert and admitted Phyllis's body was never examined to determine the cause of death.

Undersheriff Gene Maxey described Buster's reenactment of the murder. He admitted that nobody followed Buster's signed confession to see if it matched or if Buster was, as the defendant later claimed, making it up as he went along.

A revolving door of testimonies followed, none producing any knockout blows. But that wasn't the point. Howe wanted to get every witness's testimony on the record to discredit the county's case, which relied solely on Buster's confession. His strategy tried Judge Edmister's tolerance, who complained that the court had been "patient and long suffering."

"We have an innocent man charged with murder," said Howe, undeterred. "I'll spend a week if necessary."

Howe's jibe was the last straw for Wheeler at the end of an exhausting day. The county attorney lost his cool and accused Howe of going on "a fishing expedition." Judge Edmister agreed.

"Darned right, I'm fishing," said Howe, refusing to be bullied by either man. "And I've caught me a couple of fish."

The day was over, but the preliminary hearing was not. Not even close. Judge Edmister recessed the case until 9:00 a.m., Monday morning. Buster would be spending at least another weekend behind bars.

$$\bullet \ \bullet \ \bullet$$

There were far less fireworks between the prosecution and the defense on Monday, April 27. But while the two sides were less confrontational, their mutual antipathy hung like a fog in the crowded courtroom.

Howe called Buster's neighbor and drinking companion Milford Williams to the stand. Williams testified that he had witnessed Phyllis's body being removed from her makeshift grave. He also said that the police pulled out a grayish, denim stocking cap, though he didn't know who the cap belonged to. By bringing up the cap, Howe was attempting to establish that this piece of evidence belonged to the real killer, not to Buster. Wheeler quickly dismembered Howe's efforts. The county attorney got Williams to admit he was far away when he saw Phyllis's body being removed and that he had never mentioned the cap until he had spoken to Howe. The implication was clear.

Wheeler wasn't finished. The county attorney got Williams to testify that while he had been drinking all day with Clarence, Ellis, and Buster Youngwolfe, he couldn't remember anything past 7:30 to 8:00 p.m., around the time Phyllis was last seen. When Wheeler asked if Buster went with the men after 8:00 p.m., Williams said, "Well, if he did, I didn't see him."

While "I didn't see him" was a far cry from "he wasn't there," Williams's testimony cast doubt on Buster's alibi. Wheeler outmaneuvered Howe, effectively turning Howe's witness into his. The public defender, however, was granted a redirect examination.

"You were pretty drunk that night, weren't you?" said Howe.

"I was pretty tight, yes, pretty drunk," said Williams.

"You don't remember much that happened that night, do you?"

"Well, I remember going home, but that's about all."

"That's all," Howe said. Williams was dismissed.

A Fishing Expedition

Howe was playing chess with a more experienced player in Wheeler. As important as Williams's testimony could have been to Howe in establishing Buster's alibi, Wheeler's cross-examination discredited Williams's memory. Howe had to think fast. In the moment, he had no choice but to sacrifice Williams before he could be used against Buster.

The county officials continued to toe the company line. Deputy Walter Whisenhunt testified that nobody promised Buster anything and that if he would "tell the truth about it he would probably help himself." County Investigator Forrest Castle added that Buster and his mother were never told they wouldn't be recorded, that Buster never said he was tired or hungry, and that nobody "in my presence" promised Buster a life sentence if he confessed. Castle had it down, sounding as if he were a college debate student discrediting each of Buster's claims.

Mae Ellen Warren, the wife of Phyllis's brother Kenneth Warren, testified about consulting Rev. Leontine Bryant. Howe's zeal and inexperience got the better of him, as he probed further than he should have. When he asked if the body was found where the spiritualist said it would be, Wheeler objected, forcing Howe to withdraw the question.

Howe's final witness, and perhaps his most important, was Roy Hanna of the *Tulsa Tribune*. Unfortunately, Hanna didn't show up. Why Howe thought a reporter who had been antagonistic to Buster's cause would be a friendly witness for the defense was unclear. However, Howe did ask that the county attorney stipulate that if Hanna were there, he would testify that Buster "was physically fatigued and even shaking with chills" on April 6, 1953. "If the county attorney's office would agree to stipulate that I will rest."

Not surprising, Wheeler refused. "You will have to get the witness in here," said Judge Edmister. "The county attorney is not required to so stipulate."

Wheeler also objected that it was "incompetent, irrelevant and immaterial, what Mr. Hanna has to say about it in the newspaper."

Judge Edmister said that the hearing hadn't gotten to the point where they would "settle things by what is said in the *Tribune*."

"Or spiritualists either," said Wheeler.

Howe ignored the snide comments from both the judge and the county attorney. He rested his defense but renewed his demurrer that the confession was obtained with promises and threats. Judge Edmister's ruling on Friday didn't matter to Howe. He wanted it on the record that the confession was coerced.

"All we have here is an uncorroborated confession," said the public defender, "and it certainly has not been corroborated by any other evidence."

Howe got what he wanted, as his statement and the witnesses' testimonies were in the record. As inexperienced as he was, Howe wasn't so naive as to think this preliminary trial was the end of Buster's case. As much as he wanted it all to end here, he knew better.

Judge Edmister said there had not been any "duress, undue influence or improper or inhuman treatment of the defendant that would force him to make this confession." The judge ruled that "the statement he [Buster] made in his confession is ample to make a case against him."

Howe still had one other card to play, however. He asked Judge Edmister if there was enough evidence to prove the girl had died by strangulation. If the county could not prove that Phyllis had been killed by strangulation, given there had been no autopsy, then Buster's confession that he had strangled her to death was worthless. It was a clever play by Howe. Clever but naive.

"You don't have to find in any such case," said Wheeler. The judge agreed.

Judge Edmister stated that the defendant would be held without bond. Buster Youngwolfe "was out on parole when this happened; there might be another crime committed if I make bond here, and I don't want to be a party to it."

Wheeler had won the first battle. As shoddy and as prejudiced as the authorities' investigation had been, the county attorney had simply out-lawyered his younger opponent at almost every turn. In many ways Howe's strategy was sunk the second Judge Edmister ruled that the confession was admissible. It was all the county had, and the judge ruled it was fair game.

Despite Howe's efforts, his client's fate would be decided before a jury of his peers, composed of men and women in a city that had already condemned him. Buster Youngwolfe was going to trial.

13

The Alibi

While Buster sat in jail, Howe was building his case. Howe's attempt to have Buster's confession stricken at the preliminary hearing had failed. He had to try a different strategy. Howe expected as much. If one judge didn't believe that Buster had been forced to confess due to "duress, undue influence or improper or inhuman treatment," why would twelve jurors? As Buster himself knew, asking twelve people to trust an ex-convict, a "21-year-old Indian," over Tulsa's county attorney and sheriff was a tall order. Howe couldn't hang Buster's case on that alone; it was too risky.

"A jury consists of twelve persons chosen to decide who has the better lawyer," the poet Robert Frost once quipped. Bill Howe would be the first to admit that the men he would be facing, County Attorney Wheeler and his assistant J. Howard Edmondson, were more skilled in the courtroom than he was. They were more experienced, more polished, and more aggressive—but not more prepared. Howe would simply outwork them. So much of an attorney's courtroom skills are based on who tells the better story. Howe had the advantage there, for his story happened to be true. After weeks spent retracing the events and interviewing the players, Howe believed Buster had an airtight alibi for Thursday, March 12, the night Phyllis was last seen alive.

• • •

On March 12 Buster had been out drinking to celebrate his twenty-first birthday the following day, March 13. Starting at noon, Buster; his brother, Clarence; and his neighbor Milford Williams headed to the bars on First and Main Streets in downtown Tulsa. While there, they ran into Buster and Clarence's father, Ellis. The four men spent the rest of the day hitting up the bars in the area, starting with the O.K. Bar on Second Street. Clarence drove, with all four men packed into Williams's old-model panel pickup.

Between 6:30 and 7:00 p.m., the men wound up back at the O.K. Bar but didn't stay long. Each had had about fifteen beers by that point, spread out over several hours; it was enough to get a good, solid buzz going, though none of them were drunk yet. The group got back home between 7:30 and 8:00 p.m. and went their separate ways. Clarence, Williams, and Williams's wife went to get water, while Buster went home to grab dinner. Everybody reconvened on the porch to visit, and Buster played in the front yard with Phyllis. It was the last time anybody saw the child alive.

About an hour later, Mrs. Williams and Clarence's wife, Lillie Mae, wanted to see a movie, so the entire group packed into the truck. About halfway to the theater, the group realized they had left Ellis behind and turned around to pick him up. Now with Ellis in tow, the group included Lillie Mae, Mrs. Williams, and Clarence in the front seat, with Clarence driving, while Buster, Ellis, and Williams were in the back.

The group arrived at the O.K. Bar around 9:00 p.m. It wasn't long before Ellis, already drunk, started a fight with a stranger named Tommy Hays. Before the fight got ugly, a nearby police officer named C. E. Tucker arrived to break it up. Ellis was so fired up by that point, Officer Tucker had to hit him in the head with his blackjack, nearly knocking him out cold. Buster followed quietly along as Officer Tucker escorted his dazed father a few blocks away before letting him go. By this point Lillie Mae and Mrs. Williams had enough, so they left to pay a speeding ticket Clarence had received earlier in the evening and then go to the movies. This speeding ticket was critical to the defense, as it corroborated Buster's alibi on March 12.

With their wives now gone, Clarence and Williams continued to drink until the bartender, Buster and Clarence's sister, Mary Youngwolfe, said they'd drunk enough and cut them both off. Undeterred, Clarence and Williams moved on to a new bar. Buster and his father, who was not finished drinking despite his run-in with the law, joined the two at a bar called the Club Arena. By this point Clarence was fed up with his father's drunken antics, while Buster was tired and just wanted to go home. The four men thought about calling it a night but decided to stop for one last round at the Oasis Bar.

It was now well past 10:00 p.m. Drunk and exhausted, the four men decided they'd finally had enough and packed into the truck. Buster wanted to walk off his buzz, so they dropped him off at the mill, just a stone's throw from his home. Clarence and Williams dropped Ellis off at his daughter Maxine's place to let her deal with him. With Buster and Ellis gone, Clarence and Williams figured they would go for a few more beers. They headed back out to resume their drinking.

Now that he was on his feet, Buster could tell he was drunker than he thought. He stumbled down the dirt road toward his home, dragging his heavy, wobbly legs with him. Somewhere along the way he slipped down an embankment, landed on his backside, turned around to plant his hands and knees, and picked himself back up. He was now covered in mud but was too drunk and cold to care. Buster stumbled through the front door of his shack, looking as if he'd been outside playing in the rain. His mother, Bessie, and her husband Jimmy Warren, Phyllis's older brother, chatted with him for a bit. There wasn't much to say, as it was pretty clear what Buster had been up to. Buster scrounged in the icebox, looking for something to eat, but there was nothing, so he went to bed hungry. Between 11:00 and 11:30 p.m., Lillie Mae Youngwolfe and Mrs. Williams stopped by the house and saw Buster passed out on his bed. Around midnight, Clarence stopped by and saw his brother sound asleep too. Nobody had seen Phyllis since earlier that evening, but nobody thought anything of it, as this was nothing unusual for her. It would be almost a full day before the Warrens reported she was missing.

This was the story Howe would be bringing to court. It was Buster's best hope of staying alive. Buster could not have kidnapped and killed Phyllis between 8:00 and 10:00 p.m. because he was not even there. It was a rock-solid alibi. But with Buster's signed confession casting doubt over everything, Howe needed equally undeniable evidence to support it.

Two pieces of information were critical to establishing Buster's whereabouts that night. First was Ellis's bar fight with Tommy Hays. This scuffle got the attention of eyewitnesses, among them Officer Tucker, who could confirm Buster was at the bar. Unfortunately, Wheeler's cross-examination had already called Officer Tucker's memory of the date into question.

Second, and even more crucially, was the speeding ticket. Earlier on March 12, Clarence had received a speeding ticket while driving with Ellis, Williams, and Buster. Later that night, Lillie Mae and Mrs. Williams went to the police station to pay the ticket. Stamped with the date and time, this ticket supported Buster's story that he was where he and his family had said he was—namely, nowhere near Phyllis when she went missing.

· · ·

While Buster's story continued to dominate the front pages throughout the spring of 1953, Tulsa was preparing to roll out the red carpet for perhaps the biggest event in its history—the International Petroleum Exposition.

The "World's Fair of Oil" would be worthy of its name. More than 300,000 attendees, including at least 20,000 oil executives from thirty-five countries, were expected for the ten-day, $10 million event beginning May 14. Hotels had been booked for months, with rooms being denied to non-oil travelers from May 14 to May 23. More than fifteen hundred homes, including some of the city's most luxurious ones, were prepared to accommodate this influx. The housing committee expected 5,000 people would stay in hotels, 12,000 in leased dwellings, and 6,000 in homes. If attendance went beyond the organizers' already ambitious predictions, additional accommodations were standing by to lodge an additional 30,000 visitors.

As massive as the crowds were, the most incredible aspect of the event was the exhibits. Of the 1,484 exhibitions, more than twenty-five displays were said to cost $100,000, and six single displays cost $1 million dollars apiece, or nearly $10 million in today's dollars.

While not the most expensive, the most spectacular display was the National Supply Company's Rotorama. This donut-shaped, plate-glass observation deck had an outer ring that was 66 feet in diameter and an inner ring that was 33 feet in diameter that surrounded the base of a 110-foot tall drilling mast. The Rotorama was the brainchild of world-famous industrial engineer Henry Dreyfuss. A Brooklyn native, Dreyfuss's contributions to twentieth-century design were many and myriad: the 20th Century Streamliner, the ss *Independence* and ss *Constitution* ocean liners, Hoover vacuum cleaners, John Deere tractors, and even the Western Electric 302 rotary dial telephone. Dreyfuss had a stern face and bookish air, making him look intellectual and unapproachable. His work was anything but, as he prided himself on designing for the masses, applying scientific techniques and common sense—not stylistic flourishes—to serve people. His Rotorama display would have certainly stolen the show at any other event. However, the most memorable and enduring feature of the IPE wasn't a display at all. It wasn't a groundbreaking design or the work of a brilliant mind. If anything, its most marked characteristic was its simplicity.

Organizers believed that the first IPE in five years needed a spectacle, a novelty, something people would talk about for years to come. The Exposition Universelle of 1889 in Paris, France, had the Eiffel Tower; the Chicago World's Fair in 1893 debuted the Ferris wheel. The 1953 International Petroleum Exposition would find its novelty in the gilded image of a humble yet proud roughneck—the *Tulsa Golden Driller*.

Sponsored by the Mid-Continent Supply Company of Fort Worth, Texas, the first *Tulsa Golden Driller* was simply a statue and not even a permanent one. The massive roughneck stood 65 feet tall, tall enough to scan the entire IPE. He was made of modeled paper-mache, meticulously bound together by two hundred pounds of paste. He weighed four tons, most of it from his reinforced steel skeleton and his 60-foot-long telephone pole backbone. It took twenty-five five men, three cranes, and countless hours to build him. Emblazoned with a wide, beaming smile, the *Golden Driller* symbolized the boundless optimism of the oil industry in mid-century America.

This optimism for the future was not shared by everyone. For even as far as the *Golden Driller* could "see," his gentle gaze did not reach the slums just a few miles to the north.

Beneath Tulsa's sterling surface, tensions from the Buster Young-wolfe case started to simmer to a boil. A stranger had finally had enough and decided to take justice into his own hands. Unable to get to Buster, he instead went after the person Buster was closest to.

On Friday, May 1, Buster's mother, Bessie, was walking southward toward her home with a friend. It was a leisurely, much-needed stroll. One can imagine the two were talking about Buster. Bessie was consumed with her son's uncertain fate. The thought that Buster, who she knew in her heart was innocent, could be put to death filled her days with heartbreak and dread. Howe told her that he could get Buster free, and she had no choice but to believe him. Faith was all she had.

What should have been a peaceful stroll turned into a nightmare. By the time Bessie felt the rumble in her feet and heard the rubber tires scrape against the road, it was too late. A sharp, excruciating pain shot into her legs and up her spine as a truck hit her from behind. The driver sped away, leaving Bessie in a heap on the ground. Dead or alive, he didn't care. Clarence Youngwolfe chased after the driver who had tried to kill his mother, but he had no hope of catching him. Clarence managed to get the license plate number before running back to find his mother's broken body lying on the road. Bessie, still alive but badly hurt, was placed in a hospital's care.

State troopers located the truck around 11:00 p.m. Early the next morning, Trooper Bill Fisher and Detective Ed Underhill arrested George Grimm, fifty-six years old. Grimm was charged with leaving the scene of an accident involving personal injury and placed in the county jail. The *Tulsa World* was the only paper that covered this vicious assault; the *Tulsa Tribune* ignored the story.

The following week, while his mother was still recovering in the hospital, Buster was found writhing in pain on his bunk. Buster wasn't the type to complain for no reason. Try as he might to keep his composure, he was in agony. Someone at the jail called an ambulance and rushed Buster to Hillcrest Memorial Hospital for an emergency appendectomy.

It was a tough time to be a part of the Youngwolfe family. And they still had a long way to go.

• • •

On Wednesday, May 13, Buster, pale and gaunt as a ghost after his emergency operation, was formally arraigned in district court and charged with first-degree murder. Judge Eben L. Taylor accepted his plea of not guilty and set a trial date of Monday, May 25, less than two weeks away.

Since he had begun to defend Buster, Howe had been pushing for an autopsy of Phyllis. While there had been a cursory examination after Phyllis was found, there had never been a formal autopsy. This was a breach of procedure. Howe reminded reporters that the authorities had failed to conduct a thorough investigation and that an autopsy was critical to establishing when and how the girl died. After weeks of constant pressure, Howe forced Wheeler's hand.

The county attorney received court permission from Tulsa and Rogers Counties to have Phyllis's body exhumed. On Thursday, May 14—the day after Buster's arraignment—Dr. Leo Low-Beer, a Tulsa pathologist, examined Phyllis's body. Howe and County Investigator Ace Lang attended the autopsy, which confirmed that Phyllis had been killed by strangulation. Closer examination revealed a horrifying sight: Maggots were growing inside her mouth. Phyllis's makeshift grave in the neighborhood was too deep for flies to lay eggs. She wasn't buried the night she was killed; her body had been moved.

Even while making strides against the prosecution, Howe's crusade wasn't winning him any friends at the courthouse. Rumors began spreading that Howe had convinced Buster to recant his confession. People said Howe was defending a child murderer for his own publicity. Even while his colleagues slandered his name, Howe kept the facts of the case close to his chest. Gossipmongers didn't know what Howe knew, and he wouldn't tell them.

Howe had gathered eyewitnesses and evidence to support Buster's story, but the prosecution still had Buster's confession. While Howe would argue it was obtained through threats, lies, and intimidation, the men who wanted to bury Buster still had seven typed pages describing the murder in detail and signed with Buster's name. It was the county's word against Buster's. Who would believe an ex-convict? The eyewitnesses and evidence weren't enough; Howe needed more.

The trial was less than two weeks away, but Howe was thinking beyond that. Even if he successfully got Buster set free, Howe knew a stigma would follow the young man all the rest of his life. And not just Buster but Buster's family too. His infant son, Buster Jr., would grow up and be targeted at school. He'd be bullied, humiliated, and told "your daddy's a murderer" and "your daddy killed a little girl." Howe knew more than most how cruel kids can be. He had to put a nail in the coffin of the prosecution's case, but even more than that, he had to bury any doubt about Buster's innocence once and for all. There was only one way: Howe was going to use the weapon that had plagued Buster from the start.

14

The Lie Detector

"Retake the lie detector test." Howe's idea must have shocked Buster. By now Buster trusted his attorney more than anyone, but this sounded risky. The first time Buster took the test, it had proved inconclusive, which the authorities then spun in the press. As Lieutenant Stege, the first test's administrator, put it: "He has knowledge of this crime. It doesn't exonerate him. The test didn't establish his innocence." This statement was clever wordplay meant to muddy the waters and confuse the public, and even after Buster recanted his confession, it left a shadow of a doubt that still lingered in the public's mind.

Retaking the lie detector test was the last thing Buster would have expected his attorney to suggest, and frankly, it was the last thing he wanted to do. Yet here was Howe, standing face-to-face with him, with the cold iron bars between them, suggesting just that. Howe knew the jurors needed a dramatic conclusion, and he believed this was it. More than that, Howe believed in his client's innocence and wanted to eliminate all doubt forever.

Innocent or not, retaking the test was still a gamble. While the first lie detector test had been a wash, Buster had proven he was bad at taking it. He could seem nervous and jittery one moment, then detached and stoic the next. It was Buster's aloofness that had contributed to the authorities' suspicions. As far as they were concerned, Buster just seemed guilty. Of course, merely appearing guilty was not enough to coerce a confession or charge a man with murder, but it should have been enough to make a defense attorney leery of taking risks. Had the rumor mill at the Tulsa County Courthouse been right all along? Was Howe a fool or, worse, a publicity-hungry lawyer eager for a dramatic end for his showpiece even if it risked Buster's case—and life?

Howe's few remaining lawyer friends tried to talk him out of it. They told Howe that Buster had an alibi, eyewitnesses, even evidence. Howe could prove Buster was innocent without a lie detector test. "Why take a chance?" they wondered.

Howe's answer was the same every time: "Because I don't want any doubts left."

In the few weeks Howe had known him, Buster was no longer the man Howe had first met in that jail cell. And Howe knew that Buster wasn't the same man who took the test in the first place. Buster had been cornered and alone then, a suspect with no attorney to defend him, set up against a system that had declared him guilty from the word "go." Buster had changed since then. Howe had watched him grow in confidence and faith. He had witnessed his withstanding a barrage of questions without flinching. He had seen the once timid young man smile, laugh, and show affection to his wife, his mother, and his child. Howe knew his client had a case. But even if he was exonerated, Howe didn't want Buster to go through life with even the stigma of guilt hung around his neck.

The lie detector test was Howe's idea, but it was Buster's decision. Take the test; destroy all doubt. Fancy lawyering wouldn't set him free. Only the truth would.

"But if you're guilty," Howe told his client, "don't take it."

Buster agreed to the test.

• • •

The polygraph test had been a source of controversy since it was first submitted as evidence in the early 1920s. Its mythic status as the final arbiter of truth and justice, of lies and deceit, has largely been dismissed in modern psychology and criminology. Even the highest court in the land, the U.S. Supreme Court, rejected its admissibility as evidence in *U.S. v. Scheffer* in 1998.

According to the American Psychological Association in 2004,

"The accuracy (i.e., validity) of polygraph testing has long been controversial. An underlying problem is theoretical: There is no evidence that any pattern of physiological reactions is unique to deception."

Yet despite its disputed accuracy, the polygraph test continues to hold a grip on the imagination. Its enduring presence in popular culture, as well as its continued use in nonjudicial settings such as screening personnel, testifies to its real power: We believe in it. Or more accurately, we want to. We want to believe that a psychophysiological connection exists between telling the truth and telling a lie and that this procedure can prove it. Though largely a fabrication, the myth endures to this day, but it was even more profound in 1953.

While the polygraph test was then considered admissible as evidence, Howe did not see it simply as the way to win his case but as to destroy the prosecution's case once and for all. Howe believed he had enough evidence to prove Buster's alibi and, more important, to show that the prosecution could not prove beyond the shadow of a doubt that Buster was guilty. But Howe also knew the public and, more specifically, the jury needed the symbolism of the polygraph test. The polygraph test had plagued Buster from the start; Howe wanted to turn Buster's enemy into his ally.

"Buster wants this test to show the world he is innocent," Howe confidently declared to the *Tulsa Tribune*. "He is asking for it, and he will take it willingly."

But Buster's go-ahead wasn't enough. For the results from the lie detector test to be admissible in court, both sides had to agree to it. Howe needed Wheeler's permission.

"I am more than willing to give Buster every opportunity to get evidence in his favor," said Wheeler. "If he wants the lie detector test under these circumstances, we want him to have it."

Wheeler's agreeing to the lie detector test poses interesting questions. Was Wheeler just as convinced of Buster's guilt as Howe was of his innocence? Did Wheeler think the county was always acting in pursuit of a worthy cause—that is, charging a guilty man with murdering a child? Did he truly believe that Buster had killed the girl and that this test would prove it beyond a shadow of a doubt?

Or were Wheeler's motivations more strategic? Buster had already taken the test twice; once he had been too nervous to finish, and the second time it had proved inconclusive. The county attorney may have believed that he had nothing to lose by going along with Howe's crazy idea. If the test failed, as it had done twice before, then Wheeler could spin it in the prosecution's favor. By agreeing to the test, he would appear confident to the jury, while Howe would look like a fool. It may have appeared to be a risky gamble, but the prosecution had every reason to believe it would convict Buster and do so easily. As far as Wheeler or anyone with the county knew, the situation for the defense was grim.

Both Howe and Wheeler signed a court order permitting the results of the lie detector test to be admitted as evidence. However, there was one condition: The results would not be revealed until both sides had rested their cases. Neither the prosecution nor the defense would know the results until the final testimony on the last day of court. It is said a smart attorney never asks a question to which he doesn't already know the answer. If so, this was a brazen act by both sides. The lie detector test would destroy one case and cement the other. Neither side would know which until the end.

Both Howe and Wheeler were taking a leap of faith, but Buster had the most to lose. Only he knew for certain if he was lying. "Buster is so convinced of his innocence, he is willing to do this in the dark," said Howe.

The lie detector machine that had been used before was in Chicago, and the next closest one was in Kansas City, Missouri, about four hours away. The last two tests, each performed by Lt. Harry Stege, had been failures. This time the test had to be perfect—no false negatives, no errant readings, no inconclusive results. The lie detector test had to determine once and for all if Buster Youngwolfe was guilty beyond all reasonable doubt of murdering Phyllis Jean Warren.

What mattered wasn't just the machine, though, but also the man operating it. This test demanded the best. His name was Capt. Phil Hoyt of the Kansas City Police Department.

• • •

Largely forgotten today, Capt. Phil Hoyt was a pioneer in American criminology and forensic science. Fascinated with technology and its application to criminology, Hoyt had created the Kansas City Police

Department's forensic laboratory seventeen years earlier in 1936. In less than two decades he had administered 6,051 lie detector tests. Buster's would be number 6,052. In all that time, across every test, Captain Hoyt said the test "never lied."

"No man who ever showed up guilty on the test ever has been proved innocent, and no man who showed innocent ever has been convicted."

Captain Hoyt carried an air of authority as credible as any machine. When he spoke, people listened. If he said something was true, then people believed him. His authority on the matter was beyond reproach. His manner was that of a man who'd sooner be struck dead than be caught in a lie.

With his stern, stony face, Captain Hoyt looked like a statue. Hoyt was shorter than one might expect, but he carried himself with the air of a much larger man. His square head resembled a judge's gavel, with his heavy jaw sinking downward under the weight of his bony chin. But most of Captain's Hoyt's personality was reflected in his deep-set eyes, which appeared to widen behind the thin spectacles he wore on his broad, pointed nose.

Captain Hoyt had no higher priority than to find the truth. The truth served justice. The truth upheld the law. The truth kept the peace. The truth put guilty men behind bars and set innocent ones free. Hoyt's passion for the truth had been ingrained ever since his first career as a newspaperman. For seventeen years he had been a reporter for the *Kansas City (MO) Star*. The only break began in 1917 when Hoyt organized the Battery E Army light artillery unit. The battery fought overseas in May 1918 and, under Hoyt's leadership, established an outstanding battlefield performance record. Honorably discharged a year later, Hoyt returned home, where he resumed his vocation by covering city hall and the state legislature.

Hoyt liked his work as a journalist and was good at it. But when Hoyt's wife became ill and her physician said that she needed a change in environment, Hoyt left his unpredictable lifestyle as a journeyman journalist for a slightly more regimented career with the police force.

But if the physician was expecting that Hoyt would slow down, the good doctor didn't know Phil Hoyt. Hoyt wasn't the type to spend his days behind a desk, doing what he was told to do and biding his time while waiting for a pension. Hoyt dived into the field headfirst. For a man of his talents, it was the perfect fit. Hoyt felt right at home on the police force. In 1933 he opened Kansas City's first police laboratory. In 1936 already fascinated with the polygraph machine, he expanded his practice to include the lie detector test. In only a matter of years, Hoyt built the Kansas City Police Department's laboratory into one of the most modern labs in the United States. Long before forensic science became a household word, Hoyt was pioneering the field.

At the time of Buster's case in 1953, Hoyt's latest pursuit was three-dimensional (3-D) imagery. Before much of Hollywood had even heard of the technology, Hoyt was advancing it. In the early 1950s, Hoyt already envisioned a future in which a camera would take 3-D pictures of a crime scene that would then be projected on a screen in the courtroom. Instead of relying on flat drawings or still images, the jury would feel as if they were actually at the crime scene, with 360 degrees of information to render their verdict. Hoyt's fascination with forensic technology went far beyond a love for fancy gadgetry. It was all in pursuit of the truth. The truth didn't care who you were or where you came from; it only wanted to know one thing: Were you guilty or innocent?

Hoyt's specialty was the lie detector test. Hoyt had been trained by Leonarde Keeler—a former assistant to John Larson, the inventor of the original polygraph machine—who was the namesake behind his own version, dubbed the Keeler polygraph. Hoyt was an apt pupil. The polygraph machine was his instrument, and he played it with the virtuosity of a master musician.

In 1936 while his career with the police department was still new, Hoyt was starting to understand nuances of the polygraph machine and his own talent in interpreting it. One of Hoyt's first assignments was testing suspects for an embezzlement case at a bank. One of the men interviewed was the vice president, an upstanding man who was well liked in the community and had a reputation beyond reproach.

Hoyt gave him a series of tests, asking him, "Did you ever steal any money?" The vice president answered no, but the test results said differently. According to the graphs, the vice president's perspiration, respiration, and blood pressure measures were all over the charts. Hoyt's interpretation of the results was loud and clear: The vice president was lying. On the next series of tests, Hoyt was more specific. "Did you steal $7,500 from the bank recently?" The vice president answered no, and the test results came out positive. He was telling the truth. Convinced the man was innocent, Hoyt concluded the tests and asked him about his reaction to the first question.

The vice president said he had started as an office boy at the bank many years before. A short time afterward, he stole $2 from the stamp drawer. "When you asked me if I ever stole anything from the bank, that occurrence rushed into my mind," the vice president said. Decades later, the case of the missing $2 from the stamp drawer had finally been solved.

False confessions were nothing new to Hoyt. Just before Buster's case, Hoyt had administered the test to eight convicts who were serving in the state prison and had each confessed to a society murder in Kansas City. Each prisoner's result came back negative, showing the confessors were not guilty and had no knowledge of the crime. So why did they confess to it? One of them was stir crazy and would have admitted anything, said Hoyt, while the other seven had sinister motives. Each prisoner thought he might have a chance to escape en route from the penitentiary to Kansas City, so he "confessed." Hoyt's test caught them in their lies.

While Hoyt's lie detector test had never been proven wrong in 6,051 procedures, it had at times been inconclusive. Hoyt's test showed its limits on March 10, a few days before Phyllis's disappearance. Hoyt administered the test to a sixteen-year-old white girl who five years before had told the Kansas City police she had been raped by a fifty-year-old black man. The man was serving a twenty-year sentence when the girl admitted she had falsely accused him. "My conscience has been bothering me," the girl said when a nun brought her in to confess her lie. The falsely accused man, Edward Oscar, had been convicted and was serving time in a Missouri prison. Following her admission, Oscar's attorney filed a motion for his release.

"I don't know why I did it, except that my brother's opinion guided me," said the girl, who was eleven when she accused Oscar of rape. "I felt here was a man to be punished for what was done to me. . . . When I was little I never had the opportunity to believe in God and I lied, now I have learned to believe in God and I want to tell the truth for His sake, for the sake of my own conscience." When Hoyt gave the girl the test, the results proved inconclusive, which was not enough to grant Oscar his release. The girl's conscience may have been cleared, but Edward Oscar remained in prison.

Now it was Buster's turn to place his fate in Hoyt's hands. Number 6,052.

• • •

On Thursday, May 14, Buster, Howe, and Deputy Sheriff E. H. King made the four-hour trip to Kansas City. Wheeler and Assistant County Attorney Edmondson would arrive the next day to supervise. The group stayed overnight, and for the first time in weeks, Buster slept in a bed that wasn't a cold cot in a jail cell. He got a good night's sleep and the next morning was ready for the test. Calling it a test, though, was misleading. There were actually four tests total in a comprehensive, lengthy process that Hoyt employed to demonstrate if the defendant was telling the truth.

Hoyt had consulted separately with the prosecution and the defense to prepare his questions. Each of the four tests would contain ten questions. The first two questions were meant to help Buster relax by asking him for answers that were already known: his age, his name, and so on. Before he got too comfortable, the third question asked directly about the case. From that point, the questions alternated between important and innocuous.

During the first series of questions, Hoyt asked Buster the following: Were you playing with Phyllis Jean Warren at your mother's home, March 12, 1953? Did you go with Phyllis into a field across the street from your home? Did you stop in the field? Did you hit Phyllis Jean Warren in the field in front of your house?

The second series of questions concerned Buster's alibi. Did you return to town at 8:45 p.m. after eating dinner on March 12? Were you at the O.K. Bar after 8:45 p.m.? Were you at the O.K. Bar when Ellis Youngwolfe fought Tommy Hays? Did you go to the Oasis Bar?

The third series covered the details of Buster's disputed confession. Did Phyllis tell you she "would make you a good wife"? Did you have sexual intercourse with Phyllis? Did Phyllis Jean threaten to tell others that you had intercourse with her? Did you strangle

Phyllis with her belt? Did you bury Phyllis beneath a brush pile in the field?

Finally, he asked the fourth series of questions. Do you know who killed Phyllis? Did you kill Phyllis? Do you know why Phyllis was killed? Were you present when she was killed?

While answering Hoyt's questions, Buster was hooked up to the polygraph machine via a series of straps. One strap was tied around Buster's upper torso, just above the abdominals, that measured his respiratory rate; another strap was tied around his right bicep to measure his heart rate and blood pressure; and a few smaller straps were affixed to some fingers on his right hand to measure galvanic skin resistance, or electrodermal activity. These straps essentially measured the sweat on his fingertips, some of the most porous places on the body.

With its seemingly countless number of knobs and dials, the polygraph machine itself looked as if it were a space-age device from a 1940s' science fiction serial. Needles undulated up and down, recording Buster's breathing, blood pressure, and perspiration rates. Forty questions in all, the arduous, tedious, and uncomfortable process was enough to exhaust any man, guilty or innocent. Throughout the tests, Buster's staid expression betrayed no emotion either way.

While Wheeler and Edmondson stayed overnight in Kansas City, Buster, Howe, and Deputy King made the long drive back home that night. Somewhere along the quiet prairie road, Howe looked over at his client and asked, "Well, Buster, are you glad you took the test?"

Buster looked back at Howe and couldn't help but smile. "Boy, I sure am."

• • •

If either side was concerned that the lie detector tests would fail once again, their fears were put to rest. Hoyt informed both Wheeler and Howe that the tests were "conclusive." Hoyt would come to Tulsa and be the last person to testify during Buster's trial. Both sides could do nothing more but wait and pray for the best.

Each had everything to gain—and everything to lose. If the tests showed Buster had "guilty knowledge" of Phyllis's murder, his alibi would be destroyed. The case Howe built was a strong one, but a guilty reading on a lie detector test would do permanent damage in the jury's eyes. Absent an alternate theory or suspect, which the defense did not have, the jury would be left with one conclusion: Buster killed the girl, just as he had confessed.

But if the test proved Buster had no knowledge, the prosecution's case would shatter, and the county's reputation might too. The girl would still be dead, her murderer would still be free, and the man charged with the crime would be publicly vindicated as an innocent victim who had been bullied into making a confession.

Howe was as confident as ever. "I don't need the tests to convince me," he said to the *Tulsa World*. "I know Buster's innocent."

Howe needed to show conviction to the public, but his anxiety was boiling beneath his calm, cool exterior. Howe was convinced of Buster's innocence, as convinced as he was about anything on heaven or earth. Howe had staked his reputation on it and sacrificed so much of his own life to save Buster's. His practice, his marriage, his name—all of Howe's life had suffered so he could get Buster free. Yet despite Howe's conviction, he was only human. And he was afraid.

Barely a day went by that Howe didn't wish that Buster had a different attorney. That someone, somewhere, would take this burden from his shoulders. Howe knew his limits. He knew that Wheeler and especially Edmondson were two of the most talented and fierce criminal litigators in the state. Howe believed Buster's story, but he doubted his own ability to tell it. Could he convince a jury what he knew in his heart to be true—that Buster Youngwolfe was an innocent man?

"Maybe I had taken too much of Buster's life in my hands," Howe began to wonder. "I had convinced his family I would get him free, and they were sleeping nights. I wasn't."

15

A Jury of His Peers

Howe served notice to the prosecution on Thursday, May 21, that he would present an alibi for Buster, as was required for any felony case. Howe had secured eight witnesses and was set to subpoena another eight to ten.

While Howe's eight to eighteen total witnesses was a lot by most measures, it would be dwarfed by the prosecution's total—twenty-nine witnesses. The trial would be a reverse of the preliminary hearing, with the prosecution's case set to dominate the proceedings. With Captain Hoyt testifying after both the prosecution and the defense had rested their cases, the total would be nearly fifty witnesses. Witness testimony would consume an entire week before the jury could even deliberate.

Even with this parade of witnesses, court observers believed the jury's verdict would be decided on two critical pieces of evidence—Buster's signed confession and the results of the lie detector test.

• • •

While Buster Youngwolfe's murder trial played out, visitors from across the nation and around the world descended on Tulsa for the thirtieth anniversary of the International Petroleum Exposition. On Thursday, May 14, opening day, thousands braved the gray skies and chilly winds to enter the gates of what the *Tulsa World* declared as "One of the 'Biggest, Finest Shows Ever.'"

The largest American flag ever flown welcomed visitors from near and far. Suspended between two 130-foot oil derricks, the 60-by-80-foot-long Stars and Stripes rippled majestically in the cool midwestern winds, its bright red, white, and blue the only colors against the slate gray sky.

Thousands of oilmen and laymen alike thronged the fairgrounds. Millions of dollars' worth of state-of-the-art machinery were on display, yet the most enduring structure at the IPE was not equipment. Standing more than six stories tall, the inaugural *Tulsa Golden Driller* watched over the whole IPE with a wide, beaming grin. He was a symbol of the unbridled optimism for an entire industry and for the city that served as its capital.

The "petroleum age has arrived," the president of the Independent Petroleum Association of America Charlton H. Lyons triumphantly declared. Lyons opened the event with Oklahoma governor Johnston Murray by his side, proclaiming the IPE was "proof that the industry is ready to meet the challenges of a new era." The governor gave a speech and ended his remarks in Spanish, which made him a hit with the South American attendees. Governor Murray was also a hit with a random trophy hunter, who stole the license plate from his car.

Both the *Tulsa World* and the *Tulsa Tribune* paid tribute to the IPE with newspaper-length program inserts dedicated exclusively to the event and the petroleum industry it celebrated. Advertisements included a smiling *Golden Driller* waving to visitors, as well as a baton twirler next to the headline "The Greatest Industrial Show on Earth" in circus-style font. The inserts even featured a letter from President Eisenhower, sending congratulations from the White House.

The opening-day crowd of 25,517 people, while massive, was down slightly from the 26,506 who opened the 1948 show. The difference between the second-day crowds was even more dramatic, with 28,316 in 1953 versus 42,504 in 1948. While this 22 percent drop over the first two days was likely due to the cloudy weather, the IPE's organizers were nevertheless concerned. The weekend crowds easily made up the difference and then some. A record-breaking 53,673 people attended on Saturday, the third day of the event. This record lasted all of one day before it was shattered on Sunday, May 17, when 58,427 people entered the gates of the IPE.

A Jury of His Peers

Sunday also continued the two-decade tradition of honoring out-standing members of the oil industry. For the first time in the IPE's thirty-year history, one of the awards was given to a woman. Earnestine Adams, the managing editor of *Petroleum Engineers* magazine, was named Oil Woman of the Year.

By its sixth day, the IPE was no longer waiting for Tulsans to visit it; the IPE went out to Tulsa. On Tuesday morning, May 19, the exposition paraded oil equipment down the streets of downtown Tulsa, as thousands of people of all ages watched from the sidewalk or from their office windows. Twenty-five flags representing oil-producing countries flew from the floats, reminding parade viewers that oil was a global commodity and that Tulsa was its capital.

The chilly, gray weather that welcomed guests was soon replaced by warm temperatures that would continue to rise for the rest of May. On Saturday, May 23, 26,577 visitors enjoyed the sunny weather to close out the event, bringing the ten-day total attendance to a record 369,835. Despite complaints from some exhibitors that the general public had interfered with sales, IPE president and prominent Tulsa oilman W. G. Skelly said the event would remain open to all. "Without the public out there, there wouldn't be much of a show."

While the IPE was an international event and owed its success to the global petroleum industry, in a more critical way it wasn't about the world; it was about Tulsa.

"The representatives of 40 nations came not so much to the United States as they did to Tulsa," one Tulsa Chamber of Commerce official said to the *Tulsa World*. "That will be their identification and they'll never forget Tulsa." A German delegate even declared that Tulsa was "by far the cleanest and prettiest city I have ever seen."

Tulsa must have seemed as if it were the center of the universe. To the people who worked in the petroleum industry, it was, for one brief shining moment. But on both the national and international stage, the spring and summer of 1953 would prove to be some of the most monumental months of the twentieth century.

Across the pond, thousands of people swarmed into London on May 25 for the coronation of Queen Elizabeth II. While the young monarch's ascendance to the throne was still a week away, mobs of people poured in from every remnant of the realm and beyond. The coronation of a queen may have seemed archaic to a world bewitched by the promise of modernity, but to a kingdom still grieving from the ravages of two world wars, it was a celebration not of one person but of a bygone era—an era of chivalry and grace, a far cry from the present world, where the specter of modern warfare threatened to burn it all down.

It was a world not only of hope but also of contradictions. A world on fire. Between March 17 and June 4, 1953, the United States conducted a series of eleven nuclear bomb tests in the Nevada desert in an operation dubbed Upshot-Knothole. The unprecedented destructive power of nuclear weapons was literally brought home when the first bomb, nicknamed "Annie," was detonated before a live, national television audience. Featuring the now-famous footage of a two-story house being incinerated, nuclear weapons were no longer a faraway, abstract concept. Americans of all ages witnessed what appeared to be the wrath of God setting fire to the Nevada desert. Only God would never do something like this; man would.

On May 19 while thousands blissfully viewed the IPE in Tulsa, the Nevada test site withstood what was then the most destructive weapon ever designed, the thirty-two-kiloton bomb "Harry." The scientists who detonated the bomb did not anticipate that it would generate more radioactive fallout than any other nuclear bomb test in the continental United States. It earned the nickname "Dirty Harry" when people living downwind of the test site, known as "downwinders," reported high rates of dead livestock and, later, cancer. The lingering threat of radiation poisoning was a grim lesson for a nation that slept securely while protected by two oceans: A nuclear weapon can kill even after the blast.

Yet modern weaponry merely exaggerated humankind's most primitive impulses. In a dangerous person's hands, the most innocuous item can be used to kill—even a little girl's blue plastic belt.

The question was, did Buster strangle and kill Phyllis Jean Warren? County Attorney Robert L. Wheeler had staked his authority in the belief that Buster did. Public Defender Elliott Howe staked his honor that Buster didn't. It would now be up to a jury to determine who was right.

• • •

The *People v. Buster Granville Youngwolfe* trial began at 9:00 a.m. on Monday, May 25, 1953. Sixty-seven potential jurors, plus the press and a parade of onlookers, packed into the courtroom of Judge Eben L. Taylor. More than a hundred people combined with the stifling heat of an Oklahoma spring turned the old, wood-paneled courtroom into a sweltering sauna. As miserable as the conditions were, nobody dared leave and risk missing what was sure to be a showdown.

After explaining the state's case, Wheeler asked prospective jurors a series of questions: Do you know Mr. Howe, the defendant, and/ or the defendant's witnesses? Do you know about this case? Most important, could you sentence Youngwolfe to death in the electric chair should you find him guilty?

None of the first twelve potential jurors survived Wheeler's questioning. By noon half of the panel had been called, and twenty-one people had been dismissed—thirteen for objecting to the death penalty and eight for already having fixed opinions about Buster.

It was impossible to find a juror who didn't know about the case, so instead the second question changed: Could you be fair and impartial? Because the grim details had circulated in Tulsa's daily papers, this too was a challenge. Several potential jurors admitted they had an opinion but insisted they could be fair and impartial. They were dismissed.

Though his life was at stake, Buster remained optimistic, even pleasant. He smiled when he told a reporter, "I'm ready to go," and watched the proceedings with the curiosity of a child. But as the tedious jury selection process wore on, Buster became as impatient as a child too. He complained that he was hot and during the noon recess changed his thick, dark blue sport coat for a lighter, white coat. Betty Youngwolfe and their ten-month-old son, Buster Jr., sat behind him most of the day. Buster hadn't seen much of his son and relished the opportunity to be near him.

"They just got the wrong man," Howe said to the jury panel. He also called Buster's signed statement an "alleged confession." The public defender took his time with the jury, arguing the state must prove its case "by competent evidence and not by imagination, conjecture and innuendo." Sentencing a man to death, as the county attorney was proposing, required an absolute certainty of guilt. Justice demanded it.

As Wheeler did before him, Howe asked the people in the panel if they knew any of the principals. He also asked if they were biased against bars, a key component to Buster's alibi, or if Buster's prior conviction of a second-degree burglary would influence their judgment. While explaining the lie detector test to the jury panel, Howe said, "Science has come a long way. But do you agree that science is not infallible because we're not infallible?" All members of the jury panel agreed.

The tension between Howe and Wheeler had not faded in the preceding weeks. If anything, it seemed to rise with the temperature. Each man objected to his opponent's questioning throughout the day, prolonging the already lengthy process. When Howe said Buster's confession was obtained by "promises," "threats," and "lies," Wheeler objected, and Judge Taylor sustained, telling Howe he had gone too far. It would not be the last time, even that day.

Without calling the *Tulsa Tribune* out by name, Howe said, "One paper has already tried and convicted the defendant." Wheeler objected, but before Judge Taylor could rule, Howe apologized and promised to refrain from making such statements.

Howe told the jury panel about "compromise verdicts" and made them promise that if they believed Youngwolfe was innocent, then they would "stay until the cows come home" before settling for a prison sentence. When Howe asked one juror if he would "either put him in the chair or turn him loose," Judge Taylor admonished him and reminded the jury that murder could carry a life sentence. Howe knew better. Wheeler did not want life in prison; he wanted Buster's life. Howe had it right: For Buster, it was either freedom or the chair.

A much-needed moment of levity broke the tedium and tension. When Howe asked potential juror Royce Rutter if he thought a person would "have to be crazy to confess to something he didn't do," Rutter pondered for a moment and replied, "No, but it would help." The courtroom erupted in laughter, an unexpected but welcome release.

Not everyone agreed with Rutter. L. G. Post, who was related to Assistant County Attorney Ed Parks—one of Wheeler's employees— said, "I don't see how anyone could confess if he was innocent." He was dismissed.

After a grueling, five-hour session in which Wheeler and Howe had questioned sixty members of the jury panel, twelve jurors were selected. Judge Taylor excused thirty-five people for objecting to capital punishment or for having formed an opinion. Howe exercised eight of his nine peremptory challenges, while Wheeler had used five.

The members of the all-white jury who would decide Buster's fate were Carl F. Barnhart, petroleum engineer; Royce R. Rutter, American Airlines employee; W. A. Adams, petroleum industry stationary engineer; Mrs. Donald W. Gilbert, housewife; Tom F. Southgate, computator; R. S. Dodd, traffic superintendent; C. W. Pitson, truck driver; W. L. Saunders, foreman; J. H. Barnard, National Supply Company employee; Mrs. Eugene McDowell, housewife; E. W. Anderson, accountant; and Harold Albitz, vacuum cleaner salesman. The alternate juror was J. E. Dotson, an employee at the Kitchen Center.

At the end of the day's session, Judge Taylor, Wheeler, Edmonson, and Howe conferred privately. Howe requested that the jury be sequestered during the trial. He believed it was necessary to keep the jurors free from outside influences. More important, after Buster's mother had been run over and his family members had been threatened, sequestration would keep the jury safe.

Wheeler objected, so Howe, surrendering to inevitability, withdrew his request. Instead, Judge Taylor instructed the jury not to form an opinion, read any newspapers, listen to the radio, or discuss the case with anyone. The court could not—or would not—keep outside influences away from members of the jury, so it had no choice but to trust them. Judge Taylor recessed the trial until the next morning. The state's opening statement would begin at 9:30 a.m.

16

The Prosecution

More than 120 spectators packed into Judge Taylor's courtroom on Tuesday, May 26, 1953. Tensions and temperatures soared, setting the stage for what was sure to be a long, hot, miserable week in May.

The wet, swampy heat of a late Oklahoma spring makes it feel as if the earth is sweating. Oklahoma has more man-made lakes than any other state, more than two hundred, with 11,611 miles of shoreline spreading across the state like veins. When the sun heats the water, the humidity swelters like a sauna. Pack a few people into a room, and it gets uncomfortable. Pack a hundred or more into a courtroom, and it becomes unbearable.

Nobody cared, though, not today. Sweltering heat they could handle. Missing this trial, what was sure to be the damnedest trial Tulsa had ever seen, was not an option.

Judge Taylor set a dark omen for the defense in his opening remarks. When instructing the jury members about their duties, he inadvertently referred to the case as "the state vs. DeWolf." Four years earlier, Judge Taylor had presided over the *State vs. Carl Austin DeWolf* for the murder of a Tulsa policeman. DeWolf was found guilty and sentenced to death. Buster was now facing the same fate.

"You will agree this is the type and kind of vicious murder which demands the death penalty," Wheeler said in his opening statement. "We are confident you will reach such a verdict."

Wheeler recounted Buster's contradictory stories for the night

Phyllis disappeared, before he finally broke and confessed to killing the girl. Wheeler described Buster's confession in grim detail, without any flourish or flare. Just the facts.

"After Youngwolfe confessed he got a lawyer," Wheeler said. "Then he repudiated his confession." The implication was clear: This was a cut-and-dry murder case that the unscrupulous public defender had turned into his personal crusade for fame. Buster sat politely, quietly, as the state described the heinous crimes he had confessed.

Without hard evidence, Wheeler relied on witness testimony to provide the circumstantial evidence about Buster's whereabouts and character. His first witness was Phyllis's mother, Josie Warren. Josie Warren had been injured in a car accident more than a week earlier on Saturday, May 16, 1953. She was riding in a side-panel truck with Milford Williams, Buster's drinking companion, when she was thrown into the windshield after Williams's truck collided with a cleaning truck. Warren suffered multiple abrasions, lacerations, and potentially a back injury.

Mrs. Warren testified the last time she saw her daughter alive, the evening of March 12, Phyllis had just eaten dinner and then rushed next door to play with Buster. She was wearing blue jeans, a red checkered blouse, and a blue plastic belt.

Wheeler showed Mrs. Warren the belt that was used to strangle her daughter. "Is this the belt Phyllis Jean Warren was wearing the last time you saw her?" said Wheeler.

"Yes, sir," Mrs. Warren said. "It sure is."

Howe had to walk a fine line during his cross-examination. While he had to discredit Mrs. Warren's testimony, he also had to avoid appearing like a bully. After weeks of interviews and investigation, Howe believed that the Wheelers were neglectful parents at best. His challenge was to prove that without accosting the murdered girl's mother.

Howe asked her when she first learned Phyllis had disappeared. Mrs. Warren said one of her sons woke her up around 11:30 p.m., and she saw that Phyllis was gone. She said she went back to sleep, assuming that Phyllis was spending the night at the Youngwolfes' or with a friend. The next morning, Mrs. Warren said she spoke with Bessie Youngwolfe—her daughter-in-law and Buster's mother—who said Phyllis hadn't spent the night with them. However, the Warrens didn't call the police until that night.

When Howe asked her when she suspected Buster was involved with Phyllis's disappearance, she said it was after her son Jimmy, Buster's stepfather, told her that Buster and Phyllis "disappeared at the same time."

As soon as Josie Warren exited the witness stand, she left the courtroom. Neither she nor her husband, Robert Warren, were seen at the trial for their daughter's murder again.

Howe and Wheeler were at each other's throats from the start, frequently objecting to each other's questions during Mrs. Wheeler's testimony and cross-examination. Yet despite everything that had been said, both in the press and the courtroom, observers noted that there was no bitterness or acrimony between the two men. They were just two passionate attorneys fighting valiantly for their own side.

Wheeler next introduced the twenty photographs that photographer Jack Moncrief had taken. Fourteen were taken at the burial site, the other six at the funeral home. The sight of Phyllis's broken body, mangled by human hands and rearranged from weeks of exposure, were shocking and appalling to even the most hardened observer. As he did at the preliminary hearing, Howe objected to the photos being introduced as evidence. Once again he was overruled.

Dr. Leo Low-Beer, a graduate of the University of Vienna, detailed Phyllis's autopsy, describing her larynx as "spread out and pressed," which "suggested" strangulation. Dr. Low-Beer described Phyllis's last meal: navy beans and an orange or grapefruit and probably carrots and onions as well. Based on a rate of digestion, Dr. Low-Beer said she had been murdered no more than three hours after eating.

By noon the combination of body heat and cruel temperatures had turned the courtroom into a furnace. Everyone had removed their coats, except for Judge Taylor. The jury was cooled by a large fan, while the county attorney and his team got a smaller one. Howe and Buster had to sweat it out.

The remainder of the state's case concerned Buster's disputed confession, so the jury was excused. Judge Taylor would hear the evidence to determine if it was admissible.

First, the county attorney's secretary, Freda Melton, testified to taking Buster's statement. Next, Sheriff Field took the stand. Sheriff Field, who was not in Tulsa when the body was found or when Buster was arrested, described the final hours of the interrogation before Buster confessed. Sheriff Field admitted they had recorded Buster's private conversations—the first time with his wife the night before his confession, the second with his mother just before he confessed.

When Howe demanded the private recordings be played, Assistant County Attorney Edmondson was sent to retrieve them. Edmondson returned with the tape machine and put it in front of Howe. After a few moments, the defense attorney remarked dryly, "I presume the sheriff has someone to operate this." When Sheriff Field failed to get the machine to work, County Investigator Ace Lang was called into the courtroom to operate it.

Most of the recording was impossible to understand, with just muffled, mumbling voices. After several moments the voices became clear, and it picked up in the middle of Youngwolfe's confession.

Howe grilled Sheriff Field, demanding to know if any "threats or promises" had been made. Sheriff Field admitted that a deputy had told Buster about a man who had confessed to murder and got a life sentence.

"Did you tell the defendant you were tired of this fooling around?" Howe asked.

"I may have told him I was going to keep him there until he told me the truth," said Sheriff Field.

When Howe asked if Buster said he was hungry, Sheriff Field said he was offered coffee and rolls, adding that he had been tired and hungry too. When Howe asked if Buster was told his fingerprints were on the belt and that an elbow print and footprint were found at the burial site, the sheriff answered yes, but he couldn't remember who said it.

It was obvious to everyone in attendance that Sheriff Field was stumbling on the stand. The county attorney asked for a ten-minute recess. When the sheriff returned, Wheeler asked him about Buster's neighbor Milford Williams's visit to his office. According to Sheriff Field, Williams had told Buster before the confession that he was not drinking with them. Sheriff Field also said that someone mentioned that plaster casts of the footprints and elbow prints were sent to the FBI but that all anybody said was that "they better not be Buster's."

Given the sheriff's suddenly confident and cogent answers, it was clear that the county attorney had coached him during the recess. Howe's cross-examination was brief.

"Did you just come from the county attorney's office during the recess?" said Howe.

"Yes, sir."

"Was your testimony discussed?"

"Yes, sir."

After a tense, two-hour testimony, Sheriff Field was dismissed. The jury was still dismissed while Judge Taylor considered the confession. Wheeler stood before the crowded courtroom and offered his most critical piece of evidence—Buster's signed confession.

Howe objected. "It is incompetent, irrelevant and immaterial and was obtained by means of threats and promises."

More than a hundred people waited in silence. Some stood, some sat, but no one made even a murmur as the mass of humanity waited for Judge Taylor's ruling. Finally, the judge spoke.

"I don't believe I'll admit it at this time," said Judge Taylor.

Howe still had time and planned to use it. He called Buster's mother, Bessie Warren, to the stand.

With a heavy plaster cast on her broken leg from the hit-and-run weeks before, Bessie was unable to take the witness stand and had to testify from her wheelchair. Bessie's soft, low voice was difficult to understand, so Judge Taylor had to move down from the bench to the witness stand to hear her.

Despite her soft-spoken manner, Bessie threw bombs at the prosecution. This was her first time to tell her story, and she was going to use it. Bessie testified that Buster told her, "I no more than get upstairs and get my shoes off than they bring me back down," and that two deputies said that if Buster confessed, then he wouldn't "get the electric chair."

Bessie testified that a "blackheaded man" in the county attorney's office said Buster's fingerprints were on the belt, as well as other pieces of evidence. This "dark-haired man" said Buster would get a life sentence if he confessed and probably would be set free by age thirty-six, in what he described as "the prime of his life." Bessie looked at the prosecutor's table. "I believe it was you," she said, pointing at Wheeler.

However, she was mistaken, as Wheeler was returning from California. She said it also could have been one of the assistant county attorneys.

Bessie's testimony described how after four days of interrogation, her son was convinced that confessing was the only way to save himself and his mother. She said that just before Buster confessed, he told her, "I'm not going to tell you I did it, because I didn't. But I'm going to say I did it. It's my only chance to get out of this."

Buster's wife, Betty, was next. She reiterated her mother-in-law's point, saying Buster was "tired and nervous" when he confessed. During his cross-examination, Wheeler got both Bessie and Betty to admit that Buster understood his constitutional rights and made his confession of his own volition.

Howe's next witness failed to show, ending the day at a standstill. It had already been a long, hot, contentious day in the Tulsa County Courthouse, and it was just getting started. Judge Taylor still had a decision to make—whether to admit Buster's disputed confession. It was a decision that could make or break either side.

• • •

With the jury excused, Howe started the following day by putting his client back on the stand. Buster testified that he was arrested on April 2. According to Buster, his arresting officer told him, "I don't want to work you over, but I will if you keep getting smart."

Buster described his four days in the county jail, answering questions at all hours.

"What questions did they ask you?" said Howe.

"They kept asking the same questions over and over, why I killed her," said Buster. "I said I didn't."

"Was anything ever said about your mother?"

"Once they said to me, 'Buster, you don't want your mother put in jail, do you?' I said, 'No.' They said they were going to if I didn't confess."

Buster said that deputies entered one after the other to force him into confessing, each with a new spin on the same story. Deputy Lewis Downing told him they found his fingerprints on the belt. Deputy Ott Lee informed him that he'd only get a life sentence if he confessed. Deputy Johnson said to him, "Buster, you know you'll get the chair."

Together the authorities produced the perfect narrative arc: We can prove you're guilty. Confess and you'll live; don't confess and you'll die.

Buster said that the entire time he was in jail, he only had two meals.

"Were you hungry?" said Howe.

"Most of the time," said Buster.

"Were you sleepy?"

"All of the time."

Following Howe's questioning, Wheeler stepped forward to cross-examine the defendant.

"Isn't it a fact that from Saturday morning until Sunday evening you weren't questioned at all?"

Buster didn't back down against the county attorney, not this time. He testified that he was questioned Saturday night in the sheriff's office and again the next morning. Wheeler had an ace up his sleeve, however. He read aloud Buster's original statement that he was out drinking. In that statement, Assistant County Attorney Edmondson had advised Buster of his constitutional rights. "In other words," said Wheeler, "as early as April 3 you were advised by J. Howard Edmondson that you did not have to make a statement, and if you did make one, it would be used against you?"

"Yes," Buster admitted.

Following Wheeler's confrontational cross-examination, the county attorney once again presented Buster's confession as evidence. Judge Taylor did not think about it for long. He said it would be up to the jury to decide what credence to give the confession. He admitted the confession into evidence. In one fell swoop, Judge Taylor saved the prosecution and landed a potentially fatal blow to the defense.

The jury returned to the box. For the first time, the twelve strangers heard Buster's confession in its entirety. The prosecution recited every word: Wheeler read the questions, while Edmondson, playing the part of Buster, read the answers. It was a sordid and uncomfortable experience, hearing the grisly murder performed as if it were a table reading of a play. Wheeler and Edmondson spoke the words in a methodical, monotonous rhythm, a chilling dialogue that only heightened the horror. The standing-room-only crowd hung on every last word. Buster did too. He said these words—that wasn't in dispute—but they didn't come from him; instead, they had come from the disembodied voice of the broken man he had been that early Monday morning. Now his chilling words were being spoken back to him, before a jury, before strangers, before his mother, his wife, and his child. He could only hope Howe could convince these twelve men and women that his own words were lies he told to save himself.

It seemed to last for hours but had only been about ten minutes. A hush fell on the courtroom. The hundred-plus gathered souls breathed in the story they had just heard. Wheeler called County Investigator Lang to the stand and asked him to describe the afternoon of April 6, when Buster was told to reenact the crime.

Howe had lost one fight today; he wasn't going to lose another. He objected, saying the reenactment happened after he was selected as counsel but that he was not taken on the trip. Once again, the jury was excused.

Edmondson was called to the stand and testified that Howe did not inform the county attorney's office that he was Buster's counsel until after the reenactment. Judge Taylor interrupted. Did the court appoint a public defender, as required by statute, or did Buster hire Howe after his arraignment?

Wheeler called Undersheriff Gene Maxey to the stand to explain. Maxey said Buster did not want a public defender and fired his first counsel. Buster tried to enter a guilty plea, Maxey said, but Judge Stanley Edmister refused it. Buster returned to the stand after Maxey and said he talked to Howe for the first time on April 6 at noon, before the reenactment.

Despite Buster's testimony, Judge Taylor ruled that the reenactment could be admitted as evidence. This severed another nerve for the defense. Both Buster's disputed confession and his forced reenactment would be used against him.

The jury returned to the box and Lang to the stand. Lang described the reenactment, saying Buster led the way throughout. He said Buster pointed out where he had raped the girl, where he had strangled her to death, and, finally, where he had buried her.

Troy Gordon, reporter for the *Tulsa World*, testified about Buster's reenactment and his repudiation of his confession the next day. D. LeRoy Randall, *Tulsa World*'s chief photographer, identified the photos taken during the reenactment. Howe objected but was once again overruled.

After more than a day and a half of testimony, the state rested its case against Buster at 2:05 p.m. Wheeler and Edmondson had done everything they could to prove Buster was guilty beyond a reasonable doubt. Now it was Howe's job to show just how much doubt there was.

17

The Defense

"Our theory of this lawsuit is just that they've got the wrong man." Howe opened his defense that afternoon with this blunt, plainspoken declaration. In one sentence, he summed up his entire crusade. The young public defender had found his voice over the past few months and now had to use it to save Buster.

Howe was nervous. Hard as he tried to hide it, he could only contain it so much. Public speaking was not in his nature, and he was terrified about having more than a hundred people—and Buster's life—hanging on his every word.

"I recalled the days when I worked my way through [the] University of Tulsa law school painting," Howe would later tell the *Tulsa World*. "I thought, 'I wish I were painting a house right now.'"

Howe battled his nerves by memorizing every syllable of his opening statement, to the point that he spoke it from muscle memory. As usual, Howe's statement was filled with the colorful language for which he had become known.

Buster "was a prime suspect from the word go," Howe declared. He proceeded to describe Buster's entire ordeal. The details were only known to a few people and just briefly touched on by the press. This was the jury's first opportunity to hear the tale in full.

Two days after Phyllis's disappearance, Howe said, Buster was arrested and held without charge. He told the authorities he went to the movies. The authorities didn't believe him, so they held Buster for two days until they were forced to let him go. Three weeks passed while the authorities continued to search for Phyllis in vain. When Phyllis's body was found on April 3, Buster knew the law was coming for him and went to clean himself at a nearby water pump. Two deputies were waiting for him on his way back. Buster never made it home. He was taken to the brush pile where Phyllis was buried and then to the county jail.

Buster had lied about going to the movies the first time he was arrested but only to avoid going to prison for breaking his probation. Now he was forced to tell the authorities where he actually was on March 12—out drinking with his friends and family. "But it was too late." While none of his drinking companions remembered if he was with them, "the ambitious and zealous" authorities recorded statements from each saying Buster wasn't there. "They never once checked a beer joint," said Howe. "Anyway they had their man and didn't need to check further."

Despite the "six known sex perverts" who lived in the neighborhood and the "suspicious circumstances" of how Robert Warren found his daughter's body, Buster was the only suspect ever considered in her murder. "Had a competent investigation been made," said Howe, "Buster would never have been charged with this crime."

Howe described how Buster was questioned by an unceasing stream of interrogators. He only ate two meals in five days and had almost no sleep at all. He was threatened with the electric chair if he didn't confess. The authorities did nothing to confirm Buster's story, nor did they ever seriously investigate any other suspects. The authorities even lied to Buster, telling him his fingerprints, elbow prints, and footprints were found at the scene. The officers "were just positive Buster was their man," said Howe, "so any means would justify the end that they wanted."

None of it worked. Buster defiantly refused to confess to killing the girl. So they tried another tactic; they interrogated and threatened his mother and wife. They even told Buster that if his mother said one thing wrong in her testimony—just one—she'd be sent to prison for perjury.

Buster had been behind bars for five days without charge, with no end in sight, and with no way out. He started to wonder if the authorities were telling the truth. If they could put him in the electric chair for something he didn't do, then maybe they could put his mother in prison. Buster lost focus and started to believe his only way out of this hell—the only way to save his mother and his own life—was to confess.

So early Monday morning, before the break of dawn, Buster asked for his mother. He told her he was going to confess. "I'm not going to tell you that I did it," he told her, "but it looks like the only way that I can save my life, so I'm going to tell them I done it." Buster was going away for a long, long time, all for something he didn't do. But at least he'd get out someday. That's what they told him—someday.

Buster signed a statement confessing to the murder of Phyllis Jean Warren. The authorities explained to Buster his constitutional rights, which they'd spent the past four days violating. They made him say he was not coerced, because "they wanted to do it up right." When Buster tried to plead guilty to get the life sentence he was promised, Judge Stanley Edmister forced him to plead not guilty. By the time Howe met Buster for the first time that day, he "didn't seem to have any spirit left." The two didn't even discuss the case.

While the original plan was to stage Buster's reenactment of the murder after the arraignment, Howe said, Sheriff Field had a better idea. Since he'd already given the story of Buster's confession to the *Tulsa Tribune*, Field cut a deal with the *Tulsa World* to delay the reenactment until after the *Tulsa Tribune* went to print. "Good politics, you know," was how Howe described it.

The authorities pulled Buster out of his cell without telling Howe, his counsel, and forced him to reenact the murder for the press. The next morning, Buster appeared on the front page of the *Tulsa World* giving his gruesome tour while bound in handcuffs. Outraged and horrified, Howe filed motions to prevent the county from violating Buster's constitutional rights any further. Even so, Howe said he still believed he was defending a guilty man. After all, Buster had confessed. But the next night, Howe finally heard Buster's side of the story. After three hours of discussion, "I became convinced that he was telling the truth," said Howe.

"You see, Buster is an Indian and he talks and acts like an Indian. A person that does not know him could easily think that he was holding back on them, it could easily be mistaken for guilt. You see, I grew up on an Indian school reservation myself—I know a lot about Indians." Howe wasn't the type to bring his biography into a public forum. But by speaking about his own life, even vaguely, Howe showed just how much of himself he had put into this case. Even so, Howe was purposefully giving the authorities too much credit by saying Buster's natural reticence could be mistaken for guilt. The public defender knew his audience—twelve white jurors in Oklahoma in the 1950s. Inferring racism was involved would get him nowhere and maybe even harm Buster.

Howe's penchant for dramatic flair got him in trouble. He picked up a copy of the confession and called it "Buster's best witness." Edmondson objected, and Judge Taylor warned Howe to "refrain from arguing the case in your opening statement." This was not Howe's first warning nor his last. The prosecution continued to make objections throughout Howe's opening statement. Most of them Judge Taylor sustained.

Howe ended by discussing the lie detector test results, which were to come. "Every time we get on an elevator, an airplane, an automobile, we place our lives in science," said Howe. "So I guess we have an infinite faith in it." Howe said asking Buster to take the test was "the most momentous decision that I ever hope to make," but it had to be done. Buster wanted the test to show the world that he was innocent. He didn't want his son to ever think that his father had committed this crime. Even if a jury turned him loose, Howe said, without the lie detector test, people would still think he did it. "This will follow Buster to his grave," Howe said, a burden the defense attorney carried as well.

"It now weighs heavily on my shoulders," Howe told the jury. "If I should fail in my task, blood would be on my hands."

• • •

Buster took the stand as the first witness for his defense. While everyone else was sweating in suits, Buster wore a black sport shirt covered in flowers. He was trying to stay comfortable for the gauntlet he was about to endure.

Buster detailed his alibi to the jury, recounting his exact whereabouts on the evening of March 12. Next he described his lengthy interrogation, saying that he was "tired, sleepy, hungry and shaking" when he signed his confession. He testified that Undersheriff Gene Maxey led the way during his reenactment, saying Maxey "was almost running." Buster said he was simply acting out his false confession.

When it was time for the county to cross-examine the witness, Wheeler stepped aside. Instead, he put his best man on the job. Short, stout, and fierce as a pitbull, Assistant County Attorney J. Howard Edmondson had earned a reputation for his confrontational, go-for-the-throat style. Sparring wasn't just his talent. He seemed to enjoy it. Edmondson didn't mind if his nose got bloody, just so long as his knuckles were bloodier.

Edmondson approached the bench slowly, a leopard moving in on his prey. Speaking slowly but forcefully, Edmondson grilled Buster about his criminal record of two burglary convictions—the first when he was twelve years old, another just a few months before in the fall of 1952. While Buster had mentioned both in his testimony, Edmonson got him to admit he was convicted for three more burglaries, plus public drunkenness and assault.

When Edmondson asked Buster why he didn't help look for Phyllis, Buster said her being gone wasn't anything out of the ordinary.

"If you're so sure in your mind there was nothing wrong," said Edmondson, "why did you go to Dawson and talk to Mr. Tucker to establish your alibi?"

"I didn't go to Dawson," said Buster.

"But you talked to Mr. Tucker. Why?"

"I just wanted to. . . . I knew if she did turn up like she did I'd be picked up."

"Why did you choose the night of March 12 to check on [your alibi]?" said Edmondson.

Buster had no answer. Of course, Buster went to check with Officer Tucker before Phyllis was found; he'd already spent the weekend in jail after she disappeared. Buster was just being prudent, not suspicious.

Buster remained calm throughout Edmondson's relentless cross-examination. It had taken the county five days to break Buster the first time. Edmondson was having no luck doing the same in one afternoon. Despite the assistant county attorney's aggressive questioning, Buster made no incriminating comments. But the ordeal was far from over.

Judge Taylor recessed the court until 9:30 a.m. the following day. They would begin where they left off—with Buster on the stand facing Edmondson.

• • •

The assistant county attorney had failed to break the defendant on Wednesday afternoon; he was going to make up for it on Thursday morning. Edmondson's reputation for relentlessness was proven with each question, as Buster spent two uninterrupted hours enduring his dogged interrogation.

Edmondson's strategy was clear—to destroy Buster's claims that the authorities had abused him and given him false promises. The prosecution didn't need evidence to make its case, because Buster had already confessed to murder. The prosecution's job was to simply defend the confession at all costs. Breaking Buster was how he'd do it.

Edmondson got Buster to testify that while he was exhausted, he wasn't mistreated in custody and that when he was offered the chance to go to a nearby café, he only asked for a glass of milk. When Edmondson asked what time Buster was returned to his cell one night, the defendant answered it was about 10:00 p.m.

"Why couldn't you sleep?" said Edmondson.

"I was too nervous," said Buster.

"Nervous about what, Youngwolfe?"

"About the questions."

When asked how many times he was allowed to see his wife and mother, Buster said four times. Buster said he asked his mother for sandwiches, but the officers wouldn't let her bring them.

The crowd sat in rapt silence, watching a master at work as the assistant county attorney tore apart Buster's claims piece by piece. Edmondson's well-honed methods of intimidation and hostility were wearing the defendant down.

Under Edmondson's barrage, Buster admitted he was advised of his constitutional rights, that he was told that he did not have to make a statement if he didn't want to, and that any statement he made would be used against him. He also admitted that he was told there would be "no deals" made whether he confessed or not. Edmondson could sense the tide was turning. He wasn't going to let up. He next questioned Buster about the night of March 12.

"How in the world if you fell down would you get mud on your seat, elbow, and knees?" Edmondson said, roaring with theatrical flair.

"I slipped down on my seat, caught myself on my elbows, rolled over on my knees, and got up."

Just as he had done the day before, Edmondson asked Buster why he sought out Officer C. E. Tucker to establish his alibi. Buster again said it was because Phyllis had disappeared that night and that he knew he might be questioned.

When Edmondson asked Buster if he believed the deputies' claim that his footprints and elbow prints were found at the brush pile, Buster said he didn't know.

"How in the world did you think they would be your prints if you didn't do it?" the county attorney said. Buster said he had been near where Phyllis was found, and he was afraid they'd found his prints.

"Were you around the grave, Youngwolfe?" said Edmondson.

"No."

"When did you put your footprints in that grave?"

"I didn't."

"Then why were you worried about that when you confessed?"

"I wasn't."

Edmondson's cross-examination was turning into a repeat of Buster's five days of interrogation and incarceration just a few weeks before. Once again, Buster was getting tripped up and contradicting himself. Though he seemed calm by outward appearances, he was struggling.

"Didn't I tell you if you were prosecuted, Mr. Wheeler and I would be the prosecutors?"

"You told me so much I don't remember," said Buster.

"Didn't I tell you we weren't promising you anything?"

"Yes, sir."

"Did I promise you a thing?"

"I don't remember."

Buster was starting to lose his composure and shot back at Edmondson, "I'm liable to have told you anything. I wanted to get some sleep."

When Edmondson asked if Buster remembered that Wheeler told him "we are going to ask [for] the electric chair," Buster said he didn't remember. When Edmondson asked how many times he and his attorney went over the confession, Howe objected. "I don't want to hide anything," said Howe, "but he is making an inference." Judge Taylor sustained.

Edmondson wasn't finished. He asked Buster if he knew his constitutional rights because he was told about them during his past arrests. Edmondson proceeded to mention each of Buster's previous charges one by one. After each charge, Howe objected, and Judge Taylor sustained him. Nevertheless, Edmondson continued, attempting to smear Buster's character for the jury.

It was now Howe's turn for redirect examination. The public defender asked Buster if anyone had told him he could get a lawyer.

"No," said Buster.

"The county attorney doesn't have to hire a lawyer for all the defendants he questions," Edmondson objected, which Judge Taylor sustained. The time of this trial, May 1953, was still thirteen years before the landmark *Miranda v. Arizona* decision, which ruled that a suspect must be informed of his or her right to an attorney.

Buster exited the bench, having survived Edmondson's grueling cross-examination but not unscathed. The assistant county attorney has done his job and planted the seed of doubt in the jury's minds. Howe now had to go back on offense.

• • •

Howe asked his next witness, Sheriff Field, if he had arranged the reenactment on April 6. While Howe had mentioned this during his opening statement, he wanted the sheriff to admit it for the record. Sheriff Field said no, because he was home in bed.

"Didn't you delay the reenactment because you had an agreement with the managing editor of the *Tulsa World*?"

"No, sir."

"Do you know that the *Tribune's* deadline is 1:30 p.m. and didn't you wait until after that for the reenactment?"

Edmondson objected, and Judge Taylor sustained, telling Howe he had to cease this line of questioning. As much as Howe wanted to tie the reenactment stunt to Sheriff Field, he had no choice but to bite his tongue.

The Defense

Howe got Sheriff Field to admit for the jury what he had said to the court on Tuesday: "I'd keep him in that chair until he told the truth."

Tulsa Tribune police reporter Roy Hanna was next. Hanna testified that while Buster admitted to signing the confession, he told Hanna, "I didn't kill her." Somehow this bombshell never made it to print in the *Tulsa Tribune.*

Max Lemmon, one of Buster's cellmates, also testified that Buster said he didn't kill Phyllis and only confessed because "they had the goods on me." Lemmon said he told this to the county attorney, but nothing was done.

Dorothy Storey, a waitress at the Missouri Bar, said she saw Buster there between 7:00 and 7:30p.m. the night Phyllis disappeared. Florence Roberts, a waitress at the Rainbow Bar, confirmed that Buster was there that night. Finally, Buster's sister Mary, a waitress at the O.K. Bar, said her brother was there around 9:00 p.m.

Betty Youngwolfe, wearing a bright blue cotton dress, confidently winked and smiled at her husband, Buster, as she took the stand. She testified that "Phyllis came in the house and asked me for a cigarette. I told her I only had one and she said she wanted it, but I didn't give it to her." She also testified that in her statement to the county attorney on April 3, she said she and Buster had sex on March 12. Betty said Buster didn't seem to be drunk, but she could tell he had been drinking. During cross-examination, Edmondson asked her if thirty-five to forty beers would get Buster drunk. Betty said, "Not if he'd ate."

Buster's brother, Clarence Youngwolfe, testified that "it seems to me that Buster was in the back [of the O.K. Bar] when I came back from taking a drink of whiskey." When Howe asked him how much he had been drinking, Clarence paused before saying, "It could have been two cases. I don't know." The courtroom roared with laughter. Edmondson's tenacity served him well. He got Clarence to admit that he'd signed a statement on April 2 saying Buster was not with the men out drinking later. Clarence clarified his comments, though, saying that he really told his interrogators he wasn't sure whether Buster was there. When asked why he signed the statement, he said, "It looked like the only way I could get home that night."

Each of the witnesses confirmed Buster's alibi that night, while Betty and Bessie also provided details on his four days of incarceration.

As Thursday drew to a close, the defense was gaining momentum. For the first time, Tulsa was discovering what Howe had known for weeks: Buster's alibi added up. This was no longer just Buster's word against that of the authorities. Piece by piece the state's case crumbled under the combined weight of Howe's witnesses. As one person after another testified to the truth, a grim, disturbing reality started to take shape for the jury: Maybe the county did set Buster up.

If true, then the powerful, ambitious prosecutors were not going down without a fight.

18

The Final Testimony

The Youngwolfe family was nervous. For two months they had experienced nothing but desperation and despair. Now on the eve of the last day of testimony, they felt something they had not known for a very long time, perhaps for all of their lives—hope.

The Youngwolfe family was not used to winning. They had spent years being battered and beaten by the cruel realities of life for the poor. The Youngwolfes were human scar tissue. They were harder than the flesh surrounding them, but they could still bleed when cut.

Now, finally, their happy ending was within reach, or so it seemed. Howe had given them that. Howe was a man who wasn't used to winning either. He was a man who wore the scars of indignity and loneliness from his boyhood and who never learned to trust people fully, a man who knew, who feared, that if not for a few lucky breaks in his life, he could have turned out as Buster had. Maybe worse.

Buster Youngwolfe and Bill Howe were two men whose similar lives had taken dramatically different turns. Now each found themselves entwined in the same story. That story was nearing its end.

Witness testimony was set to conclude that Friday, May 29, and with it, the Youngwolfe family and Howe hoped, Buster's long march to freedom. But the Youngwolfes' suffering was not over. Not yet.

Buster's sister Mary Youngwolfe was staying in the nearby Oxford Hotel during the trial. Between 4:00 and 5:00 a.m., a man broke into her room and said, "I want you." The man began beating her savagely with closed fists. He didn't try to rape her; he was there to kill her. With a devil's strength, he tried to throw Mary out of the window, but she was able to hit him in the head with an iron. Bleeding from his forehead, the man fled in pain, leaving Mary lying bruised and battered on her hotel room floor. She had no serious injuries, save the mental scars from nearly being thrown to her death. First someone tried to kill her mother with a car; now someone else tried to kill her with his bare hands. Both times, the culprits failed. The Youngwolfe family was still standing.

Bessie and Mary Youngwolfe had survived the attempts on their lives. A jury would decide whether Buster would survive the attempt on his.

• • •

Howe had complete confidence in Buster's innocence. He had just as much confidence that a truly fair and impartial jury would believe the same. He told his story. He could feel the tide turning. But he still had to present one more critical piece of evidence before resting his defense.

Mrs. Milford Williams, the defense's next witness, testified that she didn't remember if Buster was with the group the night Buster disappeared. This wasn't a setback, for Howe had already presented the testimony of several other witnesses who confirmed Buster's whereabouts. Mrs. Williams was there for a much more important reason.

Following Ellis Youngwolfe's bar fight, Mrs. Williams and Clarence Youngwolfe's wife, Lillie Mae, left the men to pay a ten-dollar traffic fine Clarence had received earlier in the day. This ticket established Buster's alibi for March 12. Howe had placed considerable weight on the speeding ticket and the bar fight, even saying in his opening statement that Buster was "fortunate" his father got into a fight. "If he hadn't, God pity this boy."

"Are you certain the fight was on the same night the speeding ticket was paid?" Wheeler asked during his cross-examination.

"Yes, sir," said Mrs. Williams. Without even realizing it, she walked right into Wheeler's trap.

Wheeler called in Louis Boyd, police records custodian, who brought Clarence's traffic ticket and a receipt book. Despite Howe's

The Final Testimony

objection, the receipt book was admitted into evidence, and Wheeler read it to the jury. According to the traffic receipt, Mrs. Williams had paid Clarence's ten-dollar traffic fine—but on March 13, the day after Phyllis disappeared. Buster's alibi for March 12 was destroyed. All of the witness testimony was worthless now too. Even if the witnesses had seen Buster at a bar, the ticket indicated it was the night after Phyllis was killed. While the prosecution still had no way to prove Buster's whereabouts on March 12, it didn't need to; it had Buster's confession. Even worse for the defense, the results of Captain Hoyt's lie detector test no longer mattered. Buster had no alibi.

Wheeler handed the receipt book to the jury, while Howe dutifully cross-examined Boyd, no doubt knowing that his efforts were wasted. Buster was a goner now, but Howe was still too stubborn to quit.

For Howe, this was a cruel end to the long journey that had consumed his life. He had devoted everything to setting Buster free, sacrificing his reputation, his career, even his family life in the process. Now in those few bitter moments, Howe tried hard to conceal his frustration, his anguish that his work had been wasted and all was lost. But more than his pride was as stake. Howe knew that with as much as he was set to lose, Buster would lose so much more.

As Boyd spoke, the receipt book made its way through the jury panel. Juror number 2, Royce Rutter, raised his hand. Judge Taylor recognized Rutter, who rose to speak.

"It appears to me the date on this receipt book has been changed," said Rutter. Where the carbon copy said twelve, Rutter noticed it had been written over in pencil to say thirteen. The date had been changed. The implication was clear: Someone had tampered with the receipt book. Evidence had been altered. Buster's alibi stood.

"This is the final proof," Howe said. "The county attorney has framed Buster all the way along and somebody caught him in the act."

The evidence was damning. The defense attorney was furious, and the county attorney's office was exposed. Wheeler claimed not to have noticed the change and told the police clerks to explain it to him during the fifteen-minute recess. Wheeler now had to find a way to save face despite this disturbing revelation.

Following the recess, Sgt. Hazel Dameron, the traffic receipt clerk, took the stand. Dameron said the dates on receipt books were often changed for bookkeeping purposes "if it's after midnight and the book is dated ahead." The receipt book, with markers to show where other dates had been changed, was returned to the jury. No other explanation was given for why the receipt book, which was evidence in a murder trial, had been altered. The officer who signed the receipt was an hour away in Pawhuska and could not testify.

Following this bombshell, Howe called Mrs. Williams and then her daughter, Geneva, to the stand. Both testified that before Phyllis's body was found, Robert Warren had visited the brush pile "several times a day." While Howe wanted to remind the jury that there were other suspects besides Buster, he did not pursue this further. His job was to free one man, not convict another.

After questioning Troy Gordon, the *Tulsa World* reporter, Howe rested for the defense following two days of testimony.

Hoping to salvage what was left of their case, the prosecutors called Tim Dowd, the *Tulsa Tribune* reporter, as a rebuttal witness. Dowd said he saw no evidence that Buster had been mistreated and that the county attorney's staff had offered him something to eat and drink.

During his cross-examination, Howe asked Dowd, "Are you the same Tim Dowd who has been writing unfavorable stories about this crime and this trial?"

"It depends on your point of view, Mr. Howe," said Dowd.

Howe had no further questions.

The trial was over, save for one last witness. He would be a witness of the court, representing neither the prosecution nor the defense, being loyal to the truth and the truth alone. He had been sworn to secrecy and had kept his information to himself for more than a week. Judge Eben Taylor called to the stand the final witness, Capt. Phil Hoyt of the Kansas City Police Department.

• • •

Captain Hoyt approached the bench wearing a heavy, dark blue suit, an act of defiance against the sweltering Oklahoma heat. Hoyt was short, perhaps shorter than the hundred-plus spectators assembled had expected. Nobody would have been surprised to see a ten-foot man enter the courtroom, so grand were the expectations. Despite his stature, he had the bearing of a giant. His walk, his gait, his marble face, and his omniscient stare commanded respect.

After Captain Hoyt took the stand and was sworn in, Judge Taylor began asking the questions. Hoyt said he had been with the Kansas City Police Department for twenty-two years and had been giving lie detector tests for sixteen years. Hoyt said he was trained by Leonarde Keeler, the inventor of the Keeler polygraph. The police captain detailed how the test worked, explaining that it monitored the suspects' blood pressure, breathing, and perspiration to determine if he or she was telling the truth.

Hoyt explained that he asked the defendant forty questions, divided into four, ten-question series. Each series included five relevant and five irrelevant questions, ensuring the defendant never got too comfortable or too nervous. Hoyt developed the questions himself after speaking with both the prosecution and the defense.

Hoyt said that the lie detector test had "never lied" in the more than six thousand tests he had administered and that he'd accurately tested 85 percent of the people questioned. He said Buster's test results were conclusive.

Captain Hoyt described the questions he had asked Buster. The first series concerned Buster's activities with Phyllis on March 12, the second series involved Buster's alibi for that night, the third series covered the details of Buster's recanted confession; and, finally, the fourth series was blunt. Hoyt had asked, Did Buster have knowledge of the murder? Did Buster kill Phyllis?

The captivated crowd sat silently during Hoyt's lengthy testimony, hanging on to every last syllable that the soft-spoken man said. The audience included attorneys and judges who had fought hundreds of cases between them. Each said they had never experienced anything like this.

Captain Hoyt pulled out a graph that was fifteen yards long and explained the test results to the jury. He pointed out where changes in blood pressure, breathing, and perspiration rates had made their marks on the graph, saying he made his judgment based on where the marks rose and fell.

After Hoyt finished explaining his process for the enthralled courtroom, Judge Taylor looked down on him from the bench. "What opinion, Captain Hoyt, have you formed from the test as to the guilt or innocence of this defendant?"

Hoyt straightened his back and spoke with a soft but clear and confident voice. "The lie detector test which I gave Buster Young-wolfe," said Hoyt, "compares with hundreds of others which I have given to innocent men."

"What was that, Captain?" said Judge Taylor. "Will you repeat that?"

Captain Hoyt did as he was instructed, repeating his statement word for word, even using the same inflections.

When Buster Youngwolfe said he did not kill Phyllis Jean Warren, Captain Hoyt said, "he was telling the truth."

The Final Testimony

19

The Verdict

"He was telling the truth."

Captain Hoyt's words cut through the courtroom. A bright smile spread across Buster's face. The defendant shook Howe's hand with all of the energy and exuberance of a young boy. Howe was thrilled, too, but subdued. Hoyt had given his testimony, but the trial was not over. A verdict still had to be reached.

The county attorney asked for a twenty-minute recess to speak with Edmondson, Howe, and Judge Taylor in private. After a few minutes, the men returned to their opposing tables.

It was now time for closing arguments. The courtroom waited with bated breath for Wheeler's next move. Wheeler stood to face the jury, summoning his every last reserve of dignity and grace.

"I want to thank you sincerely for your consideration during this long, hot and uncomfortable trial," said Wheeler. "Captain Hoyt has 16 years experience in giving lie detector tests. I have all the faith and confidence in the world in his integrity and ability.

"You have heard the evidence. You are its judges. I cannot conscientiously ask you to convict this defendant. I can only tell you it is not the duty of the county attorney to decide whether this man is guilty or innocent. It is my duty only to present the evidence which I have. It is your duty to return a verdict."

Wheeler returned to his seat. Howe rose to face the jury. Howe had spent the past two months seeking freedom for his client, not glory for himself. This was not a movie, play, or novel; this was real life. The public defender did not deliver a flourishing, dramatic, final courtroom speech. Howe simply thanked the jury and waived his final argument.

"I cannot conscientiously ask you to convict this defendant."

It was perhaps the strangest closing statement ever uttered by a prosecutor in Tulsa County or anywhere else. Wheeler, a newly elected official, made essentially a public declaration of failure. It was astounding. Wheeler had staked the county's time, resources, and reputation to pursue Buster Youngwolfe's conviction to the bitter end. Now the bitter end had arrived but with an outcome Wheeler never anticipated. Wheeler assumed Buster's conviction was a fait accompli. Buster had confessed. The public defender was supposed to stand down. Wheeler had the government, the press, and the public on his side. None of this was supposed to happen. Yet here he was, now asking the jury to free the man he had sworn to convict.

Perhaps Wheeler had no choice. Perhaps Wheeler hadn't been determining strategy in that twenty-minute recess with Howe, Edmondson, and Judge Taylor but had been coming to terms with what he had to do—to save his office's reputation and his credibility with the public. And in exchange for Wheeler's white flag, perhaps Howe had agreed to waive his closing argument. After all he and his client had been through, Howe could have buried the county attorney deep under the dirt of his own incompetence and corruption. But he did not. The fight was won. Justice had prevailed. Howe let it go.

Despite Wheeler's final statement, releasing Buster was not his decision to make. Buster's fate—guilty or not guilty, death or life— would be decided by twelve strangers in an isolated room. With all of the evidence, their decision seemed simple. But nothing about this case had been simple. Who could say what twelve strangers would do? The jury retired at 2:38 p.m. to make their decision.

During the interval, Buster held his son on his lap and close to his heart. Nobody was going to take his son away from him. His wife and mother surrounded him, while a succession of relatives, friends, and strangers approached him to offer congratulations.

"I knew the truth would come out," Buster told a reporter. "I didn't do it."

Howe received a string of congratulations as well, which he accepted graciously but modestly, reminding well-wishers the verdict was not in yet. Howe had learned in his long thirty-three years to take nothing for granted.

Wheeler received congratulations as well and was commended for showing courage in his closing statement to the jury. One of the people congratulating him was Howe.

The twelve jurors deliberated for one hour and fifty-two minutes. They returned with their verdict at 4:30 p.m. The jury foreman handed the verdict to Judge Taylor, the only one who was sitting in a room of more than a hundred people. The judge scanned the verdict in silence and then read it aloud.

"In the case of the People v. Buster Granville Youngwolfe of the murder of Phyllis Jean Warren," Judge Taylor said, "the jury finds the defendant 'not guilty.'"

• • •

While the jury deliberated for less than two hours, a remarkably short time, the discussion among the twelve was not cut and dried. On the first ballot, one person, who was unnamed, voted guilty. The members of the jury spent most of their time debating what was meant by "reasonable doubt." But as the discussion wore on, the conclusion was clear. "The lie detector test just made it easier to reach a decision most of us had been inclined toward," one jury member said. "The state hadn't proved him guilty."

Despite the onslaught from the press and the authorities, despite Buster's being publicly slandered with accusations of guilt from the start, the purpose of trial by jury had prevailed: Buster had been found innocent and not proven guilty. The verdict was a foregone conclusion from the moment Hoyt's testimony left his lips. But if this trial had proven anything, it was that anything could happen. Yet in their hearts and minds, the jury knew that if justice was to be served, then Buster had to go free.

Except he didn't. Buster was returned to the county jail on a hold order by Chauncey Moore, the probation officer. According to Moore, Buster's testimony proved he had "loitered in beer joints and remained idle"—two violations against his probation. Moore said he planned to institute proceedings to revoke Buster's probation. Buster was going back to jail, but for how long nobody knew.

An innocent man's being set free was cause for celebration, but buried beneath the revelry was a disturbing reality: Phyllis was still dead, and her real murderer was still out there. In the past two months that the authorities had spent trying to convict an innocent man, the true killer remained free. The trail had gone cold. Was her murderer even still around? Was there enough evidence to charge someone else? It hard was hard to say. With their battle to convict Buster now lost, the county attorney and the sheriff pledged to reopen the investigation.

The following Monday, Sheriff Field told the *Tulsa World* he was laying the groundwork for an investigation. He said he had assigned men to the case, though he did not say who. Wheeler likewise said he hoped to give lie detector tests to persons of interest who might have knowledge of the killing. The county attorney and sheriff were trying to assure an anxious public that yes, they were prepared to find the murderer of Phyllis Jean Warren.

They never did.

• • •

Howe was not given a hero's celebration—no parade, no fanfare. But he wouldn't have allowed any of that anyway.

There were plenty of handshakes, back slaps, and smiles, many from people who would not even look him in the eye only a few hours before the verdict. Folks said they knew he had it won the whole time. Some even said Howe should run for office. Ike was in the White House, and Howe's Republican Party was gaining traction among Oklahoma's historically yellow dog Democrats. Some even said he should try to take Wheeler's seat.

Howe took it all in stride. Whatever personal glory there was to be gained from Buster's victory, Howe wasn't interested. If nobody ever remembered the name Elliott Howe, so be it. He'd done his job. He'd gotten an innocent man set free.

The truth was, the trial shocked Howe. He never doubted his case, his evidence, and certainly not his client's innocence, but he did doubt himself. Just two years out of law school and a few months from being laid off from the county attorney's office, the public defender was on his fourth case after losing his first; suddenly he was defending a falsely accused man in one of the highest-profile murder cases in Tulsa's history. Howe was in over his head, and he knew it.

"I looked at the jury and I thought to myself, 'I wish Buster had an attorney,'" Howe said in a profile for the *Tulsa World*. "I'm very, very mindful of my inadequacies."

Written by Troy Gordon, the *Tulsa World* profile was titled "Real Story of Youngwolfe Trial Shows Attorney with Full Belief in Client." Featuring a picture of Howe and his wife, Imelda, playing with their six-month-old daughter, Sally Jane, the article paints a portrait of a man more focused on his family than on fame.

"I'm no hero, and don't you forget it," said Howe. "I had an innocent client and that's the most any attorney can ask for."

In that same profile, Howe said he gave Buster some "fatherly advice" and that Buster promised him he'd be "a law-abiding citizen the rest of his life." Buster was going to move his family out of the neighborhood and find stable work. "As bad an experience as the ordeal was for Buster," said Howe, "I think it might be the making of him."

On Friday, June 12, Buster left the county jail without handcuffs or a deputy escort for the first time in seventy-one days. His wife, Betty, waited in the jail's corridors for three days for his release. Buster made his two-thousand-dollar bond, pending appeal on the revocation of his probation. "We really have scraped to raise the money to pay the bondsmen," Betty told the *Tulsa World*. "We practically haven't eaten in the past week."

Free for the first time in more than two months, Buster promised Howe he would now follow the "straight-and-narrow" path.

• • •

The coverage of the trial in the *Tulsa World* and *Tulsa Tribune* reads as if they were reporting two separate events. While the *Tulsa World* produced fairly balanced coverage of the trial, especially once Troy Gordon had heard Buster's side of the story, the *Tulsa Tribune*'s coverage so favored the prosecution that its readership was probably shocked to see Buster go free. Thirty-two years after the *Tulsa Tribune* had told its readers to "Nab Negro for Attacking Girl in an Elevator," the paper had once again chosen sides when a man of color was accused of attacking a white girl. Now that the case was over and Buster was set free, the *Tulsa Tribune* did not do a follow-up story on the defendant or his attorney. Within a few weeks, both papers had moved on.

National publications picked up the story. Pulpy true-crime magazines *Inside Detective* and *Official Detective Stories* published accounts in June 1953, though they only covered the story up to Buster's arrest. *Newsweek* covered the story in June 1953 in its national affairs section, giving a nationwide audience a glimpse into the drama that had unfolded in the heartland. The *Newsweek* piece was titled "Lie Detector Indian," a peculiar title that seemed to imply Howe's Native American heritage gave him supernatural powers of deduction.

A year later, *Redbook* magazine covered the story in Ralph G. Martin's "The Ordeal of an Innocent Man." Published in 1954, Martin used Buster's case as a soapbox to warn readers about the crisis in American public defense. The subtitle read: "A young father confesses the brutal murder of a neighbor's child—and then claims he didn't do it. This is how a young public defender fought for him—and, in a real way, for you."

Martin's piece informed readers that there were only eighty-four public defenders in the United States at that time, and of those only sixty-four were full time. Howe was quoted at length in the piece and, as usual, was blunt: "What the folks here don't realize is that Buster was just one of my cases that month—I had 50. Sure a lot of them are guilty, but they still deserve a properly prepared and a fair trial. And if they don't get it, then we're making a mockery of the Constitution."

Howe was surprisingly candid about himself, opening up to Martin—and, by extension, *Redbook* magazine's national readership—about the personal strain the case caused him. "I couldn't do a job like this for too long," Howe said. "I just can't walk out of a courtroom every day and say, 'Oh, well, it's too bad I didn't have the time, help or money to prepare this case properly . . .' And this shouldn't bother my conscience; it should bother everybody."

Howe argued that a public defender was everybody's defender—not just for the poor, not just for ex-criminals, but for everybody. Howe also described his days at the Chilocco Indian School, saying he was "bitter, rebellious; I lost all respect for authority." Further, his headmaster had told him, "'Howe, you'll be in the penitentiary before you're 21.'"

"Maybe that's why I feel so deeply about this public defender job—because I might have been a Buster Youngwolfe," said Howe. "But then, I guess anybody could."

Buster Youngwolfe's story would not be covered again for nearly twenty years, until the *Tulsa Tribune* published a lengthy retrospective titled "The Strange Case of Buster Youngwolfe" on Wednesday, September 23, 1970. Reporter Nolen Bulloch detailed the story's key events, starting from Phyllis's disappearance and ending with the jury's final not guilty verdict. This *Tulsa Tribune* article would be the last published account of Buster Youngwolfe's story for nearly fifty years.

• • •

Howe didn't have to believe Buster. Buster didn't have to trust Howe. But each man's fateful decision had a profound impact on both of their lives. Even in his darkest moments, when all hope seemed lost, Howe never doubted that he was doing the right thing. But he never saw himself as a hero. He had a job to do, and he was going to do it well, simple as that. Even so, Buster was more than Howe's client; he was Howe's doppelgänger, a what-if scenario in the flesh. Howe saw in his client what he easily could have become himself—a life left behind simply because no one believed in him.

What if Howe had never met that Baptist missionary? What if he had stayed on the path he had been on? What if he had remained just one of the thousands of poor Indian kids who were abandoned by a system that had no use for them?

What if . . .

What if . . .

What if?

Howe knew the answer. He could have been Buster Youngwolfe.

Whatever mistakes Buster had made in life, he deserved a defense. He deserved justice. He found both in Elliott Howe, a man who if not for a few moments of grace might have turned out just as Buster did—or worse. Instead, Howe saved Buster's life.

"I'm no hero, and don't you forget it. I had an innocent client and that's the most any attorney can ask for."

Youngwolfe Confesses Killing, Burying Young Warren Girl

'She Was Always Pestering Me About My Wife,' Indian Tells Sheriff, Deputies

By ROY HANNA

"Yes, I killed her."

Thus, in a simple statement, Buster Granville Youngwolfe, 21-year-old Cherokee Indian, today admitted the March 12 murder of 11-year-old Phyllis Jean Warren.

Sheriff W. W. Field said Youngwolfe confessed to sheriff's deputies about 5 a. m., following an hours-long questioning session.

Youngwolfe attempted to plead guilty to a charge of murder about noon today at his arraignment before Pleas Judge Stanley Edmister. However, Judge Edmister refused his plea because Youngwolfe had refused to accept a court-appointed attorney as his defender. Public Defender Quinn Dickason had been named by the judge as the Indian's attorney.

A not guilty plea was expected for Youngwolfe.

Preliminary hearing was set for April 16 and Youngwolfe was ordered held without bond.

The belt-strangled body of Phyllis was found buried beneath a tree stump about three blocks from her home last Thursday morning, three weeks to the day after she had been reported missing.

Youngwolfe, married and the father of an infant son, was ar-

didn't love Betty. Saying that she'd make a lot better wife than Betty if I'd wait for her to grow up.

"I told her she was crazy. But Phyllis is from a family, well, you know, where she'd learned things a lot faster than she would if she was just a regular kind of a girl," he said.

Youngwolfe said the sexual act took place after the girl finished the cigaret. "And I wasn't the first man, either," he asserted.

It was then Youngwolfe said Phyllis "threatened to go home just like I am." Questioned about what she meant by the statement, the young Indian said: "She was just wearing her panties and told me she was going home like that."

Youngwolfe said "she started off after telling me that, and I grabbed her. She started hollering and I put my hand over her mouth and held her for awhile. She went limp.

—Tribune Staff Photo

Fig. 14. "Youngwolfe Confesses," *Tulsa Tribune*, April 6, 1953. Buster's confession after five days of incarceration made the front page. COURTESY OF TULSA WORLD MEDIA CO.

GIRL SLAYING IS RE-ENACTED FOR OFFICERS

Youngwolfe Conducts Group to Scene After Confessing to Killing

By TROY GORDON
Of The World Staff

Buster Youngwolfe, the 21-year-old confessed murderer of an 11-year-old neighbor girl, calmly conducted county authorities through a re-enactment of the killing Monday afternoon in a muddy field north of Tulsa.

His only show of emotion was near the end of the tour, when he remarked bitterly to Undersheriff Gene Maxey:

"I should have killed the whole Warren family and left the girl alive. It would have been good riddance."

Youngwolfe, an Indian on probation from a burglary conviction, referred to the parents of his victim, Phyllis Jean Warren, who was strangled Mar. 12 on a creek bank about 400 yards from her home. The youth confessed to the slaying early Monday morning after all-night questioning by Sheriff W. W. (Bill) Field, County Attorney Robert L. Wheeler and members of their staffs.

Fig. 15. "Girl Slaying Is Re-Enacted for Officers," *Tulsa World*, April 7, 1953. Buster was forced to reenact the crime. The *Tulsa World* was invited; Buster's attorney Elliott Howe was not. COURTESY OF TULSA WORLD MEDIA CO.

Fig. 16. The sordid story of Buster Youngwolfe was a natural sell for readers of the national publication *Inside Detective*, July 1953. COURTESY OF THE AUTHOR.

Fig. 17. Buster's story from *Inside Detective*, July 1953. COURTESY OF THE AUTHOR.

Suspect shows police spot where Phyllis Jean Warren was attacked, strangled.

Fig. 18. Pictures of Buster reenacting the crime with the authorities from *Inside Detective*, July 1953. COURTESY OF THE AUTHOR.

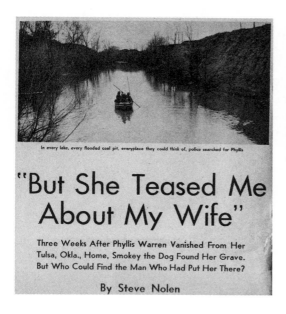

In every lake, every flooded coal pit, everyplace they could think of, police searched for Phyllis

"But She Teased Me About My Wife"

Three Weeks After Phyllis Warren Vanished From Her Tulsa, Okla., Home, Smokey the Dog Found Her Grave. But Who Could Find the Man Who Had Put Her There?

By Steve Nolen

Fig. 19. The popular national pulp magazine *Official Detective Stories* in June 1953 detailed the murder investigation, ending with Buster recanting his confession. Here, officials search the strip pits. COURTESY OF THE AUTHOR.

Only a dog could have spotted
the body in this tangled maze

where the family did their trading. Once there, he looked up the number of the school, but was told when he telephoned that Phyllis Jean's teacher already had left.

He was given her home number. He called, but the news was not good.

"No," the teacher told him, "Phyllis Jean wasn't at school today. I thought she might have been ill, or—"

The father interrupted: "I don't think she played hookey, either. Well, thanks, anyway."

Seriously concerned, he waited for a bus to take him to the downtown area where he went to the sheriff's office in the courthouse. An officer on the desk listened to him, then called, "J. B."

Deputy J. B. Manley joined them and Warren repeated his story. Manley then called another officer, Houston Johnson, and for the third time Warren related how Phyllis Jean had failed to return home.

"We'll drive you home," Manley offered, "and take a look around."

But the deputies could not uncover much additional information. The girl, an attractive blonde, had been seen last at her brother's home. They could not find a resident of the neighborhood who had seen her after nine p. m. when her brother thought she had started to her father's house.

The deputies made a round of schoolmates. Not one had seen the girl since she left school on the afternoon of Thursday, March 12.

"Run away?" the mother repeated in reply to the deputies' questions. "I can't imagine such a thing. She has stayed away overnight, but—no. I'm sure she wouldn't run away."

Mrs. Warren explained that on her return from school Phyllis had changed to blue jeans, a shirtwaist and sweat-

Spring comes early to the Okla-

"She could have run away," the other replied, "but you would think she would have made some preparations. She didn't even take a clean dress or—"

telephoned a description of the girl to the Missing Persons Bureau of the Tulsa Metropolitan Police Department and

Fig. 20. The spot where Phyllis was found, from *Official Detective Stories*, June 1953. COURTESY OF THE AUTHOR.

Fig. 21. Buster and his mother, Bessie, in *Official Detective Stories*, June 1953. COURTESY OF THE AUTHOR.

Fig. 22. Hundreds of spectators hoped to see the body of the missing girl, from *Official Detective Stories*, June 1953. COURTESY OF THE AUTHOR.

Fig. 23. Undersheriff Gene Maxey in *Official Detective Stories*, June 1953. COURTESY OF THE AUTHOR.

Fig. 24. "Elimination of Crime-Breeding Slum Areas Essential," *Tulsa World*, April 12, 1953. Reporter Troy Gordon showed everyday Tulsans the depths of poverty that existed in their city. COURTESY OF TULSA WORLD MEDIA CO.

Should These Shacks Be Razed?

—World Staff Photos

These are four of the 10 houses in the 1600 block on N. Yale ave., which county officials claim produced the murderer of 11-year-old Phyllis Jean Warren. Buster Youngwolfe, 21-year-old Indian ac-cused of the slaying, lives in the house on the lower right. There has been some talk of destroying these and other such "tumble-down shacks," but no one has the answer to: "Where would the people go?"

SLAYING CASE AIDE CHOSEN

Ex-Deputy to Assist in Youngwolfe Defense

Elimination of Crime-Breeding Slum Areas Essential, Authorities Agree

By TROY GORDON
Of The World Staff

Unless you live there, you can't imagine what it would be since Phyllis' body was found in a brushpile in a field across the street, they have been stared at, photographed and pointed at fre- shacks, old, unsafe and sagging. All but a few of the occupants keep them as clean as they can, but that

oungwolfe Found Innocent In Slaying of Girl After Lie Detector Tests Back Story

They Knew It All the Time

—*World Staff Photo*

Buster Youngwolfe and his attorney, Public Defender Elliott Howe, shook hands happily Friday after the 21-year-old Indian was nd innocent of a charge of murdering Phyllis Jean Warren, ·ar-old neighbor girl. Despite a signed confession, Youngwolfe ·d he was innocent of the charge, and Howe believed in him. detector test introduced as evidence just before the case went : jury supported his claim he was innocent.

REPORT OF KC OFFICER RUINS STATE'S CASE

Wheeler Fails to Press for Conviction After Policeman's Testimony

By TROY GORDON
Of The World Staff

Buster Youngwolfe was found innocent Friday of the murder of Phyllis Jean Warren by a jury which deliberated 1 hour and 52 minutes after hearing dramatic testimony of a Kansas City expert that lie detector tests indicated he was not guilty.

The week-long trial ended as spectacularly as a Grade B movie. The crowded courtroom had been sure all the time the jury was out the verdict would be innocent.

For all practical purposes, the trial ended when Capt. Phil Hoyt of the Kansas City police department testified that a series of eight lie detector tests given Youngwolfe May 15 in the Missouri city showed "he was telling the truth" when he said he didn't kill the 11-year-old neighbor girl.

Shows First Emotion

Youngwolfe, 21-year-old Indian, showed his first emotion of the trial at that point. He grinned widely and shook hands with Elliott Howe, the public defender who spent innumerable hours attempting to prove his client's innocence.

Youngwolfe's comment to a newsman was brief: "I knew how the test would come out. I didn't do it."

After Hoyt's climactic statement, County Attorney Robert L. Wheeler asked for a 20-minute recess. He, his chief assistant, J. Howard

Fig. 25. "Youngwolfe Found Innocent," *Tulsa World*, May 26, 1953. According to the paper, the trial of Buster Youngwolfe ended "as spectacularly as a Grade B movie" when the defendant was declared innocent. Here he shakes hands with Elliott Howe. COURTESY OF TULSA WORLD MEDIA CO.

Epilogue

Robert L. Wheeler did not seek reelection after his two-year term as county attorney ended in 1954. He briefly served as a district judge, then he returned to private practice, practicing law out of the First National Bank Building in downtown Tulsa with his brother John.

On Friday, December 18, 1964, Wheeler was killed in a plane crash with his brother while attempting to land at El Monte Airport, just east of Los Angeles. John, the owner and pilot of the plane, is believed to have gotten lost in stormy weather near Pomona and went off course in the mountainous region. Helicopter crews found Wheeler and his brother the following Monday in the San Gabriel Mountains. They were flown to Tulsa on Tuesday and buried on Thursday. Robert Wheeler was forty-five years old when he died.

• • •

Sheriff W. W. Field, like Wheeler, also did not seek reelection when his term ended in 1954. From 1969 to 1974, Field was an investigator for the Oklahoma Insurance Fund. In 1971 Field moved to Lake Tenkiller, an hour and a half southeast of Tulsa, and retired from the U.S. Army as a chief warrant officer in 1973. Sheriff Field spent his remaining days at the lake, dying of an apparent heart attack on April 15, 1977, at age sixty-three.

• • •

Lt. Harry L. Stege served in the Tulsa Police Department for more than thirty years. In 1961 when Stege was recovering from an undisclosed surgery, he dropped a match on his bed. Bedridden and weakened from his surgery, Stege was unable to put out the match before he was engulfed in flames. He was sent to a Tulsa hospital but died soon afterward from his severe burns. Stege was fifty-three.

• • •

When his boss Robert Wheeler chose not to run again, James Howard Edmondson ran to replace him as Tulsa County attorney, winning the office in 1954 and reelection in 1956. After a series of high-profile victories, Edmondson sought to capitalize on his growing grassroots support by seeking higher office, and on December 7, 1957, he announced his candidacy for governor of Oklahoma. The prairie populist secured the Democratic primary and won election as governor by the largest margin in Oklahoma's history. Edmondson was only thirty-three years old, becoming the youngest governor in Oklahoma history and at the time the youngest in the United States.

Believing his election was a mandate for change, Edmondson pursued numerous reforms. His crowning achievement was sending a vote to repeal the prohibition of alcohol sales to the people; it passed overwhelmingly. It was the most monumental of his many victories from the longest legislative session in Oklahoma history. Besides repealing prohibition, Governor Edmondson's other proposals during the historic 1959 legislative session included a merit system, central purchasing, a tax-withholding plan, several measures to ease the strain on state finances, a financing plan for two state turnpikes, and the creation of the Oklahoma Capitol Improvement Authority. Many of Governor Edmondson's other proposals—a constitutional highway commission, a legislative apportionment proposal, and the removal of gasoline tax revenues from the control of county commissioners—were rejected by the legislature. Governor Edmondson then went straight to the people through initiative petitions. All failed. By pushing for their adoption, Edmondson alienated vital parts of the Democratic Party, and by 1960, only halfway through his term, his mandate evaporated. Unable to run for reelection in 1963 due to term limits,

Governor Edmonson stood on the sidelines as Henry Bellmon was elected Oklahoma's first Republican governor in 1962.

On January 1, 1963, two weeks before Edmondson's term ended, Oklahoma U.S. senator Robert S. Kerr died. Edmondson resigned five days later, and his lieutenant governor, now governor George Nigh, appointed him to the seat. Governor Edmondson became Senator Edmondson, and for sixteen months sought to rebuild his political support from Washington, but he had burned too many bridges back home. The late Democratic senator Kerr's family and friends were especially irked that Edmondson didn't appoint Robert Kerr Jr. to fill his father's seat. In 1964 the Kerr organization raised money to oppose him, and Edmondson's brief senate career ended when he was defeated in the Democratic primary by state senator Fred R. Harris.

Edmondson's final years were spent practicing law in Oklahoma City and Washington DC. He died of an apparent heart attack on November 17, 1971, at age forty-six.

• • •

Capt. Phil Hoyt retired at sixty-five from the Kansas City Police Department on April 22, 1954; however, the department retained his services as a civilian. Hoyt had run the police laboratory he founded until May 23, 1953, just a week before his dramatic testimony in Buster's trial; then he was promoted to head a new intelligence unit in the chief's office. Hoyt continued to lead the unit until his official retirement in 1959. On November 8, 1967, Captain Hoyt and the Battery E Army light artillery unit he had organized was honored on its fiftieth anniversary.

Captain Hoyt died in January 1975. He was eighty-six years old.

• • •

Troy Gordon continued to cover the Tulsa County Courthouse until 1956, when his managing editor approached him about writing a column. While Gordon was trained to be a reporter, he was born to be a columnist. For nearly a quarter of a century, Tulsans opened their papers to read 'Round the Clock for Gordon's anecdotes, humor, and homespun wisdom. His column appeared on the left-hand side of the page, with a 'Round the Clock logo above his picture, a perk few in the newsroom received. Gordon became so popular in his adopted hometown, people would recognize him on the street.

'Round the Clock was more than friendly banter. Gordon commented on the defining issues of his time, from President John F. Kennedy's assassination in 1963 to the United States' landing the first men on the moon in 1969. In many ways, Gordon was Tulsa's moral compass, a role for which the Buster Youngwolfe case had prepared him. He was never preachy or snide, just a decent man who wasn't afraid to say what he thought was right.

"He acted as a mirror to Tulsa," *Tulsa World* city editor Wayne Greene wrote in a 1998 memorial piece. "And perhaps that's why Tulsans who loved Tulsa loved Troy."

Gordon continued to write for the *Tulsa World* until the early 1980s when his life ended in mystery and tragedy. Gordon had long battled a debilitating illness. Speculation around the newsroom was that he had dementia, though nobody knew for sure. Gordon continued to turn in his column, though some suspected that his wife, Joanne, who was also an accomplished reporter, was ghostwriting for her husband.

On January 16, 1981, Joanne called the *Tulsa World* newsroom to tell the executive editor that her husband had died. According to her, Gordon, then sixty years old, had stumbled into venetian blinds and strangled himself, a shocking end for someone who had been so strong and athletic all of his life. While the medical examiner ruled his death a suicide, Joanne insisted that he had died in an accident. Gordon was a legend in the *Tulsa World* newsroom and the city itself. Nobody wanted to disturb his legacy, so nobody pried further. Gordon's influence in Tulsa was so profound that Oral Roberts, famed evangelist and founder of his namesake university, delivered the eulogy at his funeral. He was just one of the thousands of Tulsans who mourned the death of Tulsa's most famous columnist.

• • •

The Tulsa Tribune had a joint operating agreement with the *Tulsa World* since 1941. The afternoon and morning newspapers shared advertising, printing, and circulation departments, but they otherwise maintained competing news divisions.

The agreement was renegotiated in 1981, with a new expiration date in 1996. By 1992 the *Tulsa Tribune's* circulation was about half that of the *Tulsa World's*. While the afternoon daily was said to be profitable, the *Tulsa World* did not renew the agreement, and the *Tulsa Tribune* closed, part of nationwide trend of disappearing daily afternoon papers. The *Tulsa Tribune* printed its last edition on September 30, 1992.

The *Tulsa World* acquired the *Tulsa Tribune's* assets for $30 million and became the primary print news source for northeastern Oklahoma. In the winter of 2013 the *Tulsa World* was purchased by Berkshire Hathaway's BH Media Group, controlled by Warren Buffett. BH Media Group maintains ownership of the *Tulsa World* as of this writing.

• • •

A new, temporary *Golden Driller* welcomed more than 300,000 attendees at the 1959 International Petroleum Exposition. In 1963 Tulsa passed a $3.5 million bond issue to build a 446,400 square foot, ten-acre exposition center, which opened on April 3, 1966, and just in time to welcome the largest crowds in the IPE's history. As massive as the crowds were, the most memorable spectacle at the 1966 IPE was the permanent Tulsa *Golden Driller*. At 43,500 pounds and 76 feet tall, it remains the largest freestanding statue in the world. More than a mascot of the oil industry, the *Golden Driller* has become a symbol for the city itself. Like the *Statue of Liberty*, the *Golden Driller* wears a blank expression. He is a reserved roughneck, a midwestern mythological character cast in steel, America's answer to the Greek heroes of antiquity. Inscribed on the plaque at the base of the statue is this statement: "Dedicated to the men of the petroleum industry who by their vision and daring have created from God's abundance a better life for mankind."

Despite crowds of more than 350,000 at the 1966 IPE, the 1971 event lost money and was deemed a failure. Affected by the oil slump of the 1970s and the increased competition from the Offshore Technology Conference in Houston, Texas, attendance in 1976 and 1979 plummeted, with only 26,000 attending the latter event. The International Petroleum Exposition was canceled in 1979, ending a fifty-six-year-old Tulsa tradition. While the IPE is long gone, the *Golden Driller* still stands. He is partly a relic of a city's gilded past, but in another way, his indomitable presence represents his city's enduring potential.

• • •

Tulsa's status as the Oil Capital of the World never recovered from the oil bust of the 1980s. Oil prices fell from forty dollars a barrel to barely ten dollars, resulting in the shuttering of dozens of businesses and the loss of thousands of jobs. Tulsa's population, which had consistently risen throughout its history, leveled off at 375,000 in the mid-1980s. The story of oil is a story of booms and busts, and Tulsans are familiar with the industry's mood swings. Today its title "Oil Capital of the World" is mere nostalgia. With so many oil hubs located across the country and around the world, no U.S. city can rightly claim to be oil's capital.

But Tulsa is more than oil. Since its founding Tulsa has welcomed the visionary and the vagabond, the people who had abandoned their past or been exiled from it, and those who came to this unsullied, unsettled territory armed with little more than a hope for something better. Wayfarers and wildcatters have been replaced by entrepreneurs and start-ups as a new generation carves out its destiny, just as the forebears did a century ago.

• • •

Besides Josie Warren's testimony on the second day of the trial, none of the Warren family attended Buster Youngwolfe's murder trial. The family did not give a statement to the press after Buster was acquitted and never spoke about Phyllis Jean Warren's death again. By all accounts, the Warren family returned to life as normal.

Josie Warren died of cancer in 1956. Robert Warren never remarried. His family remembers him as being quiet and reserved. While he had a drinking problem most of his life, Warren kept himself together and mostly just stayed to himself. In 1973 Warren died of "spider cancer," an informal term for cancer that spreads out with an arachnoid growth pattern via lymphatic channels or blood vessels. While being treated, physicians made an incision that caused his cancer to spread throughout his body.

The Warren boys never spoke of their sister's death or of their father's moonshining operation. If one of their wives said something, someone would shut her up and change the subject. As of this writing, only Phyllis's brother Billy Dale Warren is still alive. His family said he would not participate in an interview. The Warren sons remain protective of the family.

As of this writing, the murder of Phyllis Jean Warren remains unsolved.

• • •

Buster Granville Youngwolfe's taste of freedom was short lived. A little over a month after his release from jail, Buster was sent to prison on July 23, 1953. Judge Elmer Adams ruled that he had violated his probation on two counts of robbery by drinking in bars and being out of work. Buster's alibi saved his life but cost him his freedom.

Howe asked the court for forty-five days to prepare Buster's appeal, but as the deadline drew near, Howe became frustrated when Buster did not heed his advice and instructions. He even began to question if Buster had any interest at all in his own freedom. Feeling heartbroken and perhaps a little let down, Howe did all he could do to secure Buster's freedom, but he let the deadline expire. Buster was sentenced on Wednesday and sent to prison on Thursday.

Buster was released from prison two years later, having served his time, and was eager to make a fresh start. The Youngwolfe family had enough of their native land. The clan moved to Colorado, but their journey out west in search of a better life did not last long. Buster's dad, Ellis, got busted for writing bad checks, so after a few years the Youngwolfes moved to Muskogee and later to Tulsa.

One person who didn't make the move to Colorado was Buster's wife, Betty. The couple loved each other, but their marriage was filled with disagreements and arguments. They divorced, and Buster moved to Colorado, while Betty stayed behind.

Buster never managed to stay out of trouble. Back living in Muskogee, Buster stole a government welfare check out of a mailbox and cashed it. When he found out the authorities were hunting him, he dyed his hair and hid out in Tulsa. He and his brother, Clarence, were arrested, but Buster said his brother was not involved in the robbery. Buster served three years in prison for the crime.

Once out of prison for the second time, Buster and Clarence opened a bar in Muskogee. One brother ran it at night; the other brother ran it during the day. When he wasn't tending bar, Buster worked as a field hand on a farm, tying greens, skinning turnips, and picking okra and pecans. Buster met and married a different Betty, and the couple were married for several years. He was finally a free man—no iron bars, no jail cells. He was in a good place but not for long.

Buster's marriage to the second Betty ended in tragedy when she suffered a heart attack while driving. She was killed in the ensuing wreck. More disappointment followed, as after his second wife's death, Buster's bar burned down.

Not long after his bar went down in flames, Buster and his first wife, Betty, ran into each other while just going about their business. While both were much older, they were both still kids in many ways, Buster especially. They started to wonder, Why not? They gave their relationship another chance. They remarried, but before too long the realities of married life once again got the better of them. When Betty found out Buster had been out drinking one night, she kicked him out of the house and presumably her life. But breaking up and getting back together came to define Buster and Betty's relationship. They loved each other and couldn't stay apart for long. They had traveled a long, grueling road together, a journey that was about to take one of its strangest turns.

In 1990 Buster pleaded not guilty to the charge of lewd molestation of a twelve-year-old girl. When the state made a notice of intent to use the girl's statements as evidence, Buster pleaded guilty and was sentenced on July 13, 1990, to seven years in prison. While Buster frequently ran afoul of the law, he had never done anything so heinous. According to Buster's family, it was all a giant misunderstanding and indicative of the strange, childlike naivete he carried all of his life.

I was aware of Buster's conviction for molestation but not the details when a member of the Youngwolfe family contacted me to say that Bessie Youngwolfe, his great-niece, wanted to speak to me. The relative said Bessie, who was named after her great aunt, was very protective of her uncle, so I went into the conversation treading lightly on what was sure to be an uncomfortable subject. Bessie and I spoke, establishing enough rapport to tackle this sensitive topic. At this time I had no idea whom Buster had been charged with molesting, only that it was a twelve-year-old girl. Finally I asked Bessie what she could tell me about Buster's molestation charge, fully expecting her to evade the question or even to hang up. Instead, without pausing for a second, she responded, "It was me." Bessie proceeded to explain the situation.

In the 1980s Buster and Betty had taken Bessie in to live with them. Then one day the twelve-year-old Bessie had come home from school when Buster told her to take off her clothes. He meant that she should take off her school clothes and change into a set of playclothes. A neighbor overheard the exchange and misunderstood the intent, and everything spiraled out of control from there. The preteen Bessie told authorities that her great-uncle had touched her, but she admitted as an adult that was not true. When the time came for Bessie to take the stand and potentially be exposed in a lie, Buster pleaded guilty. According to Bessie, Buster chose to serve time for a hideous crime he did not commit rather than put her through that ordeal. Being in prison Buster could handle, but seeing his great-niece suffer he could not. After his release in 1997, Buster forgave her and remained a second dad to her, as if nothing had ever happened. Buster's great-niece Bessie Youngwolfe passed away on May 19, 2018, two months shy of her thirty-seventh birthday and only seven months after we had spoken for the last time.

Not long after he was released from prison, Buster lost the person who had been by his side most of his life. Betty had beaten lung cancer once before, but the second time she developed the disease, she was not so lucky. When she needed an emergency blood transfusion, she was rushed to the hospital, but it was too late. Betty Youngwolfe died of a throat hemorrhage on June 26, 1998. She was sixty-three years old.

Now a widower, Buster spent his later years in Chelsea, Oklahoma, about an hour north of Tulsa, with his nephew Clarence and his wife. Buster had lived a hard life, some of it due to his own making and much due to circumstances beyond his control. Now, finally, Buster was at peace. His family was close, and he read constantly. No matter how old he became, Buster never lost his love of learning or his lifelong fear of being labeled a "dumb Indian."

Near the end he could hardly walk and had started to lose his mind to dementia. Buster Jr., after retiring from the U.S. Air Force, took his dad in to live with him and his wife about thirty miles away in Inola, Oklahoma. But Buster was stubborn about the arrangement and made no secret that he wanted to be closer to his family in Chelsea. Buster became so cantankerous about it that his son gave in and said he'd him take him back to Chelsea in a week, but a week was too long for Buster.

One blistering summer day, Buster went missing. His family searched for him, but when he was gone for two days, they began to fear the worst. While some stranger in town gave him a ride partway, he tried to walk the rest of the way home to Chelsea himself. The brutal Oklahoma heat got the best of him. His niece found him dead in a ditch about a mile and a half from his family's home on July 6, 2008. Buster Youngwolfe was seventy-six years old.

• • •

Elliott Howe had a long, honorable law career in private practice. He was a dedicated member of the Muscogee-Creek Nation and served as the first Chief Justice of the Creek Nation Supreme Court. He was also a member of the Sons of the American Revolution, the Sons of the Confederacy, the Tulsa County Bar Association, and the Oklahoma Bar Association.

Despite his many affiliations, Howe never pursued politics. He never had any desire. Howe preferred to spend his time with his family. Elliott and Imelda were married for fifty-seven years and had two more children after Sally Jane Howe: Elliott Howe Jr., born October 31, 1954, and Nancy Haven Howe, born January 5, 1961. Howe also enjoyed spending his time outside, raising vegetables and growing pecan trees in his backyard, or raising horses on his farm just outside Coweta, Oklahoma. He tried to raise livestock, too, but had to stop. After his children named the animals, he couldn't bring himself to kill them.

Howe never had anything more to do with Buster Youngwolfe. Howe had saved his life; what Buster did or didn't do with it was not up to him. Howe no longer had the appetite for criminal law and spent the rest of his career in general practice.

Howe retired in 1989. He felt the legal profession had changed too much since he started. When Howe began practicing law, the profession was about helping people, but he believed it degenerated into a game focused on winning at all costs—or, more accurately, on not losing. Howe had done his job, provided for his family, and knew it was time to close shop and turn out the lights. Retirement meant more time for the things that really mattered to him—namely, teaching his grandkids how to garden.

As with many men of his age and era, Howe's mind began to fade in old age and, in its place, was an anger and resentment that had never been there before. But on rare, blessed occasions, Howe would come back from the void, back to what he was before his mind began to drift. You'd never have seen a happier or more compassionate person than he was. For all that the world had taken away from him, for all the bitterness he could have carried, nobody cared more deeply about his fellow man than Elliott Howe. That was the man he was—the man who risked everything to defend a young man falsely accused of murder when the whole world had convicted him to death.

Howe never saw himself as a hero; he was just a man doing his job. What mattered to him was never the accolades or the honors. All he wanted from life was what he had—a family, such as the one that was taken from him when he was just a boy. His family was by his side when he died of lung cancer on January 21, 2007—the same day as Imelda's eighty-second birthday. She followed him merely ten months later on October 18, 2007.

Afterword

Who Killed Phyllis Jean Warren?

County Attorney Robert L. Wheeler and Sheriff W. W. Field reopened Phyllis's murder investigation, but they never formally charged another person.

What happened?

Who killed Phyllis Jean Warren?

Before we confront this question, I must present a primer.

The purpose of this book can be summed up in a single statement: The presumption of innocence—the notion that a person is innocent until proven guilty—is a fundamental right. It is not granted by any government or principality but is the birthright of every person. This is not fidelity to an abstract principle, for this right is essential for the safety of the individual accused and for society as a whole. It is as true today as it ever was or ever will be.

This principle should not be limited to the court of law but should extend to the court of public opinion. In the world of ubiquitous media, the presumption of innocence in the public square matters now more than ever. In the court of public opinion, accusations can be made, reputations destroyed, and lives ruined before the accused even knows he or she has been charged, let alone before the accused can defend himself or herself. Laws protect people against lies, but laws cannot wipe away the stain of slander or libel from people's minds and hearts. Human nature will not allow it.

With this in mind, I tread carefully before addressing the question of who killed Phyllis Jean Warren. I am not making an accusation, for to do so would violate the purpose and principle of this book. Nor am I in a position to bring about a legal charge. Yet I am also aware that what follows is enough to plant a seed in the reader's mind and heart, as it was planted in mine. This is inevitable. Even if the players are dead, their reputations live on, so I ask the reader to proceed with caution. I am not making a formal charge, but I am reporting what my grandfather believed and why.

Phyllis Jean Warren's body was found three weeks to the day after she disappeared, hastily buried in a place that people in the neighborhood passed on nearly a daily basis, an area that had even been thoroughly searched. Yet on the morning of April 2, 1953, when the hope of finding Phyllis had been all but lost, her body was discovered buried in a brush pile just a few blocks from her home. The person who found her was her father, Robert Warren.

My grandfather believed Robert Warren killed his daughter, Phyllis Jean Warren. During my grandfather's interviews with other residents and his personal investigation of the neighborhood, he learned that Robert Warren had frequently visited the location where he later found his daughter's body, as if he had been checking on something. My grandfather also found that the dirt where Phyllis was buried was packed tightly and would have been even tighter on a crisp spring night. It would have been difficult, if not impossible, for anyone to dig the hole, especially in haste. But for a person who had buried the girl days or even weeks after March 12, who had plenty of time and could have used a shovel, it was possible. The maggots found in Phyllis's mouth once she was exhumed and properly autopsied only furthered my grandfather's conviction that the girl was not buried on the same day she was killed.

My grandfather suspected Robert Warren was the actual killer before Buster's trial, and that is why he questioned witnesses on the stand about Warren's bizarre behavior. However, my grandfather was not there to charge another suspect but to prove Buster Youngwolfe's innocence. My grandfather's defense strategy, and his only option given the circumstances, was to destroy the credibility of Buster's coerced confession. Any detours he took while questioning witnesses on the stand demonstrated that he was, by his own admission, a bit in over his head.

So the question is, why? If Robert Warren killed his daughter, why did he do it? What could his motive have possibly been? I don't know. If incestuous rape occurred, then he could have killed her for any number of reasons, such as to keep her from telling the truth. Or maybe he was acting out in a fit of rage. Or maybe he was just a strange, demented man who was not sure what he was doing. I don't know.

For that matter, I do not know that Robert Warren killed Phyllis Jean Warren. I only know that is what my grandfather believed because of the evidence; thus, that is what I believe too. But I am not a prosecutor or an investigator. I am not sworn to uphold public safety or to prosecute criminals. And I do not wish to slander a deceased man's reputation. The simple fact is I do not know and I may never know who killed Phyllis Jean Warren.

Her murder, which occurred more than sixty years ago, remains unsolved. There is little doubt that Phyllis's actual killer is dead by now, as are most of the key players in her story. Instead of wondering who might have killed her, the reader might ask, Who cares? Fair enough.

But since when has murder had a statute of limitations? If we can agree that murder, especially the murder of a child, is the most heinous of crimes, then we can also agree that it should not and cannot be ignored or simply forgotten. Justice demands more. Safe, civil society requires it. I ask you to consider: What if Phyllis Warren was your loved one? Your daughter, your sister, your friend? What if she wasn't somebody's else's child but your child? What life might she have lived if someone had not taken it away from her? Might she have become a wife or mother? Might she have crawled out of the slums and made something of herself? We'll never know. She never had the chance.

For this reason I am calling on the authorities to reopen the investigation of Phyllis Jean Warren's murder. She was murdered and buried when she was only a child. Her life was taken away before she ever had a chance to live it. Let her finally rest in peace.

• • •

My grandfather never claimed to be a great trial lawyer; he was just the one person in an entire city who cared about saving an innocent man's life. Tragically, Buster's story is all too common, even today.

Poor people, people of color especially, are the victims of injustice more often than a free society such as ours should tolerate. What can you or I do about it?

Buster Youngwolfe was vindicated and is now dead. Phyllis Jean Warren was murdered, and her killer was never found. You and I can do nothing for them, but we can do something for the thousands of innocents who sit behind bars for crimes they did not commit. I encourage readers to research and support the Innocence Project. Founded in 1992 the Innocence Project seeks to exonerate the wrongly convicted through the use of DNA testing, a modern technique that was not available in 1953. Perhaps even more important, this group seeks to reform the criminal justice system to prevent further injustice and wrongful incarceration.

Researchers have proposed several reform measures to help eliminate false confessions and the resulting wrongful convictions, including electronically recording all police interrogations, improving police training about false confessions, prohibiting certain interrogation techniques, and establishing safeguards for protecting vulnerable populations, such as the developmentally disabled and juveniles. For those interested in the science behind false confessions, I encourage further reading of the work of Dr. Richard A. Leo, particularly his "False Confessions: Causes, Consequences and Implications," published by the *Journal of the American Academy of Psychiatry and the Law* in 2009.

The victims of wrongful incarceration have predominantly been poor people of color, but justice is blind for a reason. Blind to color, blind to status, blind to wealth, justice is concerned only with the truth. Yet this standard has been denied to far too many people for far too long. Justice must be shared equally and without bias, not only because civil society demands it, but also because it is simply the right thing to do. Because if injustice can happen to him or her, it can happen to you or me. And if it can happen to you or me, none of us is truly free.

As my grandfather once said, "Maybe that's why I feel so deeply about this public defender job—because I might have been a Buster Youngwolfe. But then, I guess anybody could."

Note on Sources

This book would not have been possible without the dedicated work of journalists, especially Troy Gordon of *Tulsa World*, Tim Dowd and Roy Hanna of *Tulsa Tribune*, and Ralph G. Martin from *Redbook*, among others. In addition to documenting the events and providing quotes from the principals, these reporters' firsthand accounts provided vital historical context and narrative structure for this book. Their newspapers, along with magazine accounts of the case and trial, were my principal sources, and I supplemented them with various other sources throughout the book. To provide the reader a proper context of the sources used, and to encourage further study, here I provide an explanation of major sources used throughout this book. This note on sources is not an exhaustive listing but an overview of the primary sources utilized.

In the first chapter and throughout the book, Troy Gordon's "Elimination of Crime-Breeding Slum Areas Essential, Experts Agree" (*Tulsa World*, April 12, 1953) provided background information on and descriptions of the north Tulsa slums. Nancy Schallner's article "Tulsa's Coal Mines" from Tulsa Gal website (www.tulsagal.net) also provided supplemental information about the Dawson area. Steve Nolen's "But She Teased Me about My Wife" (*Official Detective Stories*, June 1953) and Paul McClung's "Tease" (*Inside Detective*, July 1953) also provided context about the neighborhood, as well as character details about the neighborhood's residents—specifically, who they were and what they were doing on the night Phyllis disappeared. Because these latter two sources were from detective magazines, I suspected they might have been prone to embellishment, especially in regard to quotations, so I avoided using either for direct quotations. However, the magazine articles were valuable for providing context, character analysis, and a chronology of events. I also interviewed Buster's nephew Eddie Youngwolfe, who grew up in the neighborhood, to provide further information about the area, his uncle Buster, and his friend Phyllis. He also provided anecdotes, such as Robert's owning a mule and being a drinker and about the billboard gunman. I also interviewed Phyllis's great-nephew Wade Warren for character information about his grandfather, Robert Warren.

For the second chapter, the body of information on Oklahoma's history came from William Butler's "Tulsa 75: A History of Tulsa, Oklahoma" (Tulsa Chamber of Commerce, 1974). For topics that required more in-depth information than I found in Butler's book, particularly on Indian removal and the Tulsa Race Massacre, I used a mix of academic, online, and firsthand newspaper accounts. For Indian removal, this research included but was not limited to "Trail of Tears," History.com, November 9, 2009, https://www.history.com/topics /native-american-history/trail-of-tears; correspondence with Daniel F. Littlefield Jr., the director of the Sequoyah National Research Center at the University of Arkansas–Little Rock; Ellen Holmes Pearson's article "A Trail of 4,000 Tears" from *Teaching History—Ask A Historian*, https://teachinghistory.org/history-content/ask-a-historian/25652; Vicki Rozema's *Footsteps of the Cherokee: A Guide to the Eastern Homelands of the Cherokee Nation* (John F. Blair, 1995); Sandra Faiman-Silva's *Choctaws at the Crossroads: The Political Economy of Class and Culture in the Oklahoma Timber Region* (University of Nebraska Press, 1997); William D. Welge's "Timeline of American Indian Removals" in the *Encyclopedia of Oklahoma History and Culture* (Oklahoma Historical Society, 2013); Thurman Wilkins's *The Cherokee Tragedy: The Ridge Family and the Decimation of a People* (University of Oklahoma Press, 1986); and Muriel H. Wright's "Contributions of the Indian People to Oklahoma" (*Chronicles of Oklahoma* 14, no. 2 [1936]). For the Tulsa Race Massacre, I used Scott Ellsworth's *Death in a Promised Land: The Tulsa Race Riot of 1921* (Louisiana State University Press, 1982).

For chapters 3–6 and 9–20, the body of information came from firsthand newspaper accounts from the *Tulsa World* and *Tulsa Tribune*. These sources provided a chronology, background information, and direct quotations on the events of these chapters, including the disappearance, investigation, and discovery of Phyllis; the arrest and interrogation of Buster Youngwolfe; the defense case built by public defender Elliott Howe in the lead-up to the trial; and, finally, the trial itself. Additionally, Ralph G. Martin's "The Ordeal of an Innocent Man" (*Redbook*, May 1954) and Nolen Bulloch's "The Strange Case of Buster Youngwolfe" (*Tulsa Tribune*, September 23, 1970) provided context, chronology, and quotations. For the exact details on Buster's alibi, I used the transcript of Elliott Howe's opening statement (chapter 13). I also used the official transcript from the preliminary trial to provide direct quotations and a chronology of events (chapter 9). In chapter 19 I also referenced the article "Lie Detector Indian," published in *Newsweek*, June 8, 1953.Unfortunately, the transcript from the trial itself has been lost, so I had to rely primarily on newspaper coverage.

The reference to Leroy Benton as a "two-time loser" in chapter 9 was from the June 11, 1945, edition of the *Taylor (TX) Daily Press* in Taylor, Texas.

For details on the accuracy of the lie detector in chapters 9 and 14, my primary source was "The Truth about Lie Detectors (aka Polygraph Tests)," published by the American Psychological Association in 2004. For details on the prevalence and causes of false confessions, my sources were Richard A. Leo's "False Confessions: Causes, Consequences, and Implications" in the *Journal of the American Academy of Psychiatry and the Law* (37, no. 3 [2009]); and "The Confessions of Innocent Men," written by Marc Bookman in the August 6, 2013, edition of the *Atlantic*. I also reference the work of social psychologists Saul Kassin and Lawrence Wrightman that appears in Leo's "False Confessions."

For details on the International Petroleum Exhibition used throughout the book, the majority of information came from firsthand newspaper accounts from the *Tulsa World* and *Tulsa Tribune*, as well as Bobby D. Weaver's "International Petroleum Exposition" in the *Encyclopedia of Oklahoma History and Culture* (Oklahoma Historical Society, 2009).

For chapter 8, I obtained the body of information on Elliott Howe's boyhood before he attended Chilocco Indian School from his older sister Elizabeth Howe Chief's memoirs, "The Spirit Breakers" (unpublished), as well as Daniel Dunbar Howe's history of the Howe family, *Listen to the Mockingbird: The Life and Times of a Pioneer Virginia Family* (Carr, 1961). For information on Elliott Howe's time at Chilocco, I used K. Tsianina Lomawaima's *They Called It Prairie Light: The Story of Chilocco Indian School* (University of Nebraska Press, 1993), in which Howe was referred to as "Edgar." Dr. Lomawaima also sent me her original transcript from her interview with Howe, conducted on January 18, 1984, for further details. To fill in any gaps and to eliminate discrepancies between sources on Elliott Howe's childhood, I interviewed his daughter Nancy Howe, who is also my mother. For information on Indian boarding schools and the Chilocco Indian School in particular, I used Lomawaima's previously mentioned *They Called It Prairie Light* and David Wallace Adams's *Education for Extinction: American Indians and the Boarding School Experience, 1875–1928* (University Press of Kansas, 1995), and I conducted an interview with Dr. Lomawaima. For details on Alexander Posey and his involvement in early Oklahoma statehood, I used Daniel F. Littlefield Jr.'s *Alex Posey: Creek Poet, Journalist and Humorist* (University of Nebraska Press, 1992).

For the epilogue, most of the information about the principal individuals' fates came from *Tulsa World* and *Tulsa Tribune* accounts, as well as coverage from other newspapers. For further information about J. Howard Edmondson, particularly his tenure as the governor of Oklahoma, I used Brad Agnew's "Twentieth-Century Oklahoma" and Billy Joe Davis's "James Howard Edmondson," both in the *Encyclopedia of Oklahoma History and Culture* (Oklahoma Historical Society, 2009). For character insights on Troy Gordon and details on the controversy surrounding his death, I interviewed Mike Jones, the former associate editor of the *Tulsa World* who knew Gordon and worked at the *Tulsa World* at the time of Gordon's mysterious death. My interview with Phyllis's great-nephew Wade Warren provided details on the posttrial lives of the Warren family. For details on Buster's life following the trial and up to his death, I conducted phone interviews with his nephew Eddie Youngwolfe and great-niece

Bessie Youngwolfe and an email interview with his great-niece Kim Youngwolfe. Bessie Youngwolfe was especially valuable in this regard and, as was mentioned in the book, provided details about how her great-uncle Buster Youngwolfe falsely confessed to molesting her.

Unless stated otherwise, all direct quotations were taken from *Tulsa World*, *Tulsa Tribune*, and magazine article accounts. When there were discrepancies between sources, in which the quotations were similar but used different wording, I selected what I felt was the most accurate and compelling quotation based on context.

In certain instances I speculate on the mind-set of certain individuals, particularly in the opening chapter. In these instances when there were no direct quotations, at least none that I viewed as especially reliable, I made speculations on the individuals' thoughts and feelings based on my knowledge of them from my other sources (newspapers, magazines, and interviews). I also acknowledge my speculations as such by including modifiers such as "probably," "most likely," "one could imagine," and so on.

Phyllis's rape and murder remains unsolved. Phyllis's niece attempted to get the trial transcripts from the Tulsa County Courthouse, but officials told her they could not find them. I likewise was unable to secure trial transcripts and relied heavily on newspaper and magazine coverage of the investigation and trial.